IMAGINED LONDONS

IMAGINED LONDONS ～

---
edited by

Pamela K. Gilbert

STATE UNIVERSITY OF NEW YORK PRESS

Published by
State University of New York Press, Albany

© 2002 State University of New York

For information, address State University of New York Press,
90 State Street, Suite 700, Albany, NY 12207

Production by Marilyn P. Semerad
Marketing by Michael Campochiaro

Library of Congress Cataloging-in-Publication Data

Imagined Londons / edited by Pamela K. Gilbert.
    p. cm.
  Includes bibliographical references and index.
   ISBN 0-7914-5501-7 (acid free paper) — ISBN 0-7914-5502-5 (pbk. : acid free paper)
    1. London (England)—Social life and customs. 2. London (England)—Historical
geography. I. Gilbert, Pamela K.

  DA688 .I43 2002
  942.1—dc21

2001057787

10 9 8 7 6 5 4 3 2 1

Contents ⌒

Illustrations ᵉ꧂

Acknowledgments ⮌

Where illustrations are courtesy of the author, that has been noted in the list of illustrations and in the text. In addition, we are indebted to the following proprietors for their courteous permissions to print the following illustrations.

London's Transport Museum, for use of the first topological Underground map by Harry Beck, 1933, in Figure 6.1.

Simon Patterson, and London's Transport Museum, for use of Simon Patterson's *The Great Bear*, 1992, in Figure 6.2.

I would also like to thank Michael Levenson and the NEH for the 1995 Summer Seminar, The Culture of London, which inspired this project.

Introduction:
Imagining Londons ⮑

PAMELA K. GILBERT

L ondon: world city, global city, capital of empire. Literary London. The East End. Jack the Ripper. The Beatles. Beefeaters. The Tower. Village London. Merry Olde London. The London of St. Paul's and the Millenium Dome, the London of the Fire, of Dickens, of Blake. The London of Elizabeth, of Victoria, of tourists, of Londoners. The Londons of the Imagination.

This book does not simply celebrate the Londons of patriotic or touristic rhapsody. However, it is not to be seen as a corrective, a dose of "realism" designed to disabuse us of our postcard images of the city, either. This book seeks to understand imagined Londons, while at the same time encouraging the realization that, while there are an infinite number of Other Londons, there are no Londons other than those of the imagination. From multiple perspectives, in diverse historical circumstances, people have turned their faces toward the city, and created it as the site and embodiment of communities of their dreams and necessities.

The topic of the metropolis currently garners much interest. Urbanists find that world economic development is leading us toward an interlacing network of "global cities" and seek to understand and control this phenomenon. Cultural studies scholars of many disciplines have turned to geography, striving to reinscribe both space and place in bodies of work which have long privileged a disembodied textualism. British historians and literary scholars are seeking to create a richly textured, geographically informed sense of British history, both domestic and imperial. Scholars of the empire engage the mythic and material history of the metropole. London—a key global city today and the metropole of the British empire of the nineteenth century—fascinates urbanists now as it has for over two centuries; for this new, larger generation of scholars and cultural commentators, it has become an essential part of the puzzle of British, European, and world urban history and culture.

Imagined Londons addresses these themes, in a collection which seeks both to represent and point the way for this new turn in scholarship. Although much excellent work in the past few decades has focused on the urban environment, relatively little has sought to respond to David Harvey's call in 1985 for a careful elaboration of the role of community in relation to urban space, especially in regard to London.[1] Many studies (including Harvey's) have focused on a fairly determinist view of the relations between capitalist urbanization and space. Others, following Benjamin and de Certeau, have focused on the city as a site of freedom and agency, like Walkowitz. Much of this work has been very properly focused on restoring space to social analysis, and has tended to oppose spatial analysis to narrative, as narrative represents the modern domination of space by time. Ultimately, however, space and time cannot, of course, be separated. Just as space determines and qualifies narrative, narratives shape people's understanding and uses of space. In their appropriate efforts to refocus on materialism, recent studies have sometimes failed to emphasize that people's perceptions—their narratives and beliefs about themselves and their environments—come often to have material force in the transformation of the built and natural landscape. Drawing on the themes implied by the title's gesture toward Benedict Anderson's *Imagined Communities*, this volume begins with the premise that London exists as multiple constructs, serving different purposes of representation connected to identity—urban, national, racial, etc.—and that such identity is imagined simultaneously as expansive over a particular space, whether of the nation, city, neighborhood or globe, and through historical time. The mid-nineteenth century through the present, the period included in this volume, is particularly marked by London's identification with modernity, and the communities that have been imagined there and then have generally been elaborated in relation to this sense of modern anxiety and possibility.

What authors, historians, and urban residents imagine when they invoke "London" as an entity has to do with the imagined communities, identities, exclusions, and inclusions which write a multiplicity of Londons into history, both local and global. Nineteenth- and twentieth-century responses to London's perceived complexity, its risks and opportunities, its heterogeneity and uncontainability, struggled to body the city forth in understandable structures; in turn those structures determined the shape that the growth of London would continue to take. In this sense, imagined Londons, like the imagined communities of nation, have enacted history as material entities.

Imagined Londons begins with the mid-nineteenth century, a time in which London was already well established as a modern city and the center of the British empire, and extends to the present "global city" of London. The chapters are organized chronologically from the mid-Victorian period to the millennium; they represent a diverse range of disciplinary approaches and methods focusing on a broad variety of materials, literary, architectural, graphic, musical, political, and journalistic. The authors hail from departments of English, history, philosophy, geography, and comparative literature from both the United States and United Kingdom. Although the volume doesn't pretend to be comprehensive—one of its arguments is that such would be impossible—it does offer a fine range of the latest and most interesting scholarship on the city. As a volume focused on representations, *Imagined Londons* pays particular regard to the intersection of history and literature, and often neglected issues of race and empire, transnational, postcolonial, and queer identities receive detailed attention.

The mid-Victorian period is also a good starting place because it marks the high point of development of an anxious sense of London's historical importance and relation to both modernity and history which remains in place today. No prior era was quite as consumed with, as Richard Altick has termed it, the "presence of the present," and arguably in no prior era was that sense of historical immediacy so mediated through various representations of the past, in narrative, architecture, the arts, and everyday discourse. The period is characterized by its sense that London is both coherent and problematic, an obscure text whose interpretive key could be located in its relation to its own history and projected future. London is the most recent of the great European megacities to take the world stage as a center of global power. Its belatedness has expressed itself as ceaseless assertions of peerless modernity, and London has, in the twentieth century, continued to be preoccupied with its Janus-faced relation to the past and future to a degree greater than its fellow European capitals. Despite its perhaps unique level of anxiety, however, London can be read as exemplary in some respects; like all cities, London must market itself and to do so, city planners, the tourist industry, architects, and so forth must make decisions about representation which forge an uneasy relationship between history, capitalism, the lived experiences of Londoners, the rich representational history of London given by such artists as Johnson, Blake, Dickens, Winterson, Whistler, the Beatles, and the *London A to Z*, and the existing environment, built and natural, among many other factors which affect the Londons we imagine. My deliberately provocative list of artists above highlights, perhaps heavy-handedly, the fundamental precept of this book: there are only imagined Londons, and the work of understanding them is not best served by easy assumptions about fictive versus factual discourse or "art" versus science, journalism, popular culture, or what-have-you. If in this volume there is a preoccupation with representation which emphasizes London's obsession with modernity, with tourism, with the process of being perceived and how it can best be manipulated, the volume is also concerned with perceptions of London as "real," lived space—overwhelming and ungraspable or conversely, eminently graspable within a grid of scientific observation and discipline—both of which extremes stem from the perception that the proper way to perceive (or construct) a city is to define its order, that the proper way to perceive London was as the teeming matrix of the urban future.

There have been many excellent volumes on the Victorian city (Briggs, Wolff and Dyos, and Mancoff and Trela leap to mind) and a good deal of work on Victorian London recently (Walkowitz, Nord, Schneer, and Wolfreys, just to name a very few). Likewise, twentieth-century London has spawned a good deal of excellent work (King, Dyos again, and many others in various disciplines). Generally, the two periods have been conceived and presented as separate. But one of the aims of *Imagined Londons* is to show, from the vantage point of the turn of the millennium, the continuities of these apparently disparate periods—their emphasis on modernity, and the city experienced through the eyes of Others (tourists and immigrants alike), their negotiation of London's identity as a national capital with an increasingly disparate population representing London's global ties, its exhilarating sense of possibility for new identities, new embodiments. To this end, the volume gives careful attention to the transitional years from 1870 to WWI, and the later pieces pick up threads initiated in the earlier ones. Late modernity, with its sense of London as an organic whole that demands representation and containment, is here seen itself very much as a period with its own continuity.

The volume, then, opens with four contributions that span the last half of the nineteenth century. My own chapter examines the social body in relation to Victorian understandings of metropolitan urban space, paying particular attention to medical and social thematic cartography, such as sanitary and medical maps and the Booth poverty maps. The construction of public medicine and social work as key to liberal government has been central to urban modernity in the "West." One way by which medics, sanitarians, and social workers sought to understand and control the urban social body was through mapping. This chapter traces some of the ways in which public medics and social workers constructed communities in London by vulnerability to disease, domestic habits, and so forth, and also how existing narratives about class disease were used to support, complicate, and challenge existing mappings of London. Visions of both London and urban life more generally continue to be influenced by this cartographic tradition, as this mapping not only represented Victorian theories of urbanism, but inscribed them on the city itself, as such maps were used for slum clearance and other urban planning projects.

Heidi Holder's chapter turns to Victorian theater for its representations of London life, which were extremely popular on the Victorian stage. As she demonstrates, London scenes and stories provided audiences with ways of understanding the urban experience, in all its heterogeneity. Key to that sense of variety were Londoners' experiences of colonial subjects living in the city, largely in the East End. Although often overlooked in scholarship of Victorian urban literature until recently, African and Indian characters frequently appeared, and were particular staples of the drama. As Holder shows, the uses of such "other Londoners" were mediated by classed geography. West End theaters used such characters almost as metonyms for the East End, often seen as a "foreign" realm within London itself by virtue of its poverty and association with immigrants and shipping. In East End drama, on the other hand, African, Indian, and other Asian characters could be more prominent and carry more complex significance, even though they were unable to cross class boundaries the way white characters might. Holder reminds us that London as "global" city has a history with deep roots, and that already in the early nineteenth century, Londoners were defining themselves through the city's internal others.

Morris B. Kaplan continues our focus on the "Other Londoners" of the Victorian age, this time turning our attention to the respectable spaces of the middle classes in the West. Ernest Boulton and Frederick Park were arrested in 1870 for cross-dressing and consorting with other men as women, and tried for "conspiracy to commit" sodomy. Kaplan traces the copious publicity that the case received and finds a complex relation between the treatment of sexual deviance and social class; he also finds that London was already well-known, at least in some circles, as a site of sexual freedom and possibility for a wider range of gendered subjectivity than, supposedly, less metropolitan areas. Boulton and Park's visibility raised the specter of sexual license, emphasizing London's status as a site of deviance and multiplicity. As Kaplan also points out, it also raised frightening questions about spectators' abilities to read the city, as both men had "passed" in various middle-class public spaces as women. As legibility is an ongoing concern in this period, as we will see in the first two chapters, "queer" public practices continually threatened to undermine urbanites' tenuous confidence in their own spatial literacies.

Michelle Sipe takes us forward into the fin de siecle, examining Arthur Symons's 1890s poetry. Replete with images of "fallen" women who are both situated in and stand in for urban settings, Symons's poetry portrays women's bodies as fragmented images that mirror the discontinuites of modern city life. Concerned with positioning himself as a literate authority on the city's difficult, fragmented codes, Symons articulates a rhetoric of urban mastery. Posing a chaotic, dangerous, but ultimately controllable city represented in images of fallen women against the cozy safety of domestic space represented by his apartment in Lincoln's Inn Fields, Symons develops his artistry through a conscious strategy of representing his movements through London, its music halls and streets, its diverse social spaces, as the movements of a detached connoisseur, a *flâneur extraordinaire,* who experiences the city as a series of sexual conquests through his ability to "capture" London's ambivalent beauties, and then retreat safely to an inviolable domestic space.

Chapters 5 and 6 span the turn of the century and focus on competing claims to the modern. Angela Woollacott's piece explores London from the view of colonial women coming to the metropole near the turn of the century from Australia. Possessed of a unique perspective on London, Australian women articulated their sense of Australian identity in relation to London's otherness, its perceived privations, its difference from both the land of their childhoods and from their expectations of the imperial center, often finding—and perhaps being pleased and proud to find—that London fell far short of their expectations and experiences. As Woollacott points out, in constructing the metropole as the marked term, deficient in comparison to an originary point of plenitude, these women reversed the typical assumption that the metropolis represented modernity, against the backward colonies, as they critique the poverty of London, its inequities, and cruelty to the dispossessed. In this way, they formulated a sense of themselves as members of a superior community defined against London, even as they challenged London's claims to represent modernity and progress—a fundamental component, not only of its imperial identity, but of its identity within the European context.

David Pike also emphasizes London's intense preoccupation with its own modernity, here, explicitly *modernist* in form, in his study of Harry Beck's schematic map of the underground railway, which is now perhaps the most well-known iconographic symbol of London. Pike argues that in portraying the railway network as beautiful, simple, and easily legible, which substituted an abstract representation of London for a much different and more complex topography, Beck's map offers London to us as a modernist conception of space, wherein abstract utility takes precedence over the messiness of lived experience. Thus, the abstract representation—and the "oneiric" experience of London primarily through its streamlined underground spaces rather than its heterogenous surfaces—could supplant the difficult and "primitive" London that Woollacott's subjects so deplored. Pike argues that recent urbanist theories have all worked with or against modernist space, of which Beck's map is a peculiarly fine example. Pike's piece leads us from the Victorian fascination with "realistic" representations of London to the twentieth-century modernist predilection for the stripped-down icon, which allows for modern and postmodern notions of the trademark as representation of—and replacement for—London's heterogeneity.

The next six chapters concentrate on London in the later twentieth century, and continue the focus on London's preoccupation with its own representation and its ambivalent relationship to its own histories. Continuing Pike's gesture toward the construction of London as a legible text for touristic consumption, David Gilbert and Fiona Henderson trace the representation of London in tourist guidebooks in the twentieth century. Following Dean MacCannell, Gilbert and Henderson read tourism as an effort to create coherence out of a fragmented experience of the modern world. As Gilbert and Henderson point out, London has been an object of tourism in the modern sense for at least 150 years: a period of working out anxieties about modernity and empire. Concentrating particularly on the post-war period to the present, they focus on the assertions of modernity involved in the transformation of the skyline and South Bank of the Thames associated with the 1951 Festival and the later positioning of the city as a center of fashion. However, this construction of London is in tension with the appeals to the city's history as ancient site of empire and the coziness of Merry Olde "village London."These tensions finally dovetail in the apparently contradictory, but actually continuous, presentation of London today as multicultural, post-imperial world city.

Alexei Monroe is also concerned with the nature of London's representation of itself through tourism. However, he approaches the question from the perspective of what resists or is elided by touristic packaging, particularly in the world of popular music for which London is well-known globally. Monroe points out that "mainstream" rock culture and its historical locations have become integral to the marketing of London to tourists. The tourist industry has absorbed sites formerly associated with the countercultures of rock and punk and packaged them as "heritage." Recent music sub- and countercultures have resisted some of this commodification, in part through their mobility and association with marginal sites, such as abandoned warehouses and squats: what Monroe, using Hakim Bey's term, designates "temporary autonomous zones." Monroe traces structural congruences between these musical genres and the spaces with which they are associated to suggest that postmodern urban life and its attendant popular art forms are evolving in forms which are not always amenable to traditional forms of representation and cooptation.

John Eade, Isabelle Fremeaux, and David Garbin bring us back to the theme of (post) colonials in London; however, by the late twentieth century, these can no longer be conceived as "Others" existing on the margins of the metropole, but must be understood as an integral, if ambivalent, part of the city's identity itself, as Gilbert and Henderson suggest in their chapter as well. Eade, Fremeaux, and Garbin trace the settlement of migrants' diasporic communities, which have forged transnational links not only with those in their countries of origin but also with other migrants globally. These groups challenge notions of "nation" or "culture" organized around tropes of purity, whether of language, race, country of origin, or religion. Examining Bangladeshi community building and presence in local London politics and urban renewal, this chapter examines how Bangladeshi activists deal with the local, state, and metropolitan structures, as well as how such structures interact with traditional leaders and institutions and how those interactions reflect on concepts of community organized through identifications with Bangladesh itself—through festivals, charitable contributions, and so forth which link the two geographically separated communities. Eade, Fremeaux, and Garbin find that these communities deploy several competing conceptions of space, the metropole, and London, paradoxically, to affirm a community which is intimately related to London yet transcends its spaces in favor of other organizing factors. As the globe comes home to London, London becomes both global itself and extremely parochial, a single node of a "village" community which is itself decentered and global in extent.

Like Eade, Fremeaux, and Garbin, Gautam Premnath uses issues of postcolonial identity and community to challenge the limitations inherent in a definition of London that depends on geographic space. His chapter attends to literary representations of these diasporic communities and their relation to the imperial metropole, especially in his study of V. S. Naipaul's Ralph Singh, the narrator of *The Mimic Men* (1967). Naipaul, Premnath argues, rejects the spatial separatism that characterizes the work of some of his contemporaries, such as Lamming, with its concomitant embrace of nationalist identity. Premnath sees Naipaul's figuration of London as site of both self-making and exclusion as central to Naipaul's rejection of a naive celebration of the promise of decolonization. Singh's disillusionment with the elusive and delusory "god of the city" associates metropolitan identity with the false promise of postcolonial independence. Locations in and movement through London's geography are used to chart Singh's journey, as the colony and metropole are shown to be inextricably imaginatively intertwined.

The last two chapters bring us to the brink of the present, while interrogating the present's investment in the past. They are appropriate conclusions to a volume that began with the Victorian tendency to propel their city into visions of the future. Julian Wolfreys gives us an overview of postmodern narrative's encounter with a city in which can be found the very vernacular of postmodern form, its fragmentary seductions, its sublime—or bathetic—juxtapositions, its frightening, exhilarating refusal to "mean" coherently. Wolfreys engages postmodern theories of space and architecture to read through work as diverse as that of poets Iain Sinclair and Allen Fisher, film-maker Patrick Keiller, and photographer Rachel Whiteread, illuminating what they have to teach us about encounters with and constructions of the city. In contemporary writers' psychotopographies of London, Wolfreys observes, there is an insistent engagement with time as palimpsestic, recursive, amalgamated with space in often surprising ways. These imagined Londons insist on history, even as they insist on historicity's fictive and subjective nature. This persistence of memory and event continually exceeds and subverts the neat packaging of London by "city planners or . . . any grand narrative," whether of modernity or otherwise.

Michael Levenson is also concerned with time and memory at the end of the twentieth century. His chapter rounds out the volume, appropriately, with a discussion of millennial celebratory architectures, whose monumentality seeks to memorialize past glories and anticipate future transcendence. The millennium was marked by the apportionment of considerable funding devoted to marking London's self-conscious march into the new era, through events, new architecture, and an overhauling of earlier structures to bring the city in line with its "new," "old" image. Beginning with conflicts over Victorian monuments in Trafalgar Square, Levenson charts discussions of public art and architecture—its meanings, aims, ambiguities, and failures, and the political and cultural stakes associated with them. The much-maligned Millennium Dome provides a case study. London, celebrating its national and (post-) imperial identity, waffled between self-gratulation and self-flagellation, as the Dome came to bear a burden of meanings far beyond its already weighty intended citation and subversion of St. Paul's, its assertion of a (post)modernity that simultaneously saluted and dismissed the past. However, despite the desire for a "legible" city marked by centralizing monuments, Levenson suggests, the true identity of contemporary London is more aptly revealed by the Docklands phenomenon, where, guided by nothing beyond capitalist individualism, a radically discontinuous profusion has become an oddly illegible, yet well-known and iconic, showpiece of urban possibility. As ever, imagined communities form as much from below as from above, and bear an unpredictable relationship to power, economic and otherwise.

So our volume ends with a beginning—a new millennium—and yet one that looks backward to the Victorian themes with which this volume itself begins. The tensions between urban profusion and coherent identity, liberal individualism and community values with which Victorian London was riven and from which it took its shape remain its most profound marker, architecturally and artistically. A multiplicity which has been relentlessly domesticated and packaged as the London "brand" is ceaselessly disrupted by new forms of the multiplicity that exceed and yet do not escape London's power to absorb them. And the most "modern" city of all—a term which now paradoxically evokes a receding past—is precisely so in its ceaseless negotiations of past, present, and its visions of the future. The following, then, are brief illuminations of some of the imagined Londons of late modernity.

NOTE

1. A notable exception is Jonathan Schneer's *London 1900: The Imperial Metropolis*.

WORKS CITED

Altick, Richard. *The Presence of the Present: Topics of the Day in the Victorian Novel*. Columbus: Ohio State UP, 1991.

Anderson, Benedict. *Imagined Communities: Reflections on the Origin and Spread of Nationalism*. Rev. ed. London and New York: Verso, 1991.

Benjamin, Walter. *The Arcades Project*. Trans. Howard Eiland and Kevin McLaughlin. Prepared on the basis of the German volume, ed. Rolf Tiedemann. Cambridge, MA: Belknap P, 1999.

Briggs, Asa. *Victorian Cities*. New York: Harper & Row, 1965.

de Certeau, Michel. *The Practice of Everyday Life*. 1984. Trans. Steven Rendall. Berkeley: U of California P, 1988.

Harvey, David. *Consciousness and the Urban Experience: Studies in the History and Theory of Capitalist Urbanization*. Baltimore, MD: John Hopkins UP, 1985.

King, Anthony D. *Global Cities: Post-Imperialism and the Internationalisation of London*. New York: Routledge, 1990.

Mancoff, Debra N., and D. J. Trela, eds. *Victorian Urban Settings*. New York: Garland, 1996.

Nord, Deborah Epstein. *Walking the Victorian Streets: Women, Representation, and the City*. Ithaca: Cornell UP, 1995.

Schneer, Jonathan. *London 1900: The Imperial Metropolis*. New Haven: Yale UP, 1999.

Walkowitz, Judith. *City of Dreadful Delight: Narratives of Sexual Danger in Late-Victorian London*. Chicago: U of Chicago P, 1992.

Wolff, Michael, and H. J. Dyos. *The Victorian City: Images and Realities*. 1973. London: Routledge, 1999.

Wolfreys, Julian. *Writing London: The Trace of the Urban Text from Blake to Dickens*. Basingstoke, Hampshire: Macmillan P, 1998. New York: St. Martin's, 1998.

CHAPTER 1 ⪜

The Victorian Social Body
and Urban Cartography

PAMELA K. GILBERT

MAPPING IN BRITAIN

*B*ritain, like other European powers, has a long history of map-making. During the Enlightenment, maps came to embody the power of the objective, scientific gaze to construct—or reflect—an accurate description of the geographic environment. The development of techniques of triangulation in the eighteenth century enabled cartographers to construct measurements with impressive precision. Matthew Edney remarks that triangulation "implicitly created . . . the perfect geographic panopticon . . . because its geography would be the same as the world's . . . it promised such an improvement that the archive became definitive" (337). Meanwhile, new developments in lithography enabled maps to be created and disseminated more cheaply than ever before. By the early to mid-nineteenth century, maps were everywhere—in schoolrooms, as frontispieces to books, in journals, and so forth. Thrower notes that a fifty-sheet hand atlas, published in 1817–22, and inexpensive wall maps made cartographic representations "available to large numbers of students and the general public. The use of globes, maps and atlases also became important school subjects for both girls and boys at this time" (125). By the time railways were in common use for business and personal travel—thus "shrinking the world"—maps were a type of spatial representation to which many Britons had some recourse in envisioning their environment.

All maps are rhetorical. That is, all maps organize information according to systems of priority and thus, in effect, operate as arguments, presenting only partial views which construct, rather than simply describe, an object of knowledge. Most maps flatten the terrain, offering a view of space as homogenous and equivalent. Maps rarely account for time, differences between day and night or the seasons, for example. In any case, these constraints don't make for bad maps, only, inevitably, ones which are limited by the purposes for which they are intended. Thematic maps—maps intended to illustrate a particular data set or argument, usually having to do with human actions or experiences in space—are, of course, persuasive in intent.

However, maps, much like anatomy, have generally been accorded a disproportionate truth-value by their readers, and often even by their makers, who should know better. Like the body, the earth seems the very stuff of materiality, the privileged referent of truth and experience. Maps, of all documents, are often read uncritically as representations of an external reality, not subject to a Platonic distrust of language. Biostatistics, "objective" numbers about corporeal bodies, and maps, "objective" representations of terra firma, were a perfect match—scientific, based in mathematics and material reality, unanswerable.

Social problems, including epidemic disease, crime and prostitution, were seen in the nineteenth century as problems especially attendant on urbanization. London and Paris drew particular attention from cartographers and those interested in social work who set about to determine the spatial relations of such problems. Social maps of crime and moral turpitude of various sorts were quite popular, and poverty maps led to the well-known verbal and cartographic mappings of London by Mayhew (maps published in 1862) and Booth (1889). Sanitary reports, of course, included many detailed maps to show the location of nuisances; most of these were pragmatic (at such and such a place, a drain is wanted), but many were intended to be persuasive, or used for such purposes in publications addressed to a larger audience, such as Chadwick's report maps of 1842.

THEMATIC MAPPING

The increasing visibility of maps, along with cheaper modes of production and dissemination, encouraged broader and more experimental uses of maps for specific purposes. 1830 to 1855 has been termed the "golden age" of thematic mapping (Robinson 440). The most typical use of thematic mapping before this period was for military/colonial purposes, although some population, linguistic, and even medical maps were created before this time. But most cartographic historians agree that thematic cartography generally, and especially medical cartography, began in the early nineteenth century, getting a boost from outbreaks of yellow fever in the United States and becoming fully established during the cholera pandemic of the early 1830s. Cholera is generally seen as responsible for establishing medical mapping as an expected, standard technique in Europe and the Americas, and certainly in Britain (E. W. Gilbert 173; Jarcho 133; Stevenson 228). Thematic mapping of this sort is essentially a statistical argument presented visually, and so was a result of the development of statistics as an important area of knowledge. However, it also comes into being as a result of the spatialized understanding of social problems in this period; before the significant use of such maps (which mapped not only disease, but also poverty, crime, religious practice, and educational access as the most common measures), written accounts tended to describe the conditions of populations spatially, street by street and sometimes house by house. As Stevenson observes, such detailed spatial descriptions cried out for visual representation (240). Thematic maps allowed readers to simultaneously situate themselves in a totality of human activity or experience and a spatial totality which was connected to, and helped define, that human community. Medical maps located human beings in a community of bodies linked by common vulnerability to disease.

Medical maps, presumably, would not have been as widely consumed across classes as, say, the Society for the Diffusion of Useful Knowledge's maps in informative books for working men. However, the following quote, taken from a sermon published in pamphlet form, implies that this minister's audience (largely middle to upper class), at least, was expected by the orator to be familiar with sanitary maps:

> Cleanliness . . . and an early application of medicine and medical skill . . . were supposed to be specifics against the contagion. . . . But pushing that truth too far, men began to map out the geographical boundaries of the malady. . . . Then the selfishness of our nature, leaving the poor in their disease or in their danger to pay the penalty of their localities, was heard to congratulate itself on the comparative safety of its better situations. (Henry Venn Elliott 9–11)

Clearly the minister speaks of both the mapping and readers' reactions as topics of common knowledge by 1855, well outside of medical circles. He also recognizes—and calls upon his auditors to recognize—the classed nature of such mapping, its social and policy investments, and deleterious effects upon the disenfranchised. This sermon implies that both familiarity with such maps and rather sophisticated map-reading practices—such as use of maps to predict one's own vulnerability to disease—were fairly widespread.

It is important to keep in mind the connections Victorians made between disease, morality, and the body. For Victorians, epidemic disease was a sign of poor sanitary practices which were tied to poor economic and moral practices; in turn, dirt *caused* immorality, by so violating the boundaries of the body and psyche as to degrade the self's tenuous ability to preserve independence from its surroundings, human and inanimate. Especially under the early sanitary movement of Chadwick, from the late forties through the mid-fifties, filth, to be carefully mapped onto the urban terrain by sanitary inspectors preparatory to intervention, was an index of moral corruption on the body social and in the individual bodies which comprised it. This index was clear to any person of ordinary sensory abilities who understood where to look. Excise the filth from the civic body, it was reasoned, and the health of the social body must follow. In this way, the individual humans who lived in slums were, by those who represented the city to the sanitary establishment in maps, drained of agency and massified. They were mapped as inert, usually dark areas, whether representing epidemic deaths or simply filthy slums, onto a city whose body would respond to treatment.

As the century wore on and gains were made in the most basic levels of sanitation—the improvement of sewerage and so forth—medical mapping and social mapping began to split off, though they still overlapped. Medical mapping began to suggest more sophisticated, hidden relationships between geography, the built environment, human activity, and disease that only the doctor and sanitary engineer could interpret. On the other hand, social geographers found that poverty and social ills could not simply be reduced to a one-to-one relationship with "deleterious places"; there came to be understood a complex and dynamic relationship between places, what was seen as inadequate social practice, and the "organic" functions of growth in a great city. However, social geographers continued to be heavily influenced by medical mapping's tendency to represent urban spaces anatomically, eliding individual bodies in a representation of the large, passive body of the city which required a medicalized intervention. Human actions were often viewed deterministically, as a result of environmental factors such as the inexorable laws of urban development. Obviously, there was a good deal of overlap between these concepts and the progression is not an unproblematically linear one. But as a broad outline of urban social geography's development in this period, it is reasonably accurate. To suggest a sense of this progression, I would like to briefly discuss three examples: Hector Gavin's sanitary work on Bethnal Green, conducted under Chadwick, John Snow's ground-breaking medical work on cholera, and, three decades later, Booth's famous work on London social geography.

THE SANITARY PROJECT: GAVIN

The comprehensive mapping of health in England was initialized under the sanitary project of Edwin Chadwick, which mapped both individual epidemics and generally "unhealthy" places (i.e., those with accumulations of filth). Many of the most widely perused sanitary maps were accompanied by text and statistics, and circulated in pamphlet form. Hector Gavin's *Sanitary Ramblings* (1848), based on data gathered in the service of Chadwick's sanitary project, was published separately from his findings in the Sanitary Reports in a little pamphlet apparently intended for a more general audience of middle-class elites bent on social improvement and, perhaps, charity, though it is difficult to tell how widely it circulated. Titled *Sanitary Ramblings, Being Sketches and Illustrations of Bethnal Green, a Type of the Condition of the Metropolis and Other Large Towns*, it is an excellent example of a convergence of discourses on the city. "Ramblings" places it in a tradition of guidebook literature, pleasant guides to picturesque walks, except, of course, here the picturesqueness is ironically alluded to. The "illustrations and sketches" are both visual and verbal; detailed sanitary narratives tend to go district by district, beginning with an overview and then proceeding street by street and court by court, and Gavin follows this model. There are also two maps, one showing sewers and open sewers and the other showing sewers and using variable shading to indicate the location of "cholera mist" in Bethnal Green. The argument is entirely sanitary; that is, it connects mortality/morbidity to cleanliness. Dirt represents poverty, and comes to stand in for economic deprivation. Dirt was a solvable problem, one which could be decoupled from economic deprivation, which is ambiguously presented as either not solvable or not important. Gavin originally wrote his report for Chadwick's Board Report, which quotes it extensively, but does not include it all (perhaps this also influenced Gavin's decision to bring it out separately). Among the points he makes that do not appear in the Chadwick report is that the "middle and upper classes" are the ones that "really cause" the "neglect of cleanliness" which destroy the lives of the poor (79), a statement which Chadwick may have thought impolitic in its bluntness. As Hamlin points out in his excellent study, Chadwick, as the architect of the New Poor Law, was highly motivated to elide "want of the necessaries of life" as a cause of disease—an elision against which the medics working under him sometimes rebelled.

But the maps here are more than a scientific representation of a specific physical phenomenon; they also serve a narratological function. The text is bracketed by two maps: the one at the beginning, which marks open sewers in strong black lines and the closed ones in double thin lines, and the map at the end, under which the details of the lines representing the terrain are just visible in areas heavily shaded by "cholera mist" (see fig. 1.1). The threatening dark shading of the mist represents a spiritual blight:

> . . . the accompanying lithographic plate of the parish exhibits the Disease Mist . . . ; the Angel of death [*sic*] not only breathes pestilence, and causes an afflicted people to render back dust for dust, but is accompanied with that destroying Angel which breathes a moral pestilence; for where the seeds of physical death are abundantly sown, and yield an abundant harvest, there moral death overshadows the land,—and sweeps with the besom of destruction to an eternal gulf! (Gavin 101)

16

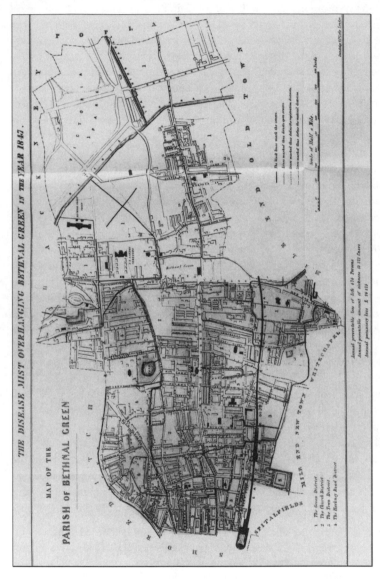

FIGURE 1.1. Hector Gavin, Map 2. Altered to show contrast in black-and-white format. Courtesy of Pamela Gilbert. Original can be found in Hector Gavin, *Sanitary Ramblings, Being Sketches and Illustrations of Bethnal Green, a Type of the Condition of the Metropolis and Other Large Towns* (London: John Churchill, 1848).

The people are mapped onto the land as soil—literally dirt comes to stand in for sinful people. It also visibly represents invisibility—in Milton's phrase, "darkness visible"—both in the cholera mist and in the dramatization of the obscurity under which Bethnal Green labors. If it can be seen and represented, it can be saved. Gavin opens his pamphlet with the following quote from the Health of Towns Reports and then explains his reasons for publishing:

> "Owing to the vastness of London," says Mr. Martin [in the "Health of Towns Reports", . . . *the rich know nothing of the poor* [his emphasis]. . . . It is true that some partial attempts have been made to display, both locally and generally, many of the remediable ills . . . of London; but no complete elucidation of the sanitary state of any one district has as yet been prominently brought forward for . . . securing the sympathy of the public. (4)

The language is replete with visual metaphors: Gavin will display and elucidate a parish lost in darkness, exemplary of a larger darkness hovering over London and other large towns. He concludes the text by observing that no one has taken an interest in or responsibility for the parish, "the very map of the parish, by which its boundaries are ascertained, is (or was a month ago), so tattered, old, and worn, as to be nearly falling to pieces" (Gavin 114). In a pragmatic way, this exemplifies the lack of care for the poor; were anyone actively taking responsibility for this parish, they would be likely to maintain an interest in the boundaries of their burden. But it also indicates, if I may put it this way, a metaphysical significance given to the map. The map "ascertains," but it also *maintains* a community as a parish, with leaders and responsibilities. The neglected map is the neglected community: ragged and ill defined. In fact, Gavin implies, it scarcely *is* a community; as he says, how can people living in such circumstances believe in "brotherly love"? It is simply a collection of human and other refuse. Should the map cease to exist, in some sense, the parish would be finally lost as a community, and as a geographic object of discourse and intervention. As the map turns to waste paper, the people are in danger of being swept, precisely, away, by that "besom of destruction," unregarded. He also implies that the map is out of date, that places (houses, people) are, quite literally, "off the map," which again intimates a lack of community care, and therefore an obligation to go, map in hand, and look at the terrain represented, remapping and reinscribing it. The map claims a certain transparency; it invites the reader to go, look for him- or herself, and see exactly what the map shows. Anyone, in Chadwick's model, with common sense, a good nose, and ordinary vision, could see and map the degenerate social and urban body, and this mapping itself is an act of recuperation.

Abstract representation is the mode by which the city can be produced as object of knowledge and, in turn, managed so as to perpetuate itself along the lines prescribed for it—to become more like the ideal mapping, fitting itself into a grid of manageability. Like a surgical diagram, the map shows illness as a dark sepia obscurity on the otherwise healthy body of the city, preparatory to a surgical excision. If Gavin's mapping invokes the coherent fate of an inadequately socialized social body, it also dramatizes the need to continually remap its terrain, in order to arrest decadence and record or invoke progress. Sanitary writers urge a continual vigilance—to look, and document, and look, and look again, as to lose sight of, or fail to oversee, a problematic district is precisely to lose control of it, to allow it to disintegrate or degenerate into that sea of wastes which forever besets the integrity of the social body.

THE MEDICAL PROJECT: SNOW

Physician Benjamin Ward Richardson, describing public reaction to the St. James's cholera epidemic, remarks, "such a panic possibly never existed in London since the days of the great plague. People fled from their homes as from instant death, leaving behind them, in their haste, all that they valued most" (xxvi). John Snow's analysis of this epidemic and his recommendation to remove the Broad Street pump handle are always cited in medical histories. Histories of medical maps cite Snow's map of the Broad Street epidemic as the most important development in medical mapping of its era. Snow positioned himself against the sanitarians, standing on the need for epidemiological expertise rather than the simple "smell is disease" test. In 1855, Snow gave evidence before the Select Committee, expressing his conviction that "he was no defender of nuisances, but . . . a bad smell cannot, simply because it is a bad smell, give rise to a specific disease" and that specific diseases were the result of specific disease agents (Richardson xxix).

Snow's *Report* begins with an argument for human transmission of the disease. The first map is of the St. James's outbreak. This is, of course, the topic of the paper, and the most impressive to the public not only because of the concentration of deaths there, but because of the fame of the parish as the location of court and metonym for aristocratic wealth of the metropolis.[1] Snow states that most deaths took place in homes very close to the drinking water pump, and shows all the deaths within a certain radius of the pump, which he defines as the "cholera field."

Additionally, he shows the locations of all other pumps in the area, and adds explanations for why some pumps were used less than others, and why some deaths apparently far from the Broad Street pump are actually related to it. All in all, the map requires a good deal of supplementary verbal explanation, totaling four pages for the basic clarification of what the reader is looking at, alone. For example, the map aims to show by the locations of the pumps that the Broad Street pump is the culprit. Yet in some heavily visited areas, other pumps are closer. This necessitates the explanation that "the water of the pump in Marlborough Street . . . was so impure that many people avoided using it," the Rupert Street pump was hard to get to, and the other scattered deaths were all somehow contracted when the victims were closer to the Broad Street pump (Snow 46–47). In short, even though Snow was right, there is nothing obvious about the way the map works, or the choices Snow made in constructing it. Yet, for all that, it is, as generations of historians have felt it to be, a striking map. Folding out of the report at a scale of thirty inches to the mile, the map marks deaths with coffin-shaped black bars. The results, in a simple black-and-white line map, are eye catching. And certainly there is a grouping around the Broad Street pump. Still, had a map reader been motivated to find fault, there is plenty here to undercut Snow's thesis—it is in the text that the objections the map might raise are nullified. It is too often forgotten that this map was widely refuted—by the investigators reporting to the Privy Council, for example—and that Snow did not use it to convince the guardians to remove the pump handle, but created it long after the fact.[2]

What the map does do, and what all disease maps of this period do to some extent, is to redefine a space, usually an urban space, by relating a certain human experience—vulnerability to disease—to some hidden or non-obvious feature of the landscape. In this way, thematic maps were very like anatomy "atlases" or pathology texts—they laid bare the "invisible" relationships between seemingly different things that only the medic/scientist's gaze could discern. In Snow's case, it was water and its flow, and the human activities around water, that defined a "field" or disease community. The community is demarcated by what we might phrase as the "furthest reach of the disease within a convenient representational area"—in other words, it does not include the cases contracted in Broad Street that terminated in the country or in hospitals in another parish. Further, it does not extend to other communities in London that suffered in the 1854–55 epidemic. However, unlike many sanitary maps, wherein communities were defined instrumentally, by boundaries of parish authority, Snow's map of the "St James's" epidemic spills considerably over into St. Anne's Soho. Parish boundaries become less important than the itineraries—the "practice of space"—which link the residents of this area in their use of a common water source. In turn, the anachronistic nature of the map freezes that human activity and figures it as a passive spatial relationship.

The next portion of the report doubles back to 1832, as Snow draws larger connections between water quality and disease. He uses tables to show parish variations in mortality, and connect them to a water supply, first in 1832 and then in 1849: "A glance at the table shows that in every district to which the supply of Southwark and Vauxhall, or the Lambeth Water Company extends, the cholera was more fatal than in any other district whatever" (64). He continues this examination through the most recent epidemic, using more than fourteen tables, mostly from William Farr's evidence, to illustrate various points about population, water purity, season, and so forth.

These tables are extensively discussed, and are themselves far more telling than the map which illustrates them and which Snow does not discuss at all. The map is quite beautiful, in three flat colors printed over a black-and-white map of Southwest London from west to east, including Putney to the Isle of Dogs to the north, and to the south of the Thames covering Wimbledon on the west to Sydenham on the east (see fig. 1.2, here in black and white). The colors include red (or pink) for areas served by the Lambeth Water Company, blue for Southwark and Vauxhall, and purple where the pipes are mingled. Obviously a commercially available map that Snow had printed over, it contains a good deal of extraneous information (railway lines and such). Deaths are marked with small square or rectangular spots, and there is no attempt to correlate them to structures such as pumps. This map is much more rarely mentioned by historians than the Broad Street map.

However, the second map is rhetorically interesting, and was interesting to its original audience, in that it shows an even less obviously visible relationship between disease and population than the first, more local map. Although Snow's maps were not important in "discovering" the causal relationships they illustrate, they were certainly important in allowing readers—guided by the expert testimony in the text—to conceptualize such relationships in a whole new way, having to do with the actions of humans in relation to the environment. The second, water company map does offer a new definition of a human community, much like the Broad Street map. The definition is based on multiple factors on a larger scale—location relative to the Thames, to particular piping, and so on, and, perhaps most importantly, on consumption. United both by access to a geographical resource and by consumption of a certain consumer good, the community achieves a certain political and legal status through this definition. (The 1866 epidemic would be marked by parliamentary investigations into the water companies and epidemiological analyses of their product and its sources.) And of course, it also shows the connectedness of a large and widely dispersed group of people through their interactions with the environment. All of these allow different ways of imagining community, and encourage them—by grounding the stakes in something as fundamental as the body and survival itself.

Perhaps most importantly, medical maps provided medics with a way to talk about populations in a way legitimated by that unique medical vision Foucault so compellingly described in *Birth of the Clinic*. Early on, sanitarians and public health legislators slighted medics, in part because the doctor was perceived as having to do only with individuals and their treatment—inevitably a private affair. For medics, it was thought, epidemics were just large numbers of individual cases. Medical mapping allowed medics to talk about populations,

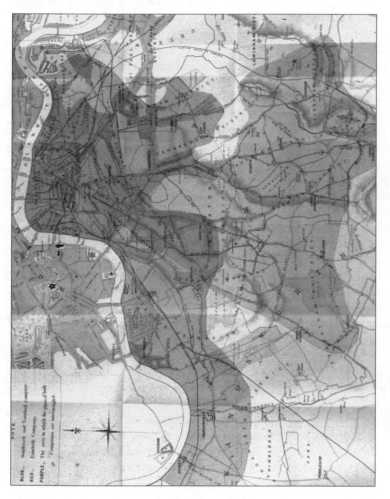

FIGURE 1.2. John Snow, Water Company Map: Detail. Altered to show contrast in black-and-white format. Courtesy of Pamela Gilbert. Original can be found in John Snow, *On the Mode of Communication of Cholera*, 2nd ed., much enlarged (London: John Churchill, 1855).

not in the borrowed terms of sanitarians, who were concerned with what the untrained eye could easily see (or nose, smell), but in terms uniquely their own, showing relationships not readily visible to the lay observer. It provided medics with a way of staking out public health as a medical, rather than simply a management, issue.

It also envisioned (and thus, in part, created) a larger spatial entity as vitally connected and participating in the same structure, and also as continuous with and affected by environment. If one portion of that entity was unhealthy, it could affect the entire organism through its circulatory mechanisms. Unlike Gavin's report, then, which emphasized the obscurity and isolation of Bethnal Green even while it gestured toward the compromised health of the urban whole, Snow's work vitally connected the visually and imaginatively isolated outbreak in St. James's with the entire urban epidemic, and portions of the city located far from each other, through water conduits. The city itself, then, could be seen anatomically as an organism, with circulatory systems vulnerable to contamination that extended throughout the entire urban "body" rather than miasmatically within a small radius; invisible, underground conduits could carry infection even to apparently "clean and sweet" areas—a point reinforced by the irony that most residents drank from the Broad Street pump because the water tasted better than that of surrounding pumps. As Snow pointed out, decaying organic matter actually aerated the water; it was precisely that which made the water dangerous that made it seem most pure to the inexpert senses. Further, it located the evil below the surface, within the "body" of the city and requiring a physician's analysis and a quasi-surgical intervention. The city itself came to be seen as a problematic organism, both because of its geography (poor drainage, water sources) and the activity of its population (drinking from particular sources, disposal of waste), which itself was in part determined by geography (people have to have water; they get it where they can). No longer could the city be seen as a basically healthy organism containing some specific problem locations, requiring local cosmetic intervention. The years of attention to morbid anatomy and the increasing importance of surgeons as a professional group since the 1830s almost certainly had a part in this shift from surface to depth, as it did in the shift from a sanitary to a medical model. This shift was also aided by the departure of Chadwick and the ascendancy of Farr.

It is hard to say what the effect of Snow's maps were initially. The *Report* was printed at Snow's expense, and, according to Richardson, he realized very little return on it. Reception was quite mixed, though Snow is generally referenced in subsequent studies as someone who must at least be refuted. On the other hand, he was widely known, and William Farr of the General Registrar's Office took a keen interest in Snow's work and data in the early 1850s, though he initially opposed his conclusions. It is not until the 1860s that he gained full credibility, when Farr himself proclaimed Snow correct. Even then, though, most medics did not subscribe to the belief in a specific disease agent, although the interaction of environmental effects and contaminated water were believed to be deleterious. In any case, by the 1860s, he is never *not* mentioned, and the first map, at least, was widely perused and imitated. Further, sanitary maps increasingly concentrated on drainage and water supply as a key feature of a site's healthfulness. This necessitated attention to land lying above the site in question, the sources and location of natural water conduits, and soil composition, as well as to the built environment. These maps also, in their "anatomical" rhetoric, treated the city as analogous to a body. The human bodies, invisible on the map of homogenous space that is the city, are represented by the personification of the city itself *as* population. Instead of the individual parishes that middle-class people must care for, as in Gavin's work, we see a large interconnected city wherein disease in one portion threatens the life of all; furthermore, remedies must be applied to the invisible, underground structure of the city through its circulatory mechanisms—its sewers and cess pits, its water conduits—rather than by the removal of obvious, superficial nuisances like dung heaps. The poverty of Golden Square dwellers is not seen as an important factor (in fact, Snow deemphasized the fact that the outbreak was in a slum, and promoted instead an image of the neighborhood as inhabited by respectable artisans, probably in order to discourage recourse to sanitary explanations).

Conceiving a geographical construct as a community and in turn as a body enabled these medics and social experts to bring the city conceptually into the domain of the social. One understanding of the city—as a region filled with private properties—was powerful in militating against centralized governmental intervention in sanitation and housing. If the city, however, were not merely a dwelling place of inappropriate bodies, but identical with them, then the city itself entered the legitimate domain of social intervention—which ultimately authorized not only sanitary, educational, and housing programs directed by government, but eventually allowed them to be government supported as well.

THE CITY AS ECONOMIC ORGANISM: BOOTH

The most famous thematic maps of London are undoubtedly those of the late nineteenth century Booth project. Booth was hailed as a "social copernicus [sic]," whose recentering of the metropolitan universe was understood to have profound effects on the understanding of the social body of London. This massive project sought to map many behaviors and aspects of life in London, but most crucially, it mapped poverty, street by street and often house by house. Booth used seven colors to distinguish levels of affluence, coding wealth as warm and light (yellow representing the wealthy and red the well-off), down through successive shades of cooler colors (pink, purple, light blue) to the very poor (dark blue), with the "vicious, criminal" level of poverty in black. In this sense, he built on the tradition of nineteenth-century iconography in the display of undesirable variables as dark shading and also the convention of conversion of economic into moral status, particularly at the lower reaches of the scale. As did Snow's map, it also enabled viewers to see the city as an organic and connected whole; unlike any map that came earlier, it worked at such a sophisticated level of particularity that it became possible to trace the trajectory of the spatial development and movement of affluence over time. It became apparent to Booth that the city developed in rings of population and that in older industrial sections where population was concentrated, poverty was sure to be found. It also displayed—though this was not frequently commented upon at the time—the proximate relationship between wealth and poverty: the wealth to the northwest of the Thames depending on the poverty of the north, the comfort of the middle classes throughout the West and central areas dependent on the poverty to the south and east. Most tellingly, it made visual knowledge of what had long been folkloric wisdom: that although extreme wealth clustered together, the upper middle class lined the fronts of large streets that backed onto and turned into side streets and courts of decreasing affluence. In short, it made the point that behind the large thoroughfare down which middle-class readers habitually walked or rode, with its evident display of health and comfort, there existed a thinly veiled reality of less fortunate, less healthy bodies upon which the display of affluence rested.

The "face" of London was deceptive; mapping laid open the corrupt body beneath the facade and could also begin to expose the laws by which it degenerated. As on an anatomical slide, the color of the stain revealed the nature of the tissue under the gaze of the scientist. Within this organic metaphor is included a corporeal model of circulation. It is clear that the middle classes represent the healthy tissue, the economic lifeblood of the city, the vibrant red following the major thoroughfares of the metropolis, backed by pink and lavender. Pockets, however, of economic corruption are vividly picked out in the colors of death. Seen overall, the west appears to be a healthy, bright orange-red with pockets of darkness. The east, however, and to some extent the south, range from a pallidly under-oxygenated pinkish-lavender to a chilling pale blue, with threateningly concentrated blotches of dark blue and black. Given the ethnic distribution of the London population, this darkness may have taken on racial overtones as well.

David Reeder provides an excellent analysis of Booth's work, arguing that "the whole point . . . was to reveal the regularities in the metropolitan condition, to expose its orderliness, and thus to make London comprehensible" (325). As Reeder observes, Booth is attentive to the movements of wealth and fascinated by what seem to operate as "rules" for the distribution in space of a particular class. Reeder notes that Booth accounts for the preponderance of wealthy in certain neighborhoods by noting the desire of the well-to-do to live on higher ground; areas that were cut off from major thoroughfares or that were cul-de-sacs susceptible of entry from only one direction tended to be inhabited by the poor (330). He states that this is part of Booth's "evolutionary and residualist" understanding of poverty: such areas form a "sump or settlement tank into which the detritus of the metropolis is poured" (Reeder 332). Reeder's metaphor—in part taken from Booth—is more telling than perhaps he realizes. Booth's understanding of poverty is profoundly informed by nineteenth-century sanitary and medical understandings of both public and individual health. Wealthy people did seek high ground, in part because it was, for at least half a century, believed to be healthier than the low terrain. Booth thus comes to his hypothesis through analysis of a medical understanding he shares with his subjects. His dislike of enclosed spaces also relates to sanitary science— enclosed spaces were thought to be dark and airless (a belief that is reflected in the anoxic tints of such sites on the map itself). But perhaps most crucially, we see again the notion of circulation which is encoded in the anatomical representation of London's body. These enclosed spaces are not connected to the circulatory vessels of the city; starved for the circulation, physically, of healthy air and water, and economically, of capital and labor, such areas wither and die, rotting and then corrupting the urban social body. Although somewhat attentive to differences between poor areas in his prose, Booth's color scheme homogenizes the poor, and, as David Englander points out, often areas were assigned to economic categories based on the inhabitants' behavior: one street was "changed from dark to light blue" because police reported that it was "not troublesome" (Englander 322), and Jewish immigrants, having social characteristics associated with several different classes of English (for example, personally clean but not conventionally "house-proud"), puzzled Booth's inspectors when they tried to assign a color to their neighborhoods (Englander 306–07). Thus, Booth's supposedly rigorous economic taxonomy was in large part actually based on the traditional categories of domestic and social behavior which had informed the mid-Victorian sanitary movement. It is not surprising, then, that both the iconography of Booth's map and (one might say therefore) the logic of his interpretations are founded on the kind of anatomical vision of the city as a body which was so powerfully instantiated in Snow's work, and on the connection of poverty and disease to immorality and domestic slovenliness inscribed by sanitarians like Gavin.

Booth's ambivalent attempt to measure economic health divorced from the social highlights a central problem of late Victorian liberalism: its contradictory affirmation of individualism and distrust of the mass, and its foundational assumption of economic interdependence. He remarks that, "When great aggregations of population are brought together, there is . . . a tendency toward uniformity of class in each section" (*Charles Booth's London* 313). Such poverty arises from "[t]he thousand opportunities for earning precarious livelihoods presented by great centres of population" (303), but it also arises from the fact that the metropolis is not a center of large-scale production, as Booth recognizes. In lamenting that large factories are mostly choosing to locate in the provinces, Booth remarks that London compensates with small workshops and sweating systems. These are "socially bad but economically advantageous," leading to irregular employment, long hours, and low wages (110). Booth is caught. On the one hand, he must acknowledge that these shops are "socially bad"—difficult for a proponent of laissez faire. On the other hand, while he admires their economic "fitness," in a passage only a page or so away, he refers to these East London trades as "a clear case of economic disease" (109). While the poverty of the East London worker is exacerbated by foreign competition and that of women home-workers, the real death blow is dealt by provincial British manufactory. The solution? Population must "adjust itself to the facts" and disperse to the new boom towns (110); in other words, the solution to the problem of the metropolis is to reduce its size.

Booth's understanding of the movement of population defined London as inhabited by concentric and centrifugal demographic rings:

> forces . . . through increased pressure at the center . . . tend to drive or draw the resident population outwards in every direction . . . generally the movement takes place gradually, from ring to ring, accompanied by a slow change of class. But the advance on new grounds shows a noticeable tendency to shoot out tongues, like the sun's corona. . . . These tongues follow the 'lie of the land' and the facilities offered for speculation in building; but the more important cause . . . is always found in the available means of communication. (*Charles Booth's London* 327)

He recommends a full-scale project to promote "improved means of communication" (which includes transportation), noting that, although some may worry that this will foster even more centralization, he believes it will have the opposite effect; small town centers will spring up in outlying areas (330). He calls for careful urban planning to avoid untrammelled building (which would lead to congestion) in favor of a more even distribution, with full communication, through roads and railways, to all parts of the urban corpus. In effect, Booth's vision of the metropolis as a monstrous organism which has outgrown its inadequate circulatory system leads him to a distrust of a city large enough to have a true urban core; such a size leads inevitably to decay and corruption, skyrocketing land prices, and overcrowding. In response to this, Booth recommends decentralization and a focus on "local life," the unreasoning and sick mass of the overgrown social body to be broken into its constituent parts. This formulation, both of urban development and decay proceeding in rings and of the healthiness of an unimpeded "flow" of labor and goods through the circulatory system of multiple bodies unified by a single communication system, has continued to be a foundation of urban planning for the past century. It still often takes its metaphoric base from the model of the city as an organic and unified body, and the metropolis as a cancerous overgrowth of the same.

There is a clear ambivalence in Booth's celebration of London—"our Jerusalem" (*Charles Booth's London* 339)—and his fear of its massiveness. Again and again, Booth's nineteenth-century liberal vision is evident in his distrust of the massive or uniform, and celebration of individualism and the domestic virtues; exasperated, he ends his chapter "Housing" in the section "Recommendations" by remarking, "I wish I could rouse in the minds of speculative builders a sense of the money value that lies in individuality, with its power of attracting the eye, rooting the affections, and arousing pride in house and home" (326). On the other hand, the metropolis is a necessary Darwinian crucible for the new England:

> Closely connected with the vitality and expansion of industry, we trace the advancement of the individual which in the aggregate is represented by the vitality and expansion of London. This is it that draws from the Provinces their best blood, and amongst Londoners selects the most fit . . . [characterized by upward mobility.] A new middle class is thus forming, which will, perhaps, hold the future in its grasp. . . . To them . . . political power will pass. (334)

According to H. Llewelyn Smith, writing for Booth, "healthy" London is a hungry organism comprised of British, and mostly English, provincials: "London is to a great extent nourished by the literal consumption of bone and sinew from the country" (in Booth *Life and Labour* 1:508). Impoverished East London, however (as yet another map graphically shows), is largely comprised of two groups: foreigners and native born Londoners. Since native Londoners are degenerate (the city causes good stock to decay in three generations), native Londoners are not desirable. Ernest Aves, also writing for Booth, cites as a "natural disadvantage" of London "the physical deterioration of Londoners" (*Life and Labour* 9:183). The "good" resident soon moves out toward the periphery; those who remain weaken and die out. London, thus, is a great beast which devours the best and brightest who are drawn in and fail to escape. "The Circe among cities," London "too often . . . exercises over her visitants her irresistible fascination only in the end to turn them into swine" (*Life and Labour* 1:554).

The good thing, however, about the London crucible, is the group of those who do leave. Charles Booth—waffling between this almost wholly anti-urban stance and admiration for the metropolis as crucible of healthy competition—amends Smith's report, adding that,

> Population flows out of, as well as into, the great cities, so that the movement, looked at nationally, is a *circulation*, which is not only healthy in itself, but essential to national health. It may be too much to say that this circulation is

caused by the deteriorating influence of city life, but the connection between the two is very close. To complain that men living in towns degenerate phys-ically is almost like complaining that the blood loses its oxygen in passing through our veins. . . . Movements of population—interchange between town and country, or between centre and extremities—are of the very essence of civilization: the word implies as much: and of these movements that between London and the provinces is the most notable example. . . . The mischief springs from the deposit which the stream of life leaves as it flows in country, no doubt, as well as in town. (emphasis in original, Booth *Life and Labour* 1:556)

Behind the healthy artery of circulation lies the anoxic capillaries clogged with the detritus of those bodies, like Dickens's Jo, who dies when he can no longer "move on."

To this end, Booth hopes for an increase in the promotion of a decentral-ized "individual responsibility." The mighty organism must be resolved into its component bodies; disconnection will eliminate both social decay and the per-ils of contagion. In this way, Booth recommends a decentered suburban ideal wherein both consumption and political identity revolve around the home: "Wherever a man may go to find his work, it is near home that he will seek his pleasure, and his wife will find her shopping . . . with brilliant shops, streets full of people, churches, and chapels certainly, perhaps a Town Hall, and prob-ably a theatre" (*Charles Booth's London* 330). These aspects of life can be sepa-rated from production ("Wherever a man may . . . find his work"). Thus the economic productivity affiliated with a great metropolis can be retained, while the dangers of its massive social body can be avoided by the creation of inde-pendent local social and political bodies based on consumption. (How this relates to his earlier observation that trade is leaving the metropolis for the provinces is unclear.) Economic interdependence becomes the principle of communication within the metropole, but Booth retreats to individualism and local identity to avoid confronting the horror of the urban social body as a mass. Whereas Gavin had noted the isolation of specific communities as cause for alarm in a radically interconnected urban body, Booth retreats to a subur-ban separatism to contain the cancerous spread of untrammelled growth. He carefully separates the economic body—a body which should operate on lais-sez faire principles enhanced by a free and open circulation system—from the political and social body which must be planned, groomed, and maintained in cellular units. Ironically, these highly "individualized" cells are all to follow the same model—a town hall, a theater, a center of consumption.

Booth, well intentioned, and deeply concerned about the high level of impoverishment, is finally limited by his liberalism. His vision both pays homage to Gavin's and Snow's emerging understanding of the urban body's permeability, the radical connectedness of economic and social factors, and its relation to health, and refuses that organic unity, attempting to cordon off that circulation by breaking down the city into homogenous and manageable units based on the bourgeois domestic individualism so often proposed as a liberal response to the culture and economy of poverty. The final disavowal of the coterminous nature of the economic and the social body fails to resolve the problems highlighted by the last thirty years of social analysis in England—that poverty produces disease and vice, rather than the other way around, and that metropolitan capitalism requires poverty, both local and peripheral, as a resource. Perhaps we can see here a dim foreshadowing of the ability of global capitalism to cloak the nature of its operations in a superficial demarcation of local markets and celebration of their "individuality."

NOTES

1. For a fuller discussion of the role of St. James's in this particular epidemic and the Snow studies, see P. Gilbert.

2. As has been recently pointed out by Howard Brody et al.

WORKS CITED

Aves, Ernest. "London as a Center of Trade and Industry." In *Life and Labour of the People in London*. Charles Booth, ed. Vol. 9. London: Macmillan and Co., 1897, 176–88.

Booth, Charles. *Charles Booth's London*. Sel. and ed. Albert Fried and Richard M. Elman. New York: Pantheon, 1968.

———, ed. *Life and Labour of the People in London*. 9 vols. London: Macmillan and Co., 1897.

Brody, Howard, Michael Russell Ripe, Peter Vinten-Johansen, Nigel Paneth, and Stephen Rachman. "Map-making and Myth-making in Broad Street: The London Cholera Epidemic, 1854." *The Lancet* 1 July 2000: 64–68.

Edney, Matthew H. *Mapping an Empire. The Geographical Construction of British India, 1765–1843*. Chicago: U of Chicago P, 1990, 1997.

Elliott, Henry Venn. "Two Sermons on the Hundred and First and Sixty-second Psalms as Applicable to the Harvest, the Cholera, and the War." London: T. Hatcherd, 1854.

Englander, David. "Booth's Jews: The Presentation of Jews and Judaism in *Life and Labour of the People in London*." In *Retrieved Riches: Social Investigation in Britain 1940–1914*. David Englander and Rosemary O'Day, eds. Ashgate: Scolar, 1995, 289–322.

Gavin, Hector. *Sanitary Ramblings, Being Sketches and Illustrations of Bethnal Green, a Type of the Condition of the Metropolis and Other Large Towns*. London: John Churchill, Princes Street, Soho (Printed at the Health of Towns Printing Office, 107 St. Martin's Lane), 1848.

Gilbert, E. W. "Pioneer Maps of Health and Disease in England." *Geographical Journal* 124 (1958): 172–83.

Gilbert, Pamela K. "'Scarcely to be Described': Urban Extremes as Real Spaces and Mythic Places in the London Cholera Epidemic of 1854." *Nineteenth Century Studies* 14 (2000): 149–72.

Hamlin, Christopher. *Public Health and Social Justice in the Age of Chadwick: Britain, 1800–1854.* Cambridge: Cambridge UP, 1998.

Harley, J. B. "Deconstructing the Map." *Cartographica* 26.2 (1989): 1–20.

Jarcho, Saul. "Yellow Fever, Cholera, and the Beginnings of Medical Cartography." *Journal of the History of Medicine and the Allied Sciences* 25 (1970): 131–42.

Reeder, David. "Representations of Metropolis: Descriptions of the Social Environment in *Life and Labour.*" In *Retrieved Riches: Social Investigation in Britain 1840–1914.* David Englander and Rosemary O'Day, eds. Ashgate: Scolar, 1995, 323–38.

Richardson, Benjamin Ward. "John Snow M.D., A Representative of Medical Science and Art of the Victorian Era." In *Snow on Cholera, Being a Reprint of Two Papers by John Snow M.D. With a Biographical Memoir by Benjamin Ward Richardson.* By John Snow. New York: Commonwealth Fund, 1936, xxiii–xlviii.

Robinson, Arthur H. "The 1834 Maps of Henry Drury Harness." *Geographical Journal* 121 (1955): 440–450.

Smith, H. Llewelyn. "Influx of Population." In *Life and Labour of the People in London.* Charles Booth, ed. Vol. 1. London: Macmillan and Co., 1897, 501–63.

Snow, John. *Snow on Cholera, Being a Reprint of Two Papers by John Snow M.D. With a Biographical Memoir by Benjamin Ward Richardson.* New York: Commonwealth Fund, 1936.

Stevenson, Lloyd G. "Putting Disease on the Map: The Early Use of Spot Maps in the Study of Yellow Fever." *Journal of the History of Medicine and the Allied Sciences* 20 (1965): 226–61.

Thrower, Norman J. W. *Maps and Civilization: Cartography in Culture and Society.* Chicago: U of Chicago P, 1996.

CHAPTER 2

Other Londoners:
Race and Class in Plays of
Nineteenth–Century London Life

HEIDI J. HOLDER

*T*he nineteenth-century British stage reflected, and helped shape, a growing fascination with urban life. As London's population rose dramatically in the first decades of the century, theater audiences demanded pieces that displayed, lampooned, celebrated, and decried the highs and lows of city life. The success of these urban comedies and dramas would depend, to a great extent, on the recreation on the boards of "authentic" London settings, more particularly a wide range of scenes designed to show *all* of London: public and private, rich and poor. A successful play such as W. T. Moncrieff's *The Scamps of London* (Sadlers' Wells, 1851) offered a panoramic tour of the city: scenes included the terminus of the Birmingham Railway in Euston Square; the dry arches of Waterloo Bridge; "a private room in a fashionable hotel in the West End"; a pleasure garden outside the city; "a room in Rat's Castle, otherwise the Dyot Street Hotel, in the Rookery, St. Giles"; and a splendid apartment in Mecklenburgh Square (playbill, Harvard Theatre Collection). As this list of sets (typical of urban plays in its inclusiveness) indicates, the characters in plays of London life would experience the city in its totality; so, by proxy, would the audience, thereby gaining a knowledge and mastery of the city's variety.

This sense of mastery, of conquering, as it were, the challenges of urban existence, is clear from the earliest of the urban plays. Consider the many adaptations of Pierce Egan's wildly popular novel *Life in London; or the Day and Night*

Adventures of Jerry Hawthorn, Esq., and His Elegant Friend Corinthian Tom, Accompanied by Bob Logic, in Their Rambles and Sprees Through the Metropolis. Egan's book tracked the adventures of "Corinthian" Tom, his country cousin Jerry, and their rowdy urban "guide" Bob Logic through London high life and low life. More a series of sketches than a novel, the book charts Jerry's "education" during his stay in London. Originally published in monthly numbers beginning in September 1820, *Life in London*—or *Tom and Jerry*, as it came to be known—appeared in a complete edition from Sherwood, Neely, and Jones in 1821. Crucial to the success of the work were the illustrations by George and Robert Cruikshank; the title page of the book promises "thirty-six scenes from real life." *Tom and Jerry* was hugely successful, so popular that the workers tinting the engravings for the books were constantly falling behind on orders. Numerous imitations sprang up in the popular press. By the end of 1821 several stage adaptations had been produced, the most notable being William Moncrieff's at the Adelphi Theatre, opening in November of 1821. (Other versions appeared in London at Sadlers' Wells, Astley's Amphitheatre, Covent Garden, the Olympic, the Royalty, and the Coburg. By one critic's account it appeared on one London stage or other every night for two full seasons.)

A key element in Egan's success was his emphasis on London's diversity. The frontispiece is the *Corinthian Capital*: a column representing a complete picture of the capital, London. From the "Roses, Pinks, and Tulips" at the top (the court), to the "bunches of turnips" and "strings of ingens" (onions) at the base (the homeless), the column shows the hierarchy of London life; in the middle, carousing, are our heroes: Tom, Jerry, and Bob. They are contained within a circle that represents a kind of wheel of fortune, connected to both the "ups" and "downs" of London high life and low life, and to images of the possible "ins" and "outs" of those worlds (on either side of Tom and Jerry are images of men imprisoned or released from incarceration).

The diversity of Egan's London was racial as well as geographic, social, and economic. The adventures of Tom, Jerry, and Bob Logic would take them, for instance, to the glittering Almack's assembly rooms in the West End, and then to All-Max ("Max" being slang for gin) in the East, where they would dance with the likes of African Sal and be entertained by the well-known black street musician Billy Waters. The African characters are firmly associated with the lower classes and the Eastern districts of London. The historian David Lorimer has argued that this association was the norm by the early nineteenth century: "Blacks became identified with labouring tasks and the lower social orders and in the process respectable people extended conventional attitudes towards their social inferiors in England to all negroes" (*Colour* 92). For the West End theater audiences, the sense of strangeness and the thrill of the classes' mingling were intensified by the presence of other races.

In Egan's own adaptation of his novel, staged at the Olympic in 1822 (and considered one of the more "genteel" adaptations), the partying in the "back slums" is more observed than participated in by Tom and Jerry, with Billy Waters directing the action:

BILLY: Now suppose 'em dance a lilly bit, it do 'em good after hearty supper.

He encourages dance between Sam and Sal:

SAM: How are you ma'am? the present company you see expects a bit of a dance from us, but I'm afraid as how you'll find me a wery awkward partender—but howsomdever I'll do my best—what shall we have? Something in wigorating?

SALLY: Me dance hornpipe.

SAM: Play the lady a nornpipe [sic]. (15)

The gentlemen arrive and observe the festivities. But in the more popular version by W. T. Moncrieff, the action is more wild, and Tom, Jerry, and Bob participate, disguised as beggars. (Jerry wears a sign that says "deaf and dumb"; Bob Logic advertises that he is the father of thirteen children.) The lady friends of the principal characters also show up, likewise disguised as beggars, in an attempt to keep track of their men. Sue, enamored of Jerry, is even approached by Billy Waters, who offers her a swig from his bottle: "I say missee, you drink eh! my Buckra Beauty?" (63) Later on, at All-Max, Tom and Jerry watch with amusement while a black infant is fed gin—"a drop of mother's milk"—then join in the merry-making and dance a wild reel with African Sal (83–87).

For the upper-class characters, such moments bring release from class boundaries. Egan makes this clear in the original All-Max scene in the novel:

It required no patronage;—a card of admission was not necessary;—no inquiries were made;—and every cove that put in his appearance was quite welcome: colour or country considered no obstacle; and *dress* and ADDRESS completely out of the question. *Ceremonies* were not in use, and, therefore, no struggle took place at ALL-MAX for the master of them. The parties *paired off* according to *fancy*; the eye was pleased in the choice, and nothing thought of about birth and distinction. All was *happiness*—everybody free and easy, and freedom of expression allowed to the very echo. The group motley indeed; —Lascars, blacks, jack tars, coal heavers, women of colour, old and young, and a sprinkling of the remnants of once fine girls, & c. were all *jigging* together. . . . (*Life in London* 227; emphasis in original)

Egan is describing a scene of exhilarating freedom. Tom, Jerry, and Bob are permitted, without consequences, to ignore—even violate—rules and norms that put Londoners in their respective places. By extension, the audience gets to enjoy the brief moment of revolutionary "leveling." Of course, this thrilling glimpse of disorder is contained within a novel (or play) that ultimately reinforces class distinctions. Still, the chaotic scene, with its challenge to social hierarchies, draws our attention, as it clearly drew the attention of some alarmed reviewers. *John Bull,* lamenting the popularity of the dramatizations of *Life in London,* put Egan's work in the context of revolutionary literature: "we would no more suffer a copy of the book whence these dramas are compiled to be seen in our house, than we would a copy of . . . *Paine's* Age of Reason" (414).

However outlandish the East End settings may sound, their effect was derived, in large measure, from their supposed authenticity. The bills insisted on the play's "truthful" images: its "twenty new scenes," we are told, were "painted from drawings [made] on the spot" (playbill, Adelphi Theatre, Harvard Theatre Collection). The figure of Billy Waters serves, in part, to heighten the play's realism. Waters was a well-known figure on the streets of London. A one-legged musician, Waters wore a plumed cocked hat and attracted audiences by playing the fiddle while dancing and whirling on his wooden peg leg. Waters survives in the historical record in part due to his representation in the many adaptations of *Life in London.* He was rumored to have been ruined by his resulting fame, and, dying in a St. Giles workhouse, was said to mutter, "Cuss him, dam Tom-mee—Tom—mee Jerry!" (see, for instance, the frontispiece of Hindley's account of the *Tom and Jerry* phenomenon).

The black beggars and musicians who appear in *Tom and Jerry* are evidence of the play's realism in its staging of the "exotic" population of the East End. These characters take no significant part in the play's action; more importantly, they do not share the chameleon-like social mobility of the central characters. While Tom, Jerry, and Bob Logic (and in some versions, their female counterparts) may wander through the various "worlds" of London, and can disguise themselves to blend in anywhere, characters such as Billy Waters and African Sal are fixed: they embody the foreign and "low" quality of the slums.

This essentialist reading of black characters would lead to a very specific kind of racial "comedy" of city life by the 1830s. Two burlesques by the highly successful comic performer Charles Mathews, staged at the Adelphi, rely for comic effect on black characters with pretensions to a higher social standing. In *Mr. Mathews' Comic Annual for 1831,* Cleopatra, the "negro nurse" employed in London by a merchant from Trinidad, is wooed by a "Black Adonis" named Caeser La Blond. Her employer strictly insists on her chaste behavior; meanwhile, she reveals to Caesar that "he . . . is a papa." The low behavior on the part of the servants is set off by their lofty names and attempts at elegant language. Caesar refers to his conquests among the local black servants as "African princesses," while Cleopatra will beg him to hide their child with "the Princess of Timbuktoo, who is a laundress of colour, living in Water Lane" (*Comic Annual* 91 *verso*).[1] While in the Egan-inspired staging of London life the upper classes could (with the correct "education") merge into any class and adopt any role, similar attempts by black servant characters such as Cleopatra and Caesar to

partake of the language, actions, and style of their betters merely serve to reinforce their "true" natures and provoke laughter.

Of course, the immense social knowledge and protean range of the
Eganesque gentlemen represent a fantasy, a dream of social power and knowledge (such "slumming" as Tom and Jerry engage in was likely to be as dangerous as it might be "fun"); likewise, the utter failure of Mathews's black servants
to step out of their prescribed roles might be read as fantasy, a reassuring picture of the absurdity of attempts to cross racial and class boundaries. Tom and
Jerry can associate with characters whose very "blackness" is a measure of the
freedom of the upper-class gentleman. At the same time, the emphasis on race
can be used to reinscribe social limitations. Many comedies from the 1830s to
1840s would focus on characters who seek upward mobility. The Adelphi, in
fact, made this kind of comedy something of a specialty. A play such as J. S.
Coyne's *How to Settle Accounts with Your Laundress* (1847) puts on display a number of working-class characters who strive for elegance and status. Even the servants are hopeless snobs: one complains wearily of the "impidence of the lower
orders" (Coyne 156). The down-to-earth laundress, who happily accepts her
place in life, humiliates her pretentious fiancé and orchestrates an ending that
puts everyone in his or her proper place. These comedies of failed social transformation often suggest something innate and inviolable in class distinctions.
Coyne's characters may desire to soar free of the bonds of class, but their very
language betrays them. Even as they aim for elegance of diction, they are tied
to the speech patterns of their rank, and often of their professions. The jealous
hairdresser Brown complains that his rival has "taken the curl out of my happiness." He plans to issue a challenge and declares, "let him choose his own
weapons—curling irons if he likes" (159). The choice of phrasing by such characters points to their status as workers or tradesmen, while the figurative language of upper-class characters is often drawn from non-laboring activities
such as the hunt. Adding race to the picture seems to strengthen the idea that
lower-class characters cannot transcend social boundaries. If their very speech
betrays them (an idea that G. B. Shaw would eventually revisit in *Pygmalion*), in
plays such as Mathews's their innate "lowness" is also cued visibly, by their race.

Mathews reworks this comic lower-class type in his burlesque *Othello, The
Moor of Fleet Street* (Adelphi, 1833), which transports Shakespeare's tragedy to
the byways of contemporary London. Here Othello is a street-sweeper, who
romances Desdemona, daughter of a brazier (brass-worker) in Bridge Street. A
good deal of the humor here relies on the (*Beggar's Opera*-style) contrast
between low characters and elevated language and theme.

There are a considerable number of theatrical in-jokes. John Reeves, who
plays Othello, was Jerry in the Adelphi production of *Tom and Jerry*. In Mathews's piece he is, on one level, continuing the fantasy of the ability of gentlemen (by definition white) to take on a role of any race or class. After all, black

actors did not, as a rule, play black roles (much of the fun seemed to be in shamming race). Later in 1833, the black American tragedian Ira Aldridge would present London with its first black Othello, when he took over the role at Covent Garden upon the death of Edmund Kean. Not all reviewers could bring themselves to take his performance seriously ("rather fair, for a black," was the response of the *Athenaeum*). Mathews's crossing sweeper gets laughs by shifting from an impression of Kean doing Othello ("Most potent, very reverend, grave / My noble and approved good masters: / Rather than speak I'll sing a stave / Relating to my strange disasters") to the kind of nonsense singing associated with the streets: "Tooral looral lay, te rol rumpti nay, / Tweedle Deedle rem! ri fol rumpti doodle em!" (55).

Again, class and racial types are conflated. Mathews's Othello bears a close resemblance to the emerging stereotype of the violent working-class husband (see Dickens's "Sketches by Boz" for other examples from this period): he tries to murder his wife with prussic acid. Additionally, as he succumbs to his jealousy, he sounds more and more like the comic black character familiar from *Tom and Jerry*. As the drunken Othello reels home, intent on murder, he sings:

> Bukra wives, dey like Old Nick,
> Very fair to face, sir.
> Very black dey do de trick
> Dere hubbies to disgrace, sir.
> Sing ching clinkqua, for woman's flaw
> De Africans have speedy law. (76)

While Othello here loses all pretence to "whiteness" in his speech, Desdemona's closing song (yes, this Desdemona lives) points up the actor's pretense of "blackness":

> Ladies I hope you'll like my love
> He's far more fair than black;
> If you applaud him, he'll improve—
> Now won't you dearest Jack? (79)

The last line clearly addresses John Reeves, who plays Othello, thus pointing to the "show" of blackness here. By drawing our attention to Reeves as an actor, the text highlights the contradictions inherent in the depiction of race in plays of city life. Again, the effect is to suggest both social restriction and freedom: the piece both mocks the lofty role playing of Othello (who ultimately lapses into a low "darky" type) and celebrates the role playing of Reeves, who can successfully portray a low and black figure, but who is ultimately, indeed *literally*, "more fair than black."

The tradition of staging race observed in Mathews and in the adaptations of Egan seems to offer scant hope for genuine dramatic characterization of London's minorities in the emerging urban drama. Plays centering on London life and continuing the tradition of "authentic" and panoramic scenery and effects begun by Egan were enormously popular throughout the century, especially in the mid-Victorian years. However, the characterization of Asians, Africans, and Indians remained limited to minor figures: servants, entertainers, and beggars (and often only in crowd scenes). While London might be home to Indian students, Lascars, African servants and artisans, and a variety of Asian workers,[2] they would be seen on-stage as Rampunkah, a "hindoo servant," in Joseph Derrick's *Twins* (Olympic Theatre, 1884); Sally Slack (a "proper negress") in *The Revolt of the Workhouse* (Victoria, 1838); Ah Luck, a comic servant, in Paul Meritt and George F. Rowe's *New Babylon* (Duke's Theatre, 1879); or "Calaban, a black attached to the Old Bailey," in one of the innumerable versions of *Jack Sheppard* (Pavilion, 1855). The devoted servant Ah Luck can stand in for many. As he shoos away the villain, who is posing as an "image" peddlar (who sells cheap pictures and engravings), he flings the man's merchandise after him, pausing when he picks up an image of the Queen; he hugs it to his breast, saying "muchee welly goodee woman—welly goodee to chinamen . . . God em blessee Queen Victolia" (Meritt 79).

Even the most inviting opportunities to expand the characterization of racial minorities in domestic and urban melodrama were resisted. Take, for example, Wilkie Collins's own adaptation of his best-selling novel *The Moonstone*. While the novel moves back and forth between the city and the countryside, all action in the play takes place at Rachel Verinder's country house. The slow sorting out of virtuous and wicked characters, which in Collins's novel is set firmly in the context of a past English crime committed against Indians, is in the drama reduced to a brief explanation of the dark history of the gem:

> BETTEREDGE: It was in the Indian wars. The moonstone was an ornament on one of the heathen images in those parts. The last place they defended against the English troops was their temple. The colonel was the first of the storming party to get in. He killed the two priests who defended their idol and he cut the diamond out of the wooden head of the image with his sword. "Loot" they call it in the army. I call it murder and robbery. And the curse of murder and robbery goes with the diamond. (15)

Notable in Collins's novel is the presence of Indian villains, who lurk both in the countryside and in London. They are a silent menace throughout. However, the crime that brings them to England (the initial theft of the gem) and the crime that occupies the narrative (the subsequent theft of the gem from Rachel Verinder) are committed by Englishmen. The novel's moral ambiguity is conveyed by several narratives that nudge us toward a revision of the obvious categories of good and evil. Take, for instance, the narrative of the obtuse but ostensibly pious Miss Clack. She recounts the shocking assault by the Indian characters on the seemingly highly moral Godfrey Ablewhite, an attack that takes place in a perfectly respectable neighborhood of London:

What did it mean? Taking the worldly point of view, it appeared to mean that
Mr. Godfrey had been the victim of some incomprehensible error, committed by certain unknown men. A dark conspiracy was on foot in the midst of
us, and our beloved and innocent friend had been entangled in its meshes.
When the Christian hero of a hundred charitable victories plunges into a pit-
fall that has been dug for him by mistake, oh what a warning it is to the rest
of us to be unceasingly on our guard! How soon may our own evil passions
prove to be Oriental noblemen who pounce on us unawares! (241)

Miss Clack, who fancies herself a good reader of character and situations, is
wrong on all counts. The Indian characters have not made a mistake, and Godfrey is no "Christian hero." The one major crime of which the Indians are,
finally, guilty—the killing in a London public house of the falsely pious Godfrey, who stole the diamond from Rachel—is clearly seen as poetic justice
("heathen" justice, perhaps, but nonetheless poetic). In fact, the novel ends in
India, with the gem's restoration to its proper place.

In the dramatic version Collins obliterates his sly use of the Indian presence. While the initial story of the diamond's tainted origins remains, there are
no Indians on the stage, and the sense that all England is, in effect, haunted by
furtive, vengeful aliens who may appear anywhere, at any time, disappears. In
the play, the villain Godfrey, caught by an English detective, will be turned over
to the English courts, not murdered near the wharfs of London. Indeed, the
diamond is not taken back to India by the triumphant descendants of the
wronged priests, as it is in the novel; Rachel, addressing the moonstone,
announces that "I shall sell you tomorrow, and the money shall be a fund for
the afflicted and the poor" (88). This ending dissipates the miasma of guilt and
doubt that hangs over virtually all of the English characters in the novel, in
which the Indian presence seems to put everyone on trial and the English system of investigation and justice proves inadequate, even irrelevant. What
remains is a rather unsurprising melodrama.

The elements of *The Moonstone* that Collins suppresses in his dramatic
adaptation—the foreign presence, its status as key to the revelation of crime,
and its role in the imposition of justice—do, in fact, surface in the Victorian
theater. But we do not find them in the theaters of the West End; we must,
rather, look to the less fashionable districts to the east and south. Here, in the
working-class theaters, we finally meet racial "others" who have key roles to
play in the dramatic action.

How We Live; or, London Labour and London Poor (author unknown), staged
at the Surrey Theatre on London's south side in 1856, is in most respects a very
typical example of the dramas of London's poor. (The poor had become a popular melodramatic subject mid-century, particularly following Henry Mayhew's
exposés of London poverty in the *Morning Chronicle*.) The opening setup, an
early morning scene in Covent Garden Market, would seem to suggest that we

will be following in the footsteps of Tom and Jerry. Arthur Townbred has been
giving a friend from the country, Charles Roseleaf, a tour. To Arthur's query,
"Well Charles what do you think of London life?," Charles replies: "bred all my
life in a quiet country town, what must I think when I behold the mighty
stream of human life that rushes past me in one continual flood?" (2). Arthur
provides the customary explanation of London types, such as costermongers,
but with a defense: "a hardworking and generally speaking honest race, who do
considerably more for the world than the world does for them" (3). The deeply
defensive quality of much of the dialogue suggests that the audiences for working-class plays knew only too well the stereotypical depiction of lower-class
characters as mendacious, alcoholic, or foolishly ostentatious.

Arthur and Charles need some assistance finding the guardian of Arthur's
fiancée, Clara, who is somewhere in the city, and must rely on a coster, Joe
Bunt, for guidance and knowledge. Here Bunt, a decidedly working-class type,
takes over the function of the worldly upper-class guide, such as Egan's Bob
Logic. In a further revision of Egan, the lessons Arthur teaches George have to
do not with safely having a good time, but with assisting one's fellow creatures.
Egan's dandies are now humanitarians.

The play offers a veritable parade of fallen and put-upon individuals, such
as Lady Mary (a "fallen woman" who attempts to kill herself in a leap from
Waterloo Bridge) and Captain George (a reduced gentleman who is now selling needles). The scourge of almost all the characters, both upper and lower
class, is the appropriately named Jasper Steelhard. But the undoing of Jasper's
villainy, and the restoration of order that is the expected conclusion of melodrama, is provided by Araxa the Hindoo. Araxa clearly recognizes Jasper, and
knows some secret from his past. He warns the goodhearted street-lad Jerry not
to inquire too closely into that past: "Bramah forbid it—my good boy my heart
clings to you as it does to my own child, for you were kind to the dark stranger,
when distress was on his path" (21). Araxa is established as part of the working-class crowd, and chats with them about the ups and downs of street business. All sorts of working-class types are here, including patterers, costers,
watercress-girls, lucifer-girls, and minstrels in blackface.

Araxa not only possesses key information (and the revelation of such
"secret" information is an expected scene in such plays), but also functions as a
critic of England's treatment of the poor. In the second act we see a pathetic
gathering before the gates of a workhouse. Araxa notes that "[t]he bitter cold,
the biting wind, and the falling snow have more pity, more feeling, than the cal-
lous welcome of the casual ward" (58). When Joe Bunt brings on a fainting
woman and sick child and tries to get assistance, Araxa observes, "There's a heart
in that man's body a nobleman might be proud of" (58). Note here the reversal
of the comedy of class inversion seen in Egan and Mathews. Rather than the
ridiculous attempt to ape "noble" manners seen in Mathews's Cleopatra and

Caesar, a genuine nobility is found in Joe Bunt. And it is Araxa, "the hindoo," who seems to be our moral guide.

Araxa's role only gains in importance. On his deathbed in the kitchen of the Travellers Rest, he makes a confession to Jerry. Once he was a confederate of Steelhard and committed forgery. Jerry the street-lad is, in fact, Steelhard's long-lost son. Araxa clarifies the relationships among a number of the characters in the play (thus, the woeful Lady Mary is Steelhard's wife and Jerry's mother). Clara, Arthur's intended wife, is saved from Steelhard by Araxa's revelation of his criminality, and Jasper Steelhard himself dies in a fire set to destroy the evidence Araxa presented to Jerry.

Such use of an Indian character to bring to light the true nature of a play's central characters and the real family ties among them appears even more spectacularly in James Willing and Frank Stainforth's *Glad Tidings*, an enormously successful play at the Standard Theatre in Shoreditch in 1883. As with the earliest London plays, such as the adaptations of Egan's *Life in London*, *Glad Tidings* banked on its highly realistic sets and stage effects, including a recreation of the recent sinking of the excursion steamer *Princess Alice* (here rechristened the *Glad Tidings*). The plot hinges on fraud and bigamy. Young Arthur Pierce has been accused of fraud (a crime actually committed by the scheming upper-class Margaret Musgrave, who in fact suffers an unrequited love for Arthur). As is often the case in melodramas from the second half of the century, the disgraced man travels to the outer reaches of the empire to prove himself in the army. Arthur goes to India, where, in a plot device that echoes *Jane Eyre*, he falls in love with and marries a "half-caste" woman who subsequently goes mad and dies in an asylum. Upon his return to England he marries the virtuous Isabel, much to Margaret's dismay. She promptly allies herself with Geoffrey Golder, who has designs on Isabel. Their joint attempt to break up the marriage of Arthur and Isabel is the focus of the play.

In *Glad Tidings*, the patterns of class-based urban realism seen in the mocking city comedies of the West End theaters have been duly noted—and reversed. In fact, the play attracted attention from West End critics and theatergoers precisely because it presumed to represent upper-class scenes and neighborhoods far distant from the environs of this particular theater (Shoreditch was a very working-class district of London's East End). While theaters such as the Adelphi could with impunity claim the right and power accurately to depict all of London, rich and poor, it was still, even in 1883, something of a novelty for an East End theater to assert this prerogative. *Glad Tidings* was very widely reviewed, and the critics, when not commenting on the questionable taste of the morgue scene on the docks that followed the "sensation" scene of the ship's destruction, homed in on the spectacular urban realism.

In particular, it was the act 2 scene in Hyde Park's Rotten Row that fascinated reviewers. As real horses canter by, upper-class characters meet, chat, and, in the case of the villains, scheme. Most of the reviewers touted the scene's success. *Vanity Fair* (6 Sept. 1883) noted that "the iron posts and rails over which we have all leant and talked, the trees, the idlers, the horses, the pony, the old gentleman on the hack, and the policemen are all here. The whole thing is an original and effective tableau." The *Referee* (2 Sept. 1883) hailed the scene as "the most wonderful bit of realism the stage has ever seen . . . it will be a treat for the East-enders who have never been in Hyde Park during 'the season' when swells and belles and equine beauties abound." The *People* (2 Sept. 1883) suggested that *Glad Tidings* was "a play that will not only in all probability for some time to come be popular with East-enders, but will likewise attract a goodly number of enthusiastic playgoers from the West End and the outlying suburban districts comprised in the term 'Greater London.'" Not all the reviewers conceded the tableau's accuracy. While the critic in *Funny Folks* insisted that this scene was "worth seeing by the most fastidious West-ender" (15 Sept. 1883) and the *Daily Chronicle* termed it a "triumph of stage management" (10 Sept. 1883), the *Echo* sniffed that "the illusion [is] sustained by horses, although their riders are certainly not good imitations of the class seen near Knightsbridge on an afternoon in May" (31 Aug. 1883).

The debate extended beyond a discussion of the Hyde Park scene to the representation of fashionable interiors. The *Referee* commented that the set of a baronet's drawing room was "quite equal to anything the West End theaters are in the habit of producing," and the *L.S.D.* (3 Sept. 1883) praised the same set, calling it "one of the most brilliant stage interiors imaginable, but in perfect good taste throughout." The *Evening News* disagreed on this point: "from Rotten Row we ride off to the home of rank and fashion, where the ladies and gentlemen disport themselves in full dress early in the morning" (30 Aug. 1883).[3] I stress this range of critical responses to illustrate the unavoidable intrusion of class into any examination of stage realism, particularly realism in depictions of urban life.

Of course, it was not only the set that mattered, but the character who appeared *in* it. Where the earlier comic plays of London life followed gentlemen on jaunts to the eastern realms of the city, or displayed and reinforced social hierarchies by lampooning lower-class black characters, *Glad Tidings*—like *How We Live; or London Labour and London Poor*—asserts the significance of working-class and minority figures, in this case by having them appear in upper-class settings. In the Rotten Row scene, one critic observes, there is a comic moment when, amid the fashionable riders, a "shaggy costermonger endeavors to drive his donkey cart up the Row" (*Illustrated News* 8 Sept. 1883). This out-of-place denizen of the east certainly got laughs; for working-class members of the audience, there was also likely to be a bit of nose-thumbing glee at this symbolic intrusion into an upper-class space.

A still more serious intrusion will follow. An Indian beggar girl is nearly run over in the Row, and is about to be ejected from the park by police, when she is recognized by Golder. The beggar turns out to be Juanna, sister to Arthur's dead "half-caste" Indian wife. Golder suggests to her a mutually advantageous scheme: Juanna will, with his coaching, claim to be the dead wife, thereby invalidating Arthur's second marriage to Isabel. Juanna, at first, is only too happy to oblige:

> GOLDER: Take this money—Come to me at this address and if you follow out my instructions you never need want for a home and money. Stay—Did you love your sister?
>
> JUANNA: Dearly. Can you ask?
>
> GOLDER: Would you care what harm you did her runaway husband?
>
> JUANNA: Care?—No. Revenge is dear to the Indian soul—I wish I could crush him as he crushed my poor sister.
>
> GOLDER: Enough—Mind, you must obey me in everything.
>
> JUANNA: Sir, you are the only being who has spoken kindly to the poor stranger in this land, show me how I can avenge my sister's wrongs and you shall find me both grateful and obedient. (Willing and Stainforth 23)

Juanna is, like Araxa, a pivotal figure. She makes a sharp statement about the cruel treatment of the poor, and she takes part in criminal schemes that she will later be instrumental in unraveling.

Both Araxa and Juanna are used to reveal acts of fraud and forgery committed by *English* characters. Juanna will eventually repent, and, after suffering mortal injury during the sinking of the steamer, give her written confession to the wife of one of the villain's associates. After a vain attempt at suppression by her husband, the truth is revealed. The unveiling of upper-class villainy was nothing new on the East End stage (Colin Hazlewood's plays at the Britannia in Hoxton offer a seemingly endless series of such moments), but the precise mechanism of society's reordering highlights the role of poor outcast Indian characters.

The emphasis on criminal acts of fraud and forgery deserves comment. Such acts propel the plotlines of many Victorian plays. Fraud or forgery can be seen as a particularly "male" crime, corresponding in melodrama to the particularly "female" crimes of the fallen woman: men sinned financially, women sexually (although, in some cases, women could sin in either context). Criminal acts involving financial chicanery (what we might see as white-collar crimes) were certainly seen on the West End stage, in urban dramas ranging from Andrew Halliday's *The Great City* (Drury Lane, 1867) to Oscar Wilde's *An Ideal Husband* (Haymarket, 1895). Perhaps one of the reasons for this plotline's popularity had to do with the nature of the crime. Fraud and forgery, in particular, are crimes not only involving cash but also *knowledge*. Victims of these crimes are not merely robbed but tricked; they are deprived of the truth, and sometimes even of identity. The multiple false charges of fraud against Arthur in *Glad Tidings* don't merely label him a felon: they expel him from his family and country, nullify his marriage, and partner him with a Doppleganger of his dead wife. The crimes in these plays disorder society and mask identity. By having Araxa and Juanna act as undoers of these crimes, as agents of enlightenment, as restorers of social order, the East End and south-side theaters are making ironic use of a character type that was already tied to issues of identity and class boundaries. The difference is that this character is now granted agency: he or she doesn't passively embody notions of class, hierarchy, and identity, but functions to impose such notions on others.

It becomes clear that the use of racial "others" in dramas of the working-class theater may, as with the earlier West End plays discussed above, be symbolic as well as "realistic." In Moncrieff and Mathews, black characters were used not only to complete a detailed and accurate picture of London's residents, but also to mark the foreign and exotic nature of lower-class areas of London. In turn, the working-class theaters presented plays that *thwart* such carefully drawn distinctions. The strange, exotic "others," such as Araxa and Juanna, can reveal connections between East and West (as in Steelhard's status as father to a street urchin). These outsiders are also granted a certain power over upper-class characters (such as Steelhard, Margaret, and Golder), unmasking their true criminal natures. And such representations do offer something beyond the hopelessly exotic, menacing, or fairy tale–like representations of Indians outside of urban melodrama (see Lahiri, chap. 3).

Ultimately, limitations in the roles granted to London's racial minorities are evident in plays from both West End and East End theaters. These "other" Londoners bear greater dramatic significance in working-class plays; however, one can't help noticing that Araxa and Juanna are both sacrificed. It is by way of their deathbed confessions that all is put right. In the end they are not fully incorporated into the world of London, but remain bound by their status as tools in a theatricalized class conflict. After playing their required roles, they are not needed. The presence of racial minorities in urban plays only *seems* realistic; these "other Londoners" are in fact deeply symbolic figures, embodying barriers or links between the classes.

NOTES

1. I am indebted to Manfred Draudt's examination of this sketch in his edition of Mathews's *Othello, The Moor of Fleet Street* (21–27).

2. For an examination of London's black population in the early part of the nineteenth century (when Egan and Mathews, for instance, were writing), see Myers, chapter 2. On the nineteenth-century Indian population of London, see Lahiri's introduction.

3. These quotations are drawn from promotional materials found in the clipping files for the Standard Theatre at the Raymond Mander and Joe Mitchenson Theatre Collection, Greenwich.

WORKS CITED

Collins, Wilkie. *The Moonstone: A Dramatic Story in Three Acts (Altered from the Novel for Performance on Stage)*. London: Charles Dickens & Evens, Crystal Palace P, 1877.

——. *The Moonstone*. J. I. M. Stewart, ed. London: Penguin, 1966.

Coyne, Joseph Stirling. *How to Settle Accounts with Your Laundress*. In *The Magistrate and Other Nineteenth-Century Plays*. Michael Booth, ed. New York: Oxford UP, 1974.

Egan, Pierce. *Life in London; or, The Day and Night Adventures of Jerry Hawthorn, Esq. and His Elegant Friend Corinthian Tom.* . . . 1821. New York: D. Appleton, 1904.

——. *Tom and Jerry; or, Life in London*. London: John Lowndes, 1822.

Hindley, Charles. *The True History of Tom and Jerry*. London: Charles Hindley, c. 1892.

How We Live; or, London Labour and London Poor. Ms. Lord Chamberlain's Plays, LCP 52958CC. British Library.

John Bull (London). 10 Dec. 1821: 414.

Lahiri, Shompa. *Indians in Britain: Anglo-Indian Encounters, Race and Identity, 1880–1930*. London and Portland, OR: Frank Cass, 2000.

Lorimer, D. *Colour, Class, and the Victorians*. Leicester: Leicester UP, 1978.

Mathews, Charles. *Mr. Mathews' Comic Annual for 1831*. Ms. Lord Chamberlain's Plays. ADD 42910. British Library.

——. *Othello, The Moor of Fleet Street*. Manfred Draudt, ed. Tübingen and Basel: Francke Verlag, 1993.

Merritt, Paul. *New Babylon*. Ms. Lord Chamberlain's Plays, LCP 53202L. British Library.

Moncrieff, W(illiam) T(homas). *Tom and Jerry; or, Life in London*. London: W. T. Moncrieff, 1826.

Myers, Norma. *Reconstructing the Black Past: Blacks in Britain c. 1780–1830*. London and Portland, OR: Frank Cass, 1996.

Standard Theatre clipping file. Mander and Mitchenson Theatre Collection, Greenwich.

Tom and Jerry Clipping File, Billy Rose Theatre Collection, New York Public Library.

Willing, James, and Frank Stainforth. *Glad Tidings*. Ms. Lord Chamberlain's Plays, LCP 53299I. British Library.

CHAPTER 3

"Men in Petticoats":
Border Crossings in the Queer Case
of Mr. Boulton and Mr. Park

MORRIS B. KAPLAN

*K*nown to their friends and to posterity as "Stella" and "Fanny," Ernest Boulton and Frederick Park, sons of a stockbroker and of a judge respectively, were arrested in 1870 for dressing in women's clothes and appearing out and about in London with other young men. The case received extensive publicity. Newspapers, journals, popular pamphlets, and correspondence among contemporaries reveal the problematic intersection between charges of sexual deviance and conceptions of masculinity intimately linked with social class. It served to focus anxieties about drawing the boundaries and policing the borders between public and private, respectable and illicit, modes of behavior. The case revealed dangers and attractions only half-concealed in London's West End, implicitly mapping an erotic underworld at the heart of the capital. Witnesses claimed to have believed Boulton and Park to be women, responding to them as especially flagrant—and especially attractive—female prostitutes. Agitation about the visibility of prostitution in England's cities and concern about the threat of venereal disease had been marked during the preceding years. The display of explicitly sexual possibilities in public spaces—literally embodied in women whose "painted faces" disguised the contagion they carried (Anderson; Nord)—was taken to threaten bourgeois domesticity and moral virtue. To these threats Fanny and Stella added subversion of the "natural" order of sex and gender. At the same time, these young men appeared in court as scions of the respectable middle class, represented by distinguished barristers who claimed they were actors and pranksters who had gone too far. Ironically, the attempt to discipline and punish these privileged miscreants became the occasion of a spectacular performance before an audience greater than any they might have imagined. The flagrant behavior of Boulton and Park confounded norms governing gender, sexuality, and social class. This chapter will map the plurality of boundary transgressions at issue in the case and examine the anomalous effects of efforts to patrol these borders.

The episode began with Boulton's and Park's arrest while leaving the Strand Theatre in late April 1870 and culminated in their trial before the Lord Chief Justice and a special jury at the Queen's Bench, Westminster Hall, in May, 1871. After an extended hearing in the Bow Street magistrate's court that attracted crowds of onlookers and was reported in detail by the press, they were indicted and tried for "conspiracy to commit the felony" of sodomy. The legal theory under which these sons of respectable middle-class families were charged was so problematic that a detailed record was made: the Public Records Office at Kew houses a two-thousand-page handwritten verbatim transcript of the trial as well as copies of all the depositions taken from witnesses at the magistrate's court, and the texts of thirty or more letters that had been entered into evidence. In recent years, the case has attracted the attention of scholars concerned with the regulation of sexuality and emergence of distinctively modern forms of sexual identity. Social historian Jeffrey Weeks has emphasized the linkage between "male prostitution and the regulation of homosexuality in England in the nineteenth and early twentieth centuries" (195), while gay novelist, playwright, and director Neil Bartlett numbers Fanny and Stella among the progenitors of modern gay identities and forms of life. More recently, William A. Cohen has provided a reading that emphasizes the multiple constructions of private and public in the case: his central focus is on the highly contested medical evidence and on the letters that police had confiscated (Cohen 23–129). My own investigation emphasizes the salience of class in the construction of Fanny and Stella and the role of London as a site of both social interaction and erotic fantasy. As Judith Walkowitz has shown, this "city of dreadful delight" could be read in terms of pervasive moral danger and enticing sexual opportunity.

The flagrant appearance of Fanny and Stella on the London scene was discomfiting enough to get them arrested. For over a year, they had been under surveillance for publicly parading in women's clothes, often followed by groups of male admirers. After taking the pair into custody as they exited a theater (in full drag and accompanied by a young swell), police searched their rooms and confiscated a large quantity of apparel, jewelry, photographs, and personal letters. The police surgeon subjected the two to intrusive physical examinations analogous to those authorized for suspected female prostitutes by the Contagious

Diseases Acts (Walkowitz, *Prostitution* 69–89).[1] Their letters seemed to reveal the existence of a coterie that shared a coded language, played fast and loose with gender identities, and raised suspicions about deviant desires and sexual practices. Police tracked two of their correspondents to Edinburgh where they conducted similar searches leading to the indictment of two other men. All these men were members of the respectable classes: "idle" gentlemen or professionals. Witnesses were produced who had seen Boulton and Park in drag at theaters and restaurants, at the annual Oxford-Cambridge boat race on the Thames, and at a fancy dress ball. On several occasions they had been ejected from the Burlington Arcade, the Alhambra Theatre, and other public places because of the commotion they created. Often mistaken for female prostitutes, Boulton and Park were characterized primarily by the ambiguity surrounding their gender. Although newspaper accounts and editorial commentary were couched in terms of righteous indignation, sometimes verging on vengeful anger, they also displayed some real confusion and did not completely disguise the authors' fascination with these exotic figures. Indeed, Hugh Alexander Mundell, the "idle" gentleman and son of a barrister who was arrested with them, testified that when first he met them, although the two wore men's clothes, he took them to be women in disguise. When they insisted they were men, this young man about town refused to believe them. (Of course, there is no reason to accept the self-serving statements of their admirers—given under the threat of legal prosecution.) Fanny's and Stella's transgression of conventional norms or, at least, their ambiguous displays of feminine and masculine characteristics, may have been among their principal charms. The cross-class character of their performance may well have enhanced their allure as well.

The presence in London of sites where men looking for sexual opportunities with other men might gather was not new, nor was the sight of men in women's clothes. However, Fanny and Stella wandered off the stage and outside the confines of a sexual underworld known only to the cognoscenti. Their enhanced visibility reflected both the proliferation of urban forms of life and the emergence of a heightened consciousness of gender transgression and erotic possibility among middle-class men able to explore the city. Their very public performances unsettled any easy division between private and public activities, domestic and commercial domains, bourgeois respectability and illicit sexuality, personal desire and social practice. Indeed, as the court proceedings and publicity about them reveal, Boulton and Park problematized the legibility of familiar public spaces. Central to the case were multiple contestations of the meanings of their promenades. The terrain they crossed was inhabited by diverse communities of interpretation: social reality pervaded by moral conflict and erotic fantasy. When figures like Fanny and Stella paraded openly on the streets of central London, they challenged conventional assumptions about gender and sexuality, respectability and transgression, business and pleasure.

"Molly clubs," established venues in which men looking for other men gathered together with like-minded fellows, may be dated back to the beginnings of the eighteenth century (Norton; Trumbach).[2] They provided venues that joined same-sex desire with gender inversion as men wore feminine drag, took women's names, and "married" other men—at least for an evening's entertainment. Something important happened when these figures emerged from these protected enclaves and began openly walking the streets of London's West End. Both the social scene and the persons who inhabited it were transformed by this "coming out." The metropolis was increasingly seen, by some at least, principally as a scene of sexual pleasures that could not be found elsewhere. Such a landscape even spawned guides for the curious visitor to the capital, not very well disguised in the language of moral condemnation. *The Yokel's Preceptor*, a London publication of the 1850s, warned newcomers of dangers lurking in the streets and whetted the appetites of those with unconventional tastes or restless desires:

> The increase of these monsters in the shape of men, commonly designated margeries, poofs, etc., of late years, in the great Metropolis, renders it necessary for the safety of the public that they should be made known. The punishment generally awarded to such miscreants is not half severe enough, and till the law is more frequently carried to the fullest extent against them, there can be no hopes of crushing the bestiality. The wretches are too well paid . . . supported by their rich companions—to care a jot about a few months' imprisonment. Why has the pillory been abolished? . . . Will the reader credit it . . . that these monsters actually walk the streets the same as whores, looking out for a chance! (in Hyde, *The Other Love* 120)

Despite the intensity of its invective, the guide identifies parts of the city that offered such sights and opportunities, including the Strand, the Quadrant, Holborn, Charing Cross, Fleet Street, and St. Martin's Court. The author mentioned individuals, one of whom, known by a woman's name, kept a "fancy woman" of his own. The guide painted a vivid portrait of their gathering places, appearance, and distinctive gestures:

> They generally congregate around the picture shops, and are to be known by their effeminate air, their fashionable dress. When they see what they imagine to be a chance, they place their fingers in a peculiar manner underneath the tails of their coats, and wag them about—their method of giving the office. A great many of them flock to the saloons, and boxes of theatres, and coffee-houses, etc. (in Hyde, *The Other Love* 121)

The spectacle of Victorian London offered and inspired a variety of erotic possibilities.

The public attention paid to Boulton and Park in 1870–1871 suggests that the appearance of men in women's clothes around the West End was still a novelty. Cross-dressing was not yet established in the public mind as an indication of same-sex sexual desire. In charging the defendants with "conspiracy to commit the felony" of sodomy rather than the less serious offense of cross-dressing, the prosecutor undertook to establish that link. The way of life and intimate relations of this coterie were subject to intense and protracted public scrutiny. They were reported in extensive detail in major newspapers, including the *Times, Daily Telegraph*, and *Reynolds'*, with headlines announcing "Men in Petticoats" or "The Young Men in Women's Attire." The illustrated papers included vivid portraits of the two, both in and out of drag. (By the time of their trial, they appeared as well-dressed young men about town; Fanny had even grown a moustache.) Quite a lot was made of assertions that Stella had lived with a young member of Parliament as his wife, carrying visiting cards that announced her as "Lady Arthur Clinton." Lord Arthur had also been charged in the case, but he died before the trial under circumstances that led to suspicions of suicide.

The case was vigorously contested, and the middle-class men were represented by some of the leading barristers of the day. They offered evidence of Boulton's and Park's longtime interest in theatrical performances, amateur and professional, in which both took women's roles. The well-financed defense team called eminent professors of medicine to testify as to the innocence of the men's bodily condition and to challenge "expert" testimony on the effects of repeated acts of sodomy. The uncertainty regarding the significance of Fanny and Stella's female impersonations permitted even the most sober accounts to dwell on their appearance and to capitalize on the interest displayed by crowds of people who flocked to the Bow Street magistrate's court to see them. The police reports came to resemble the society and fashion pages:

> When placed in the dock, Boulton wore a cherry-coloured evening dress trimmed with white lace; his arms were bare, and he had on bracelets. He wore a wig and a plaited chignon. Park's costume consisted of a dark green satin dress, low-necked, trimmed in black lace, of which he also had a shawl around his shoulders. His hair was flaxened and in curls. He had on a pair of white kid gloves. (*Times*, 30 April 30 1870: 11)

The pair's second court appearance proved a different matter: "the Bow-street Police-court and its approaches were literally besieged by the public. . . . The prisoners appeared in male apparel on this occasion, much to the disappointment of the crowds assembled to see them." The paper accompanied this apparent fascination with a moral gloss: "The case excited unusual interest, probably owing to the notoriety acquired by certain young men who, for years past have been in the habit of visiting places of public resort in feminine attire, and who have been occasionally turned out or compelled to retire to avoid the consequences of the public indignation excited by their presence when detected" (*Times*, 7 May 1870: 11). People's responses were more ambivalent than the *Times's* surmise, suggesting that any unitary "public indignation" was a journalistic fiction that cloaked a far more diverse range of reactions. The popularity of the court proceedings gives the game away: a week later, "[t]here was the usual rabble outside but ample provision had been made . . . to prevent the inconvenient crowding of the court. Nevertheless, the small area of the building was quite full, the audience including many persons of rank, besides many literary and theatrical celebrities" (*Times*, 14 May 1870: 10). The next week, the courtroom was again filled to capacity with crowds outside in the street: "Boulton and Park . . . appeared to be as cool and collected as on each former occasion, although looking somewhat the worse for their three weeks confinement in prison" (*Times*, 21 May 1870: 11). As more details emerged about the lives of the defendants and their circle of friends, a more complex "public opinion" was articulated:

> During the reading of the letters the audience in the body of the court appeared to be exceedingly amused, and the prisoners themselves smile occasionally. Certain expressions of endearment addressed by one man to another, caused such an outburst of laughter that Mr. Poland [for the Crown] begged that such unseemly demonstrations might be checked . . . but neither the admonition of the Bench nor the repeated remonstrance of . . . officers of the Court had any appreciable effect upon a certain portion of the public. (*Times*, 30 May 1871: 13)

Recall that the "rabble" has been kept outside; this indoors "portion" may well include "celebrities" and "persons of rank." In trying to contain Fanny and Stella's performances by arresting them, the authorities got more than they bargained for.

For a month or so in the spring of 1870, the Bow Street magistrate's court offered one of London's most beguiling entertainments. The newspaper accounts, and those in the penny pamphlets that began to circulate, relied heavily on the details of testimony offered at Bow Street. Only the medical evidence, which does not concern us here, was suppressed. In reconstructing some "tales of the city" that emerged in this queer case, I will rely on the depositions submitted to the court reflecting testimony at Bow Street.[3] The first will be the hapless Mr. Mundell, who was arrested with the defendants, but eventually appeared as a witness for the prosecution. His testimony provides glimpses of urban social life as well as the ambiguous charms of Boulton and Park. The former quite captured his interest:

> I knew the prisoner Boulton by the name of "Stella," no other name till I was in the Surrey Theatre. I made his acquaintance on the 22nd of April at that theatre, the two prisoners were there together in the dress circle. . . . I went there alone. I was principally in the stalls, my attention called to them, as being two women dressed in men's clothes, and I believed them to be women. They

went together to an adjoining public house. I followed them, and they afterwards went back to their seats. . . . I followed them again. They said, I think
you're following us. That was said in a joking manner. I said I think we are.
They said nothing but returned to the dress circle, where they stood looking
over. We got into conversation, after which I asked them if they would like
to go behind the scenes. (10)

The play itself was eclipsed by the flirtatious sociability that marked the Victorian theater; Fanny and Stella in their balcony box provided part of the spectacle for Mundell in the orchestra below. The threesome entertained themselves
so well during and after the intermissions that they decided to return together
at a later date to see what they had missed of the play. Mundell accompanied
the pair across Waterloo Bridge: "As we were walking, I chaffed them, thinking
they were women dressed in men's clothes, I told them, when they walked they
had better swing their arms about a little more. We parted at the Strand end of
Waterloo Bridge, they going toward the City. I went home" (12). Their next
encounter was again at the Surrey Theatre where, dressed in women's clothes,
they handed him a letter: "the handwriting appeared to me like a woman's, the
substance of the letter was that they were men, and I told them I did not believe
it. They said it was quite true, we are men. I believed that they had written the
letter as a joke" (14). There they were joined by another man. All four went
back to finish the play, then off to supper at the Globe Restaurant. When
briefly alone with the object of his affection, Mundell sought an advantage: "I
treated them as ladies. Stella/Boulton keeping me off whenever I made any
advances. I put my arm around her back once, sure would have gone on, but
the strange gentleman returned to the box, which prevented me. Boulton kept
me off as much as he could" (16). The dance of proper names and pronouns
reflects the pervasive uncertainty about how to refer to his companions after
their arrest had disclosed their male sex.

The trip to the Strand Theatre was the culmination of Mundell's pursuit
of Stella. He had secured an invitation to join them at Park's rooms, complaining that he had failed to get Boulton's address. There, once again he found
them in men's clothes, but Mundell insisted he had continued to believe them
women. The visit was musical: his hosts played the piano and talked about their
theatrical performances. They agreed to go to the theater that evening, where
Park had reserved a box for "Mrs. Graham." In the interim, Mundell accompanied them to Chancery Lane for a visit to friends, after which they all went
shopping. They took a cab to a glover's on Oxford Street and a jeweller's in
Portland Place. Mundell claimed that he had paid for nothing: "nor did I give
money to either of the prisoners." At the Strand, his companions dressed as
women: "I saw Park's dress was torn when in the box, a few stitches in the
flounce. . . . There was nothing wrong in the box at the Strand, they behaved
themselves as ladies" (21). Although told that they were men by another man

in the box, Mundell continued to resist: "I said, I had my doubts very much about one, but I was certain Boulton was a woman, and I was never taken in so in my life."

It is difficult to evaluate the young gentleman's testimony. He succeeded in avoiding prosecution as party to the "conspiracy to commit the felony" of sodomy, but admitted at trial that he had assumed Fanny and Stella were not at all ladies in the proper sense, but female prostitutes. Was that all there was to it? Or did Mundell enjoy the ambiguities of their gender more than he admitted? Was his refusal to accept their announcement of masculinity a way of protecting his own status while continuing to flirt with pleasure and danger? We cannot know, since his pursuit of Stella ended with the arrest of all three of them. Police Superintendent James Jacob Thomson testified that he had arrived at the Strand at about ten o'clock that night, where he saw the prisoners in a private box dressed as women: "Boulton was pointed out to me as supposed to be the Duchess of Manchester" (1). Officer William Chamberlain, who had followed Fanny and Stella to the theater from their rooms at 13 Wakefield Street, testified that "Park . . . went into the Ladies room and asked a female there to pin up a portion of the dress he was wearing which had come undone. The female did so, and Park gave her something for her trouble" (5). Eventually the attendant herself would be called to corroborate this offense. The resolution of Mundell's doubts about his companions' gender was finally effected, not by a "joking" note or sexual liaison, but by the evidence of a police surgeon who attested in court to Boulton's and Park's biological sex, as well as to other anatomical details that the papers chose not to report.

The hearings at Bow Street that so engaged various portions of the London public revealed that the police had Stella and Fanny under surveillance for over a year. Their own observations were augmented by reports from theater managers and security personnel at the Burlington Arcade. After the arrest, police received evidence from others who had seen Fanny and Stella promenade about the town: the coachman who drove them in drag to the Oxford-Cambridge boat race; the young man who invited them to a fancy dress ball the next night, as well as two of his female guests; an outraged gentleman who had stolen a kiss from Stella in a restaurant and felt humiliated by the eventual disclosure of her sex. The prosecutors and police were not satisfied with this evidence of public display, but searched out intimate details of the defendants' private lives. The multiple arenas of interaction displayed in this case confound standard dichotomies between private and public spheres. The evidence conveys a complex picture of distinctively urban forms of life. London is revealed as a site of individual freedom, public performance, and social surveillance. John Reeves, who worked as staff superintendent at the Alhambra Theatre, testified that he had known Boulton and Park for over two years, having many times seen them at the theater. Their first meeting ended with his ejecting them from the premises:

My attention was first drawn to them two years ago when they were dressed as women. They were there together. I went to them and desired them to leave, as the public believed they were dressed as women. A person who was in their company and who I had often seen before, told me not to interfere, it was a mistake. I said it's no mistake with me. I believe they are men dressed as women and they'll have to leave. I called assistance then and we marched them out of the place and their friends followed them. (39)

Reeves reported that the pair had been "walking about as women looking over their shoulders as if enticing men." When they left, three or four men followed them. A few months later, they returned to a less friendly reception. Reeves found them surrounded by a hostile group: "they were creating a disturbance, and persons believed them to be men" (40). Later they varied their theater-going routine. They appeared dressed as men, but with their face and neck painted and powdered: "their shirt collars [were] much lower than they are now, their waistcoats were very open. They looked at people as they passed, and their manners were more feminine than masculine" (40–41). Their femininity was not that of proper ladies: "I had heard them make noises with their lips, the same that I have heard made by females when passing gentlemen on the street" (42). The general impression was the same as that made by street-walkers, but with a difference: "I could not tell whether they were men or women. Sometimes I thought they were women, sometimes I thought they were men. Whenever I have seen them, their faces have been painted" (43). Once, they took a private box: "I saw people looking up at the boxes they were in, and saw that they were playing all sorts of frivolous games with each other. They were looking in front of the box, handing cigarettes backwards and forwards to each other and lighting them by gaslight" (43). When Reeves asked them to leave this time, they offered him a brandy and soda. He not only refused their offer, but also saw that the guinea they had paid for the box was returned. Reeves claimed to have seen Boulton and Park at the Alhambra over twenty times, but only twice in women's clothes. He had also observed them in Regent Street, dressed as men, with their faces painted.

It is not far from Regent Street to the Burlington Arcade on Piccadilly. Historian Erika Diana Rappaport describes the stores in this early shopping mall as "dedicated to an aristocratic and upper-middle-class market. . . . [T]ypically [they] remained quite small, rarely advertised, and spent little effort on window display" (Rappaport 151). Maintaining a milieu congenial to an elite clientele required a private security staff, working with police, to exclude undesirable elements. This was not so easy to do, as George Smith, formerly the beadle in the Burlington Arcade, revealed. Called to testify about his own encounters with Boulton and Park, he disclosed that he had been sacked for routinely accepting payment from female prostitutes. In exchange he would allow them to walk freely within the sanctuary. Smith, a former policeman, defended his conduct on the grounds that it was good for business. He insisted that the shop owners themselves knew that "gay ladies" were among their best customers and adamantly denied the insinuation that he later ejected women from whom he had accepted payment (53). As to Fanny and Stella, that was another matter entirely. Smith allows us briefly to hear the voice of Stella, who tartly resisted the beadle's relentless discipline:

> I went up to Boulton and said, "I have received several complaints about you. . . . I have seen enough of your conduct to consider you to be an improper person to be in the Arcade, you must leave at once. . . ." Boulton said [to a companion named Cumming], "Take no notice of that fellow" in a feminine manner. . . . I forcibly took hold of Boulton and ejected him at the Piccadilly end. Cumming followed us down to the end of the Arcade and said something. I took hold of him saying, "You are as bad as the other. You leave the Arcade at once." and I put him out on to the pavement. There were a good many gentlemen present at the time and some of them hissed Boulton and Cumming. Holden the Constable stood there and saw me eject them. . . . I saw the prisoner Boulton and Cumming about a fortnight after this coming down the Arcade towards Piccadilly. I was in uniform and they saw me, and I went towards them. On seeing me, they directly rushed into a hosier's shop. . . . I stood at the door till they came out. I said to Boulton "I have cautioned you not to come here, you'll leave the Arcade at once." He said, "I shall go where I like." I replied, "You'll do nothing of the sort, you'll go out." He tried to pass me to go up the Arcade, and I again ejected him. (49–51)

What was all this fuss about? Smith offered this account: "I noticed his face. It was painted very thickly with rouge and everything else on. He always caused such commotion, everybody was looking at him. I watched them and saw Boulton turn his head to two gentlemen who passed them, smile at them, and make a noise with his lips, the same as a woman would for inducement" (49). The crowning moment occurred when Boulton addressed the beadle as "Oh, you sweet little dear": "I made a note of that. It was about January or February 1869, when Boulton looked at the two gentlemen" (52). Smith refused to answer questions about his current means of support. His admission to accepting money from "gay ladies" raised the suspicion that his determination to exclude Boulton, Park, and Cumming from the arcade may have resulted from their teasing attempts to resist or to charm him rather than offer a bribe.

London offered many opportunities for Fanny and Stella to display their charms. In addition to theaters and shopping arcades, there were public festivities and private celebrations. The Oxford-Cambridge boat race, held on April 6 in 1870, offered a chance to go out for a riverside picnic and to attend a fancy dress ball at a hotel in the Strand. Boulton and Park hired a coach to take them to Hammersmith Bridge; by the time they got there, it was too crowded actually to get onto the bridge. They watched the race in the crowd along the bank while their brougham waited. Henry Holland, who drove the coach, was among those who testified at Bow Street. He had been told his customer was a "Mrs. Parker," and he patiently ferried the pair and a changing roster of male companions around the city before and after the race. Park appeared first, reporting that "her" sister was not yet ready, so they went off to get a hamper of food, stopping at a few public houses for refreshment along the way. Later they collected Boulton as well. After the race, they visited several more pubs, as well as a pastry shop. Fanny and Stella were generous in providing food and drink for their driver as well as themselves. The arrangement worked well enough for Holland to be engaged again later in the month. Told this time he was employed by "Mrs. Graham," he took the pair and their friends (including Mundell) to the Surrey Theatre and afterwards to dinner at the Globe Restaurant. Holland claimed he had no idea that Boulton and Park were men, as on both occasions they were dressed as women. In response to a question about all those stops along the way, he stated that "They appeared sober when they went into the different public houses" (38).

On the day of the boat race, the driver had left them at the Royal Exeter Hotel in the Strand, where Park had discharged him. A gentleman called Amos Westrop Gibbings had invited Boulton and Park to be his guests at the hotel and to attend a ball there the next evening. Gibbings cut quite a figure when he appeared in the magistrate's court, creating a stir that was reported in the papers. He returned from Calais when he had heard of his friends' arrest and voluntarily came forward to testify on their behalf. He calmly announced that he himself had often performed female parts in theatricals, usually for charity, but also more generally. He listed a number of his roles, including Lady Teazle in Sheridan's *The School for Scandal*. Having seen Boulton perform as Mrs. Chillington in *The Morning Call* at the Egyptian Hall (in which Lord Arthur Clinton played opposite), Gibbings wrote, inviting him to be his special guest at the Royal Exeter Hotel. Before the ball, Gibbings, Boulton, and Park, dressed as ladies, enjoyed supper together. Then:

> It was to have been a very small party but it swelled to 45. There were many gentlemen but only myself, the two prisoners, Thomas, Cumming, and Peel were dressed as females. Several ladies were there, eight ladies. There was no impropriety that I saw in the room the whole night. There was no conceal-ment as to the gentlemen who were dressed as ladies. . . . The servants and attendants knew all about it. The servants came to see us when we were dressed in the ball room. (162)

Two of the lady guests were called to testify at Bow Street: Maria Cavendish more or less confirmed Gibbings's view of the event, although she told of some conflict among the members of her own party, having nothing to do with Boulton, Park, or cross-dressing. Her companion Agnes Earl seemed more confused about the whole thing, protesting in court that she did not wish to attend such a party again. Gibbings himself admitted that "There was a squabble towards the end of the evening and I shut up everything" (162). Still it had been a social success for the host and his entourage: "We who were dressed as women at the Ball, danced with men. The prisoners also danced with men. . . . Nearly all the gentlemen who were at the ball called on the following afternoon" (169).

Mr. Gibbings almost stole the show from Fanny and Stella, who were not permitted under the law of the time to testify on their own behalf. He was quite forthcoming about his cross-dressing: "1 went to several theaters during the week. I can't remember to which I went in female attire. Boulton went with me twice to Highbury Barn, a Bal Masque, dressed as a man." Although manifestly unconventional in his style of life, this young man of twenty-one carefully drew his own lines of propriety: "I have gone about dressed as a woman in the day time in a carriage not more than three times. I never went out so dressed in the day time with the intention of walking in the street. On one occasion I was in a carriage which broke down in the Haymarket, and I was then compelled to walk down half the street, much against my will" (171). Given the reactions to Fanny and Stella's public promenades, it would seem Gibbings was eager not to be mistaken for a streetwalker. He explained to the court: "Going about in drag is a slang term for men going about in women's clothes" (172). Drag might be defensible in theatrical and social contexts but walking the streets seemed to cross a line, even for Mr. Gibbings. Violating gender norms may have been less serious than the cross-class performance of street prostitution. Edward Nelson Haxell, landlord of the hotel which was also known as Haxell's, gave added weight to Gibbings's testimony. He described the latter as "a very old customer of mine" and "a gentleman of independent fortune, and not in any employment to my knowledge." Gibbings had introduced Boulton to Haxell as "the best amateur actress off the Boards, and I knew he was a man." Haxell saw the defendant half-a-dozen times in women's clothes during his stay at the hotel. He testified that Gibbings had explained to him the meaning of "going about in drag" and swore "on his oath" that "every gentleman at the ball knew that the young men in female attire were really men." At this point, the *Times* reported, "[t]here was a most indecent manifestation of applause expressed by stomping and cheering: which the court had to reprimand." Young Gibbings must have been a man of commanding self-assurance. The marks of class privilege inflected the unconventional style of dress and gender performance that he so matter-of-factly described and enacted. His aristocratic bearing impressed audience, court, and reporter alike:

> His appearance in the witness box was regarded with intense curiosity and created quite a sensation in court. The young man stepped into the witness-box without any sign of diffidence, and gave his evidence with remarkable

clearness and self-possession. His voice and manner were decidedly effeminate. He spoke in a slight lisp and with an air of simplicity and candour which impressed the court materially in his favour. He appeared to regard the modern pastime of "going about in drag" as perfectly harmless and repudiated with indignation the notion that he was being made the dupe of others, or that he was in any way implicated in the nefarious actions sought to be established by the prosecution.

The *Times* also reported an application to the court by a Mr. Collette on behalf of the Society for the Suppression of Vice: "He said that a great many letters had been addressed to the Society and deputations had waited upon him, urging the Society to interfere to prevent the publication of any further evidence in the case in the newspapers ... for the sake of public decency." The sources of their concern were made evident by a concluding note: "A large portion of the crowd outside the Court cheered the prisoners as they were stepping into the van, while others booed and hissed at them. Boulton took off his hat, and both the prisoners bowed to the mob in return" (*Times*, 23 May 1870: 13). The case of Boulton and Park turned the Bow Street magistrate's court into an urban spectacle where moral and cultural conflicts were dramatized and played out.

The scene at Queen's Bench, Westminster, where the pair and their alleged co-conspirators were tried about a year later before the Lord Chief Justice was rather more dignified but no less widely publicized. Once again, newspapers reported on Mundell's ill-fated flirtation and the attempts to discipline the cross-dressers in their visits to theaters and the Burlington Arcade. Gibbings's ball at Haxell's Hotel was no longer on offer. The prosecution relied heavily on the medical evidence, which self-destructed in the course of the trial, and on a very detailed examination of the letters and living arrangements of the group (Cohen 77–84, 110–120). Charles Upchurch has argued that people high up in the government had seen from the earlier proceedings that the police intervention energized hitherto quiet minorities and brought out a display of unorthodox forms of life that undermined efforts to contain them. Although it is hard to prove deliberate agency, the case of Boulton and Park did evoke serious divisions not only among the diverse communities of London, but also within the forces charged with maintaining order and decency. In the end, the prosecution failed to make its case; even the summation of evidence by the Lord Chief Justice inclined toward the defense. Boulton and Park were acquitted by the special jury of all but the charge of cross-dressing, the least serious they had faced: "The announcement was received with a burst of applause" (*Times*, 16 May 1871: 11). In the spirit of earlier coverage, the *Penny Illustrated Paper* reported the climax under the headline "The Female Impersonators": "They did not display their light-coloured kid-gloves, as on former days, and the familiar bouquet was dispensed with. Boulton fainted upon the verdict being returned, and upon his recovery, the prisoners left the court with their friends" (20 May 1871: 31).

Who were these friends, unembarrassed to show their solidarity with the notorious pair? Why did the crowd cheer? Were they convinced of the innocence of the young men? Or were they complicit in a successful subversion of legal authority? Contemporary readers find it hard to accept that Boulton and Park were just ordinary young men with an extravagant sense of fun. Neil Bartlett comes close to regretting their acquittal as a refusal by society to recognize the reality of their alternative form of life: "The verdict seems unbelievable. The evidence of Fanny and Stella's visibility was converted into proof that they didn't exist" (Bartlett 142). Their letters reveal a complicated nexus of relations among men with a shared sensibility and appreciation of sexual ambiguity. An admirer praises Fanny as "Lais and Antinuous in one," invoking both the classical courtesan and the beloved of the Emperor Hadrian. Stella apologizes to a friend for her "campish ways" (Cohen 112–13). We do have the report of one rather interested contemporary witness. The painter Simeon Solomon, soon afterwards to be arrested with another man for sexual offenses in a public toilet, wrote to Algernon Swinburne after a day at the trial: "There were some very funny things said but nothing improper except the disgusting and silly medical evidence of which I heard but very little." He reported that "I saw the writer of those highly effusive letters. He looks rather humdrum." After the morning session, Solomon "was ravenous and went to the nearest restaurant" where he met the defendants and their lawyers. "Knowing the solicitor, I sat down with them, which as it was a public crowded room, I had no hesitation in doing. B——n is very remarkable. He is not quite beautiful but supremely pretty, a perfect figure, manner and voice altogether. I was agreeably surprised at him." Despite the fear implicit in his explaining why he "didn't hesitate" to join them for a very public lunch, Solomon predicted: "Of course they will be acquitted" (in Lang 143–44). Clearly, the trial did not evoke a unitary response. Much of the drama derived from the publicity given to forms of life enjoyed by a minority at odds with dominant mores, displaying a distinct community in collision with society at large. We cannot say how large or small the minority may have been; moreover, its members also participated in the amorphous "general public" (Cohen 97–110). In fact, there were multiple audiences for the Boulton and Park trial with their own perspectives and interests. Nancy Fraser's conception of "subaltern publics" captures the social realities at work here better than any notion of homogeneous popular opinion (Fraser 109–42).

Some of the early publicity illustrates the fascination and confusion Stella and Fanny inspired. Consider a penny pamphlet entitled "The Lives of Boulton and Park. Extraordinary Revelations." Its eight pages primarily reproduce newspaper coverage of the proceedings at Bow Street. On the cover is a drawing of "The toilet at the station" in which two uniformed policemen surround and ogle an apparently female figure in her underwear, while another in full fancy ball gown looks on in horror with another bobby, more stern than his fellows, standing behind "her" chair. The first page of the document bears yet another title (my favorite), "Stella, Star of the Strand." The text begins with the ritual excoriation: "the social crime, for so it is, which they have openly perpetrated, cannot be too strongly condemned. We speak firmly, and without the slightest hesitation, when we say that the proceedings of these misguided young men deserve the heaviest punishment which the law can possibly award." One act in particular reveals "the base and prurient natures which these misguided youths (for they are but little more) must possess":

> We refer to the entrance of Park into the retiring room, which is set apart for ladies at the Strand Theatre, where he had the unblushing impudence to apply to the female attendant to fasten up the gathers of his skirt, which he alleged had come unfastened. . . . We can now ask, and with a just cause too, what protection have those who are nearest and dearest to our hearts and hearths: these loved ones whom we recognize by the endearing titles of mother, sister, wife or daughter. Is it right, moral, or just, that their sacred privacy should thus be ruthlessly violated. If every debauched *roué* can by assuming feminine garb enforce his way with impunity into the chambers set apart for our countrywomen, then we call upon law and justice to aid us in exposing these outrages upon decency. ("Lives" 1)

Shades of Horner in *The Country Wife*! Park's offense jeopardizes the privacy, and perhaps more, of the women of England. His feminine garb may cloak an aggressively masculine ambition to penetrate the secrets of the fairer sex. The excesses of urban life are descried as a threat to English civilization: "the most revolting profligacy of the guilty cities of the plain, or the debauchery of ancient Rome during the days of Messalina and Theodora, could not possibly outvie with many of the atrocious phrases of London life as they exist in the nineteenth century" ("Lives" 2). Having juxtaposed the sins of Sodom with classical figures of uncontrolled feminine desire, the pamphlet goes on to recite a catalogue of recent cases, including orgies at a "house of ill-fame" on Panton Street, the unnamed crime against a woman by a "vagabond Haymarket café house keeper," a celebrated divorce, and "Mrs. Beecher Stowe's Byron scandal." After rehearsing the incomplete details of the first few days' testimony (the pamphlet must have been rushed to publication), it calls for parliamentary action to compel "the idle and disreputable to seek some means of employment, and not to haunt low taverns, live upon the prostitution of the unfortunate class, or glean a livelihood by billiard marking and sharping." These latter activities are far from any offenses alleged against the young men in women's clothes, whose case had become a condensation of diverse urban ills. Stella and Fanny are represented as symptomatic as well as specific figures: "There are few families who have not a black sheep in their flock; and these black sheep form a very large portion of the community, and the injury which they do to society is immense." The social injury at issue here is both overdetermined by allusions to diverse forms of historical and contemporary corruption and somewhat indeterminate in its reference to deviant sexuality:

> We only hint at the picture we could draw if we dare . . . we point below our breath to other signs of commandments broken which are too sacred to be written; of man metamorphosized, not to "beasts that perish," but to beasts procuring their own perishment, body and soul together, of abominations by which lust defies disease as well as heaven and all many instinct; of houses —, but we cannot, indeed, tell the truth; and less than the truth is nothing in presence of the frightful vices that mock Christianity and poison society in our midst. ("Lives" 7)

Would readers of this flight into hell-fire sermonizing conjoin "abomination" with the earlier "cities of the plain" to suspect that "sodomy" is the threat? If they did, how specific a meaning might they associate with "the sin not fit to be named among Christians"? As we have seen, the trial before Queen's Bench the following year singularly failed to prove any "conspiracy to commit the felony" of sodomy, or any other sexual offense.

The proliferation of dangers, named and unnamed, recited in "The Lives of Boulton and Park" is identified with their distinctly urban context. Returning to its eponymous figures, the pamphlet concludes with the pervasive ambiguity surrounding their gender: "These young men appear to be very unfortunate, for whenever they dressed in men's clothes they were always taken for women, and when they were attired in the dress of the fair sex they were always taken for men, under such circumstances what were they to do?" ("Lives" 8). This formulation seeks to contain the confusion by portraying a consistent failure in their gender performance. However, the evidence displays an almost dizzying proliferation of possibilities, in which both performers often succeeded in their impersonations. Their audiences may have included some who were fooled by the disguises, some who saw right through them, and others who enjoyed their inability quite to decide. The pamphlet concludes with quotations from provincial press accounts of Boulton's and Park's successes acting feminine roles on the stage and the former's as a singer who "brought down the house." The theatrical activities which the defense advanced to demonstrate they were guilty of nothing but a frivolous extension of their stage impersonations are themselves numbered among the guilty pleasures of urban life. The pamphlet characterizes as "ludicrous" the ways in which the papers treated the play of gender: in one account, the masculine identities of Boulton and Park are emphasized; in another, the former's disguise as "Miss Edwards" is not detected; while a third actually comments on nature's handiwork in crafting a man who can sing and act so much like "a really charming girl." The performances of Boulton and Park, Stella and Fanny, received multiple and divergent receptions—on stage, and in the theaters, shopping arcades, and streets of London. Wherever they appeared, they caught the attention of onlookers, inspiring fascination, disapproval, surveillance, finally arrest, and this spectacular court case.

Fanny and Stella traverse a domain where social reality and erotic fantasy intersect. The trial testimony did not touch on the question of actual sexual conduct, except for the highly problematic and ultimately rejected medical evidence. The jury was asked to infer illicit sex from the defendants' public behavior and the expressions of affection contained in their correspondence with male friends. In the end the jury chose not to take that leap. The newspaper accounts, which omitted all of the medical evidence, left their readers to fill in the details from their own imaginations. There can be little doubt, however, that many who observed them and interacted with them were erotically engaged. Fanny and Stella were even immortalized in a limerick:

> There was an old person of Sark
> Who buggered a pig in the dark
> The swine in surprise
> Murmured: "God blast your eyes,
> Do you take me for Boulton or Park?" (Simpson et al. 59)

Despite the explicit reference to buggery and identification with bestiality here, for many the ambiguity of their gender performances was an integral element of their attraction. Remember the hapless Hugh Mundell who, after his arrest with them at the Strand Theatre, testified that they were dressed in male attire when he first met them. He "assumed" that they were women in disguise. When they insisted they were men, he refused to believe them. Despite its self-serving character, this account resonates with much of the testimony regarding reactions to their public display. It suggests some of the ways that the "men in petticoats" mobilized the desires and fantasies of those who observed them.

Stella and Fanny are among the few figures in social history to appear in a published work of pornography. Characters based on Boulton and Park play a prominent role in *The Sins of the Cities of the Plain; or, Confessions of a Mary-ann*, privately printed in London in 1881.[4] That work opens with the narrator's account of his encounter with John Saul of Lisle Street, the eponymous "Mary-ann," whom he met in Leicester Square. The succeeding chapters purport to be based on Saul's account of his life. In the Cleveland Street affair of 1889–90, a man with that name came forward to give statements to police and to testify in court. On the witness stand he described himself as a "professional sodomite." There is rather more than a passing resemblance between the historical individual represented in official papers and press accounts and the character of that name in the novel. H. Montgomery Hyde, the assiduous historian of English homosexuality (as he sees it), regards the novel as a generally reliable portrayal of social realities: "Although some of the details of the incidents described in *The Sins of the Cities of the Plains* may be exaggerated, the work is based upon fact and no doubt gives a faithful enough picture of a seamy side of contemporary London life" (*The Other Love* 123). However, I would not take these fantastic *Confessions of a Mary-ann* as the accurate rendering of anyone's life story.[5]

The work maps a Victorian sexual underworld in which representations of erotic life are permeated by the exaggerations and projections of fantasy. The fact of its publication demonstrates the existence of an audience willing to pay well to cross its imaginary landscape, some high in the hope that it would guide them in fact to some of London's dreadful delights.[6] The book opens with a scene of urban cruising, in a locale where similar encounters may still be observed today, albeit with less discretion: "The writer of these notes was walking through Leicester Square one sunny afternoon last November, when his attention was particularly taken by an effeminate, but very good-looking young fellow, who was walking in front of him, looking in shop-windows from time to time, and now and then looking around as if to attract my attention" (*Sins*, 1881, I:7 [7]).[7] Despite the attribution of effeminacy, it is the bulge in the fork of his trousers that attracts interest: "evidently he was favoured by nature by a very extraordinary development of the male appendage." Saul combines features of femininity and hyper-masculinity. In part this expresses a Victorian tendency to see flagrant sexuality as itself a feminine characteristic.[8] However, the conjunction of apparently contradictory marks of gender should not surprise the student of Boulton and Park, or the admirer of Stella and Fanny. In this case, the narrator follows the ambiguous object of his desire into a picture shop, where he makes his move; soon they are off in a cab to his chambers.[9] Their meeting is free from the constraints of social class and economic status; it occurs in a largely male world, where each is free to gaze openly upon the other and act on agreements negotiated between them. The narrator conflates his sexual interest with the pursuit of truth, which slides from getting a look and feel of that endowment toward discovering what makes the Mary-ann tick. Eventually he will pay Saul to write the story of his life. The narrator's account of the genesis of his text ends on a note that should give pause to the historian in search of verisimilitude: "at each visit we had a delicious turn at bottom-fucking, but as the recital of the same kind of thing over and over again is likely to pall upon my readers, I shall omit a repetition of our numerous orgies of lust, all very similar to the foregoing, and content myself by a simple recital of his adventures" (*Sins*, I:25–26 [23]). Like a campy latter-day Scheherazade, Saul must entertain his patron (and *his* readers) with tales of erotic adventure and "orgies of lust" so diverse and imaginative that their prurient interest will not pall.

Saul's narrative moves from the country and suburbs to London and presents its hero in ever more complex and transgressive situations. However fantasmatic the elaboration, the scene is recognizably the London of the 1870s.
The transition to the city is accomplished when our hero's mother succeeds in
getting him placed at the house of Cygnet and Ego, a West End firm specializ-
ing in fine linen and silk with a most aristocratic clientele. When Saul is sent
with a delivery to Churton House, Piccadilly, his erotic adventures continue in
a *menage à trois* with the marquis and his sister the Hon. Lady Diana Firbelow.[10]
There follows an incestuous and polymorphous threesome that includes Saul's
penetrating the marquis while he enjoys vaginal intercourse with his sister.

However Saul's life is not all adventure; the young employees of the firm
are subject to a strict moral regimen. When he stays out all night providing
additional services for one of the clients, our hero loses his position. The client
is all too willing to help out, referring Saul to a secret club where the members "would only be too glad of my services at their salacious seances, and my
fortune would be at once assured." The place was run by "Mr. Inslip—a rather
suggestive name you will think considering the practices of the members."
These well-placed gentlemen paid one hundred guineas before they were
admitted, and were expected in addition to provide generously for the "street
Mary-anns, soldiers, and youths like myself" whom the proprietor procured.
Inslip is happy to find a new recruit; Saul reports he "was soon very favorably
impressed by my feminine appearance and well-furnished implement of love"
(*Sins,* I:81–83 [78–79]). The neophyte is introduced to Fred Jones, a former
guardsman now employed full-time as a prostitute; "by the time we put on our
hats to go to the club he had fairly told me all that he knew, and considerably
opened my eyes as to how the sin of Sodom was regularly practised in the
Modern Babylon" (*Sins*, I:87–88 [83]). At the club, Fred acts as lady's maid,
assisting Jack in donning women's attire in which he then dresses himself. Their
mutual smooching is interrupted by Mr. Inslip who christens them for the
evening "Isabel" and "Eviline." The guests at the club are divided between
elderly gentlemen and youthful cross-dressers. When the lights go out, the pretense of genteel sociability is dropped, as well as a lot of other barriers: "Before
time was called about 6 A.M., I had had six different gentlemen, besides one of
those dressed up as a girl. We sucked; we frigged and gamahuched, and generally finished off by the orthodox buggery in a tight asshole" (*Sins*, I:92 [86]).

Throughout *The Sins of the Cities of the Plain*, narratives of sexual adventure confound expectations linked to gender and class: the pornographic novel
presents itself as revealing the truth of desire underlying conventional society,
revealing a world of deviant practices at the heart of the capital. Fanny and
Stella appear to vindicate the historical veracity of the tale: "The extent to
which sodomy is carried on in London between gentlemen and young fellows
is little dreamed of by the outside public. You remember the Boulton and Park

scandal court case? Well; I was present at the ball given at Haxell's Hotel in the Strand." In a gesture designed perhaps to protect the actual landlord while opening the way to further titillation packaged as historical truth, Saul reports: "No doubt the proprietor was quite innocent of what our fun really was; but there were two or three dressing rooms into which the company might retire at pleasure" (*Sins*, I:96 [89]). What would the proper Mr. Gibbings have said? Was this the cause of Agnes Earl's distress? Of the altercation that caused Gibbings to end the party prematurely? Or have we stumbled onto the cause of its success despite those mishaps? Oddly enough, the explicit pornography does illuminate questions implied by the historical record. We're told that Boulton "was superbly got up as a beautiful lady and Lord Arthur was very spooney upon her" (*Sins*, I:97 [89]). At the trial Lord Arthur Clinton was said to share a household with Boulton, who styled himself his lady. In the novel, Saul follows the couple to one of the dressing rooms where he spies through the keyhole on their amorous doings. Saul leaves before the encounter reaches its climax, but is later introduced to the couple and to Park. (Fanny and Stella have been renamed Laura and Selina in the novel.) Introduced as "Miss Eveline," Saul is invited to join the group afterwards at their rooms (*Sins* I:105 [93]). However, the sexual enterprise of the guests is not restricted to encounters in private rooms behind closed doors: "soon after the lights were turned out and a general lark in the dark took place. I do not for a moment believe there was one real female in the room, for I groped ever so many of them, and always found a nice little cock under their petticoats" (*Sins*, I:106 [94]). At the end of the evening, Eveline goes off with Laura and Selina to their flat, where "I believe the people of the house thought that we were gay ladies" (*Sins*, II:8 [94]). Of course, a threesome is in the offing: their orgy includes mutual masturbation, birching, and anal sex during which Saul penetrates Park while himself being penetrated by Boulton.

The fantasmatic urban landscape mapped by *The Sins of the Cities of the Plain* is one of polymorphous pansexuality and pervasive gender fuck. It moves through scenes of increasingly exotic and transgressive activity, adding incest, miscegenation, pedophilia, and bestiality to those already enumerated. Many of these scenes include both men and women; there is even one with a cow. They emphasize the mixing of aristocratic and middle-class clients of apparent respectability with male prostitutes who may be got up in full feminine drag or military uniform—with some doing both. The extent to which this material reflects actual social practices is highly questionable, but it does illuminate the erotic imaginary of Victorian gentlemen seeking alternatives to a more domestic sexual regime. Most of these scenes cross boundaries defining gender and sexual propriety, age cohorts, and social classes. Schoolmasters have sex with their pupils; employers with servants; customers with clerks; brothers with sisters; noble lords with rough lads; respectable bourgeois with drag queens. Border patrols are nowhere in sight. But the historical Boulton and Park were arrested and prosecuted. Their trial became an arena of cultural contestation in which accepted lines between private and public were continually crossed and confounded. The prosecution argued vigorously that the pair's cross-dressing, flirtatious interactions, and epistolary effusions manifested criminal desires and a propensity to vicious conduct. The defense contended that the very publicity of the offensive conduct was proof of its innocence: anyone engaged in the pursuit of such guilty private pleasures would hardly call so much attention to himself. Between the innermost privacy of accused mental states and the general publicity of legal and social judgment, we find a plurality of intermediate zones: households, clubs, parties, restaurants, theaters, streets, and arcades. Testimony from landladies and domestic servants revealed the privacy of the home as itself a site of discipline and surveillance. Fellow guests invited to Gibbings's ball and companions at restaurant meals opened the doors on these social occasions. The police themselves had searched flats and confiscated clothes, photographs, and personal correspondence. The only act of anal penetration proved in this case of alleged conspiracy to commit sodomy was that performed by the police surgeon to establish whether or not the accused had performed forbidden acts. To rebut the charges, Boulton and Park introduced personal revelations of their own. Park's father testified about his finances while Boulton's mother offered a portrait of her son's lifelong pleasure in playing dress-up games. The defense presented medical evidence as to the condition of their most intimate bodily spaces. The involvement of both in theatricals was documented with testimony, photographs, and newspaper clippings. The court proceedings and news accounts enacted multiple conflicts over the public rendering of the private lives of the two men. Fanny and Stella got into trouble because they had flouted social norms regarding the proper boundaries between public display and private desire. However, the effort to police their activities culminated in the licensing of private acts of medical sodomy and the staging of a public spectacle beyond their wildest dreams.

NOTES

This chapter is based on research begun during the NEH summer seminar entitled the Culture of London, 1850–92, directed by Michael Levenson in 1995; research continued with the aid of an NEH summer grant in 1998. I have received continuing support from the Faculty Support Funds of the academic vice president and of the humanities divison at Purchase College, State University of New York. This historical project pursues issues I first approached in *Sexual Justice*, especially chapters two, four, and five (Kaplan 47–78, 115–76). It will culminate in *Sodom on the Thames: Love, Lust, and Scandal in Wilde Times*, to be published by Cornell University Press in 2003. I am indebted to far too many friends and fellow scholars to name all here. However, I must mention

William Cohen, Geoffrey Field, and Michael O'Loughlin who helped me prepare myself to pursue archival research. Thanks to all those mentioned and not, but especially to Michael Levenson and to my fellow Londonist Pamela Gilbert for her interest and patience with this contribution.

1. However, at the trial of Boulton and Park, the Lord Chief Justice made clear his disapproval of the police surgeon's initiative regarding the two middle-class men.

2. Although Norton is not persuasive in his assimilation of these phenomena to a perennial "gay subculture" and the writing is often over the top, he has gathered a great deal of useful material. For historically and theoretically sophisticated reflections on these phenomena, see Trumbach.

3. The records of the Boulton and Park case are found in two separate files in the Public Records Office. The transcript of the trial in May 1871 is found in DPP 4/6, along with copies of thirty letters offered into evidence. The signed depositions reflecting testimony offered at Bow Street are in KB 6/3. All quotations in the text are from the latter. The numbers in parentheses indicate the pagination of these documents as given by the archivists. I have modernized the punctuation but otherwise left the texts unaltered.

4. The contemporary version (*Sins of the Cities*, 1992) is based on this text but revises it in major respects, some of which are discussed below. These differences are explored more fully in Kaplan "Who's Afraid of John Saul?" Thus far this important document in the history of sexuality has not received much careful attention from contemporary scholars. In his landmark study of Victorian pornography, *The Other Victorians*, Steven Marcus misses it completely, which leads him to argue that homosexual conduct between men was largely absent from that material and displaced onto flagellation scenes. The most important exception to this general failure is the reading of John Saul's spying on Boulton and Lord Arthur Clinton in Cohen, pp. 123–29.

5. Hyde seems to me to be even further off the mark when he writes regarding the historical John Saul who testified at the Euston libel case in the Cleveland Street affair: "he had given a detailed account of his homosexual activities to the author of The Sins" (Hyde, *Their Good Names* 107). For a detailed examination of the novel and of the Cleveland Street affair in which the historical John Saul subsequently appeared, see Kaplan, "Who's Afraid of John Saul?" 283–301.

6. According to a French bookseller named Charles Hirsch, he sold Oscar Wilde "certain licentious works of a special genre which he euphemistically called 'socratic.'" Most of these were in French, but at least one, he recalled was in English. This was *The Sins of the Cities of the Plain*" (Hyde, *A History* 149–50).

7. All quotations are taken from the two-volume 1881 edition which I examined at the British Library. In brackets, I have provided page references to comparable passages in Masquerade Books's 1992 Badboy edition, which is more easily available but not reliable. I discuss the revisions in the contemporary version in Kaplan, 1999, p. 290.

8. The discourses on prostitution tended to divide women into those who were totally asexual and in need of protection, "angels in the house," and loose or fallen women who carried the contagion of sexual excess as well as venereal disease.

9. The historical Saul testified at Ernest Parke's libel trial in the Cleveland Street affair that Lord Euston took him in a cab to the male brothel at 19 Cleveland Street after picking him in Piccadilly (Kaplan, "Who's Afraid of John Saul?" 297–98).

10. In the Badboy edition, she becomes the marquis' friend, Sir Dennis Firbelow, eliminating the incestuous and bisexual elements of the original as well as the pun in the name (*Sins of the Cities*, 1992, 68).

WORKS CITED

Anderson, Amanda. *Tainted Souls and Painted Faces: The Rhetoric of Fallenness in Victorian Culture*. Ithaca, NY: Cornell UP, 1993.

Bartlett, Neil. *Who Was That Man?* London: Penguin, 1988.

Calhoun, Craig, ed. *Habermas and the Public Sphere*. Cambridge, MA: MIT P, 1989.

Cohen, William A. *Sex Scandal*. Durham: Duke UP, 1996.

Duberman, Martin, Martha Vicinus, and George Chauncey. *Hidden from History*. New York: NAL Books, 1989.

Fraser, Nancy. "Rethinking the Public Sphere." In *Habermas and the Public Sphere*. Calhoun, ed. Cambridge, MA: MIT P, 1989. 109–42.

Hyde, H. Montgomery. *A History of Pornography*. London: Heinemann, 1964.

———. *The Other Love*. London: Mayflower, 1970.

———. *Their Good Names*. London: Hamilton, 1970.

Kaplan, Morris B. *Sexual Justice*. New York: Routledge, 1997.

———. "Who's Afraid of John Saul?" *GLQ* 5.3 (1999): 267–314.

Lang, Cecil, ed. *The Swinburne Letters*. New Haven: Yale UP, 1962.

"Lives of Boulton and Park. Extraordinary Revelations." London: George Clarke, 1870.

Nord, Deborah Epstein. *Walking the Victorian Streets*. Ithaca, NY: Cornell UP, 1995.

Norton, Rictor. *Mother Clap's Molly House*. London: InBook, 1992.

Public Records Office. London, KB 6/3, 1870.

———. London, DPP 4/6, 1871.

Rappaport, Erika Diana. *Shopping for Pleasure*. Princeton, NJ: Princeton UP, 2000.

Simpson, Colin, Lewis Chester, and David Leitch. *The Cleveland Street Affair*. Boston: Little, Brown, 1976.

Sins of the Cities of the Plain. New York: Masquerade Books, 1992.

Sins of the Cities of the Plains; or, the Confessions of a Mary-ann. 2 vol. London: Erotic Biblion Society of London and New York, 1881.

The Times. London, 1870–1871. Microfilm. British Library.

Trumbach, Randolph. "The Birth of the Queen." In *Hidden from History*. Duberman et al., eds. New York: NAL Books, 1989. 129–40.

Upchurch, Charles. "Forgetting the Unthinkable." *Gender and History* 121 (2000): 127–157.

Walkowitz, Judith R. *Prostitution and Victorian Society*. Cambridge, UK: Cambridge UP, 1980.

———. *City of Dreadful Delight*. Chicago: U of Chicago P, 1992.

Weeks, Jeffrey. "Inverts, Perverts, and Mary-Annes." In *Hidden from History*. Duberman et al., eds. New York: NAL Books, 1989. 195–211.

CHAPTER 4

Romancing the City: Arthur Symons and the Spatial Politics of Aesthetics in 1890s London

MICHELLE SIPE

> In the city setting legibility is crucial.
> —Kevin Lynch, *The Image of the City*

*I*n his most successful and controversial collections of poems, *Silhouettes* (1892) and *London Nights* (1895), Arthur Symons creates images of women who are often caught in or fractured into a series of poses that mirror the seemingly disjointed experience of modern city life. Indeed, the corpus of Arthur Symons's 1890s poetry and fiction focuses on the alluring icon of the "fallen" woman, who was often found in London's streets and the music halls the writer frequented for both personal pleasure and income (as a critic for the *Star*). His chief biographer, Karl Beckson, and critics of late Victorian literature like Murray Pittock and Tom Gibbons, have read Symons's poems primarily as enactments or reflections of symbolism, the mid- to late-nineteenth-century nexus of aesthetic theories and styles that includes aestheticism, impressionism, and, most infamously, decadence.[1] In response to literary history's general marginalization of 1890s aesthetics as "a muddled aesthetic doctrine," many of these same critics have championed symbolism as the dominant, unifying frame for British fin de siècle literature, stressing its value as an essential contribution to modernist aesthetics (Whittington-Egan

155). Karl Beckson has wryly observed, in his introduction to Holbrook Jackson's *The Eighteen Nineties*, that "it is a commonplace of literary history that the 1890s—with their dazzling array of creative genius, their astonishing personalities, and their significant effect upon the ensuing century—do not mark a historical climax or signal the beginning of modern literature" (v). As Beckson suggests, it is the "astonishing" images and personalities of the writers associated with literary decadence, as much as their risqué subject matter and unconventional styles, that have obscured their place in British literary history. Against this critical feminization, with its emphasis on artificial appearance and decadent, unmanly behavior, the restoration of 1890s British aesthetics has tended to celebrate the flâneur poet as a reassuringly masculine figure that moves through the modern metropolis and gathers fleeting "sensations" and impressions of modern life while remaining emotionally and physically detached. Muting the ambiguous social and sexual nature of the flâneur figure, criticism of Symons has generally emphasized his mastery and control over urban landscape and marginalized his associations with literary decadence. The wandering poet's alienation from the city, and the association of urbanism with the spiritual loss and empty materialism that signified cultural decline for the avante-garde, paradoxically provides the flâneur with the raw material for art that transcends the monotony and vicious materialism of everyday life.

Tom Gibbons has argued along these lines in his survey of Symons's literary criticism. In his reading of Symons's seminal essay on the subject, "The Decadent Movement in Literature" (1893), Gibbons sees a controlled urban impressionism that seeks to represent "the complex inner life of man in the modern city," rather than the artificial poses and stylistic excesses of decadence (75). Gibbons takes Symons at his word when he quotes the writer's claim to a modern aesthetic that will be realized "through the more difficult poetry of the disagreeable," in which the measure of artistic ability is "the capacity for dealing with London, indoors or out" (72–73). But what constitutes "the disagreeable" is taken for granted in this mythology. Gibbons's easy placement of Symons's aesthetic in a modern urban context assumes, rightly, the essential consumption of space needed to maintain the artist's vision, but overlooks the ways in which middle-class ideologies of class and gender in general and domestic ideology in particular shape his images of London. Of course, "the difficult poetry of the disagreeable" belies the proximity of the working classes, immigrants, the indeterminate gradations of lower- and middle-class men meeting the city's burgeoning commercial, civic, and professional demands, and the women of all social levels who daily jostled the financially pressed man of letters. But Symons's proclaimed relationship to the city has not only obscured those who constitute "the disagreeable": it has also mystified middle-class domestic ideologies of space that figure home as the antithesis and antidote to the city's heterogeneity. For the man of letters whose creativity and livelihood require the successful navigation of the city's continually shifting boundaries, his living quarters and domestic life become essential to his identity and productivity.

Against the fluidity of London life, its spatial and social complexity, Arthur Symons's aesthetic stance towards the city is crucial to his status as a man of letters. But his use of Decadent poetics as the means to read the city's more illegitimate, exotic, or Eastern(ized) regions is an expression of a long literary tradition of urban exploration, in which ramblers like Pierce Egan's Tom and Jerry delight in the carnivalesque pleasures of the East End and then return uncorrupted to the West End. In addition to such popular tales of East End "slumming," Dickens's wide-ranging urban realism, as well as Henry Mayhew's and Charles Booth's more factual accounts of London poverty, share or assume the unifying perspective of a man of leisure whose discriminating gaze organizes and makes sense of an otherwise bewildering metropolis.[2]

But these visions are neither exhaustive nor sustainable. As feminist critics of the Victorian city have argued, the late-nineteenth-century flâneur and his cool objectivity was increasingly compromised by modern urban life. Despite their rhetorical persistence, the East and West Ends no longer successfully framed imaginative visions or experiences of London. Judith Walkowitz identifies an "epistemological crisis" that erodes male writers' sense of "being at home in the city":

> Social investigation, serious fiction, and "shilling shockers" of the 1880's all bear witness to a growing skepticism among men of letters about their capacity to read the city and to sustain a coherent vision of a structured public landscape. They expressed this unease by constructing a mental map of London marked by fragmentation, complexity and introspection, all of which imperiled the *flâneur's* ability to experience the city as a totalizing force. Forces inside and outside of bourgeois culture provoked this epistemological crisis, for while it undoubtedly mirrored the self doubts of professional and literary men, the crisis was also precipitated by the actions and energies of different social actors making claims on city space and impinging on the prerogatives of privileged men. (39)

According to Walkowitz's account, the city's complexity no longer provides a satisfying panorama of urban characters and picturesque scenes; rather, London has become an amalgam of confusing forces that weaken the male writer's ability to sustain an objective, coherent view of urban space. While her interest lies in the wide range of women that more visibly occupy the city, her analysis of the male spectator also points to the tensions and struggles within bourgeois culture over what kinds of professions and types of work signify respectable masculine pursuits.

Though it does not address the city directly, James Eli Adams's study of Victorian masculinity posits men's anxieties about spectatorship and performance in

public space as part of a broader crisis over male intellectual labor in the nineteenth century. In response to this crisis, middle-class male writers' competing
"styles of masculinity" appropriate a limited number of figures of self-discipline:

> Those rhetorics [of masculinity] are persistently related in their appeal to a
> small number of models of masculine identity: the gentleman, the prophet, the
> dandy, the priest, and the soldier. Each of these models is typically understood
> as the incarnation of an ascetic regimen, an elaborately articulated program of
> self-discipline. As such, they lay claim to the capacity for self-discipline as a
> distinctly masculine attribute and in their different ways embody masculinity
> as a virtuoso asceticism. (2)

Even the most "effeminate" styles, such as decadence and aestheticism, incorporate models representing an "ascetic regimen," models which, Adams argues,
are intended to offset the loss of older, more stable forms of masculine authority and identity. More specifically, he demonstrates how decadent writers like
Walter Pater worked "to reinscribe norms of masculinity within the ethos of
aestheticism—to present even spectatorship as an exercise in eminently virile
self-discipline" (185). Extending Adams's emphasis on ascetic models, Thaïs
Morgan has pointed out the persistence of "classical republican discourse" in
the Victorian imagination, which measures the health of the nation-state by the
degree to which its male members conform to masculine standards of self-
restraint. According to republican discourse, men's virtue "comprises both a
private practice of managing one's desires and a public discourse in which 'law'
regulates the male body in the best interests of the polity" (111). While high-
lighting the management of male desire, Morgan's dual focus on "private practice" and "public discourse" marks the interdependence of private and public
spaces in the maintenance of male virtue, spaces that are mediated, ultimately,
by Victorian models of domesticity.

The separation of home and work, while shoring up segregated spheres
of masculine and feminine identity and influence, also contributes to the fractured nature of masculinity and male intellectual labor in Victorian culture.
That is, while Victorian domestic ideology intended to maintain men's and
women's essential differences through the spatial separation of work and
home, the home to which men must return is coded as a feminine space. To
compensate for the softening, potentially emasculating effects of home, men
must also seek out more dangerous, "bracing" spaces to prove their virility and
exhibit self-restraint. Thus, middle-class masculinity is a tense negotiation of
both private and public spaces; manhood requires the ability to afford and
maintain a respectable level of privacy as well as the energy to perform one's
masculinity within a variety of spaces away from home, whether institutional-
ized places of work, a train or a busy London street, the café, club, or the music
hall. For the avante-garde poet in London, "being at home in the city"

includes two distinct, but interdependent, poles: comfortable living quarters and the places of leisure that provide limited, surveyable spaces for literary (re)production of the city.

URBAN POETICS

Ultimately, Arthur Symons's artistic development in London is inseparable from his peripatetic wanderings, his consciously authoritative movement between and among multiple and diverse social spaces: the East End and West, music hall and club, cabman's shelter and café, street and respectable apartment. In addition to his poetry, his letters to friends and to popular publications like the *Star* foster an image of confident mobility, of unlimited access to legitimate and illegitimate urban spaces, and the ability to move between them unscathed. In his poetry and prose, Symons cultivates an urban romance, staging himself as the virile hero who sees the essence of London in the women who move through its streets and dance in its music halls. Symons's embrace of virility is essential to his particular urban poetics, and is a quality that he mythologizes early in his career, as seen in a study of Shakespeare he undertook. Karl Beckson's biography documents the young author's imaginative investment in the "provincial" Shakespeare's erotic relationship to London:

> In tracing the biographical background the provincial young author undoubtedly associated himself with the provincial Shakespeare, but, unlike the Bard, Arthur had not gone up to London where Shakespeare at the age of 22 found himself in "a swarming medley of vice and valour, grime and splendour, finicking daintiness and brutal coarseness; everywhere a vigourous stirring of life and striking out of literature, with all the evils consequent on such an awakening." (Beckson, quoting Symons 24)

The image of the city as an ambiguous, "swarming medley" that stimulates the male poet's sexual and artistic awakening persists in Symons's later literary adventures, after his move to London at the age of twenty-five. Undoubtedly, the young writer's early mentor, Walter Pater, and the latter's emphasis on a virile aesthetic temperament, shaped Symons's poetic relationship to the city. In his 1873 preface to *Studies in the History of the Renaissance*, Pater locates the virtue of Wordsworth's poetry in the "heat of his genius" and the "active principle" that "penetrates his verse" (xi). Symons applies similar principles of aesthetic virility to the ephemeral movements of his poems "Nora on the Pavement" and "Stella Maris," demonstrating his ability to draw from or gesture towards essential truths in an otherwise troubling, urban landscape. By figuring the city as feminine vagueness and fragment, he puts a decadent spin on the rather familiar trope of woman as the fictional ground from which to write and affirm a coherent masculine identity.

The subject of Symons's poetry as well as his short stories is often an anonymous woman encountered or glimpsed on a city street or stage who leaves a haunting impression on the narrator. The poems begin with phrases, seemingly unattached and free floating. "Javanese Dancers" begins without a clear subject or object, observer or observed: "Twitched strings, the clang of metal, beaten drums," introduces the poem, while the dancer emerges in the third line, already thoroughly entwined in a series of impressions, as well as formally contained within the quatrain itself. Even her smile is detached from its supposed source, diffused in the very syntax and structure of the poetry: "Smiling between her painted lids a smile" (*Silhouettes* 33). Despite the dancer's movements, the poem's emphasis is on her stillness, as "motionless, unintelligible, she twines," "with smiles inanimate." Just as the dancer's actions are frozen into timeless artistic gestures, so too is the dancer's agency diffused into vagueness. Similarly, in "Renee," the spectator describes Renee as "calm with that vague unrest, / Sad with that sensitive, vaguely ironical mouth" (*London Nights* 6). The possibility of a shared gaze is rhetorically softened by her "vaguely ironical mouth." The dancer of "La Melinite: Moulin-Rouge" is also characterized by "her morbid, vague ambiguous grace" (24). Even Nora of "Nora on the Pavement," who leaps free at the end of the poem, is portrayed as "petulant and bewildered," qualities that enable the narrator's "Thronging desires and longing looks" to "re-incarnate her." She is portrayed as part of the fabric of the image:

> There where the ballet circles,
> See her, but ah! not free her from the race
> of glittering lines that link and interlace
> This colour now, now that, may be her
> In the bright web of those harmonious circles. (7)

The dancer's movements are paradoxically dispersed and contained by the dance and the aestheticization of it through "harmonious circles." In these impressions of urban life, women's bodies and movements are separated out and diffused into the symbolic wholeness of the poems. Overall, the descriptions of women seem relatively innocuous, while the narrator seems to occupy a corrupt position, separate from the beautiful impressions he repeatedly describes. However, the repeated fetishization of the dancers' features and gestures and the stress on their artificiality displace the materiality of women, as well as the bodies, sounds, and smells that are part of the city landscape. (The "disagreeable," is, however, more realistically depicted in his London sketch, "East and West End Silhouettes": "Odors of stale meat . . . the pleasant savor of hot chestnuts . . . the shrill voices of women rise from the green grocers . . . mingle in inexpressible confusion" [*Memoirs* 79].) The abstraction and transformation of materiality into artificiality feminizes the landscape, and empowers the observer, who is able to perform poetic acts of enclosure in an otherwise chaotic urban environment.

In his essay "The World as Ballet," the true test of the artist's virtuosity is, again, the ability to abstract and neutralize the subjectivity of the music hall and ballet dancers who inhabit his fiction:

> And now, look at the dance, on the stage, a mere spectator. Here are all these young bodies, made more alluring by an artificial heightening of whites and reds on the face, displaying, employing, all their natural beauty, themselves, full of the sense of joy of motion, or affecting that enjoyment, offered to our eyes like a bouquet of flowers, a bouquet of living flowers, which have all the glitter of artificial ones. As they dance, so human, so remote, so desirable, so evasive, . . . they seem to sum up in themselves the appeal of everything in the world that is passing, and coloured and to be enjoyed. (*Memoirs* 245)

The "mere spectator" takes what he sees as the "artificial heightening of whites and reds" and creates an abstract portrait in which discrete women's bodies are dissolved into patterns and colors; what is threateningly real or "natural" (the disturbing notion that the dancers may be participating in the manufacture of affect and "affecting that enjoyment") is checked by the observer's enjoyment of the spectacle. The overriding emphasis on artistic harmony and visual pleasure that envelops the women obscures the troubling spatial arrangement of looking, his passive role as spectator.

In his preface to *Silhouettes*, "Being a Word on Behalf of Patchouli," Symons elaborates the artist's choice of the artificial over the natural and posits the city as the source and site of the artificial:

> If you prefer your "new mown hay" in the hayfield, and I, it may be, in a scent-bottle, why may not my individual caprice be allowed to find expression as well as yours? . . . I am always charmed to read beautiful poems about nature in the country. Only, personally, I prefer town to country; and in the town we have to find for ourselves, as best we may, the *décor* which is the town equivalent of the great natural *décor* of fields and hills. Here it is that artificiality comes in; and if anyone sees not beauty in the effects of artificial light, in all the variable, most human, and yet most factitious town landscape, I can only pity him, and go my own way. (xv)

This passage's emphasis on the natural and the artificial foregrounds the gendered infrastructure of Symons's urban poetics. His mock dialogue dismisses the pastoral mode and the poet who adopts it as well as his choice of "natural decor." By privileging the city over the country, the artificial over the natural, individual selection and choice over a passive receptivity, he is participating in a definition of art and culture as constructed, and locates value in that construction. The preference that Symons asserts, however, figures both country and city as the (feminized) ground for (masculine) cultivation, a figuration that collapses "the natural" and "the artificial" as competing sources or grounds for the performance of a virile aesthetic.

Despite Symons's decadent celebration of London's artificiality, it is not portrayed as particularly hospitable to masculine aesthetics and the literati. His descriptions of the Rhymers' Club and meetings with writers and artists in London's cafés and taverns portray an anxious group of intellectual men marginalized by the general public. In contrast with Paris, London is perceived as hostile to artistic movements; in London, "art has to be protected . . . by a kind of affected modesty which is the Englishman's natural pose, half pride and half distrust" (*Memoirs* 83). His definition of the Englishman's ambivalent pose captures the slippery, anxious nature of fin de siècle modes of masculinity that must be husbanded in "semi-literary" taverns where men of letters gather to share their work.

In "East and West End Silhouettes," Symons describes his chance encounter with friends, other intellectuals, and artists who decide to have a drink at the Café Royal. In the café, safely and respectably located in the West End, "We talked of London, of the impressions the streets gave us," but then he recalls a colleague's confession: "'I feel as I walk along the Strand,' said Saint Just, 'how kind it would be if I were to stab every second man I meet'" (*Memoirs* 80). The absence of narrative explanation or commentary implies Symons's implicit agreement with St. Just, that the multitude of others, the indecipherable crowd, has become a source of disillusionment that dehumanizes relations between men. Finally, we are told, "when the problems had been examined in all their angles," Symons "rejoiced to find the conversation was slipping round towards art," adding, "And we were soon confessing to one another that each of us had written a poem about the Café Royal—something modern, modernity in poetry. Saint Just's was about a lady with amber gloves; my lady was in black, black from head to feet" (81).

His poem for this occasion is entitled "Ambiguë," and is another instance in which femininity as vagueness, or "passionate ambiguity," becomes the artistic occasion for the expression of modernity, an extraction of meaning that will give a contour or shape to the dehumanizing experience of London's overwhelming size and complexity of indeterminate spaces:

> Is there a meaning in your mystery
>   Strange eyes, so cold, so mirror-like, whose smile
>   Lures, but declares not? What determinate wile
> Lurks in that passionate ambiguity? (*Memoirs* 81)

The narrative structure of "East and West End Silhouettes" begins with the chance urban encounter and ends with the aesthetic impression that collapses the heterogeneous quality of London, the heat and disillusionment, and the hostile, pressing crowds into a single woman's "passionate ambiguity." The Café Royal, as a briefly illuminated space within the vagueness of London, underscores the defensive nature of the semi-private space of the café where men gather to share their impressions.

Despite his many friendships and literary associations with men, Symons reveals more precisely the everyday pressures of living in London to a female friend. In a letter to Katherine Willard, he complains of the stress of working as a writer in the city, where the vicissitudes of publishing are tempered by fellow artists' acceptance and praise. In reality, Symons was not a man of leisure: he worked obsessively, publishing articles and reviews for literary circles and the popular press alike—often several a week during the height of his career—in addition to his poetry. Though prolific, his residence and penchant for entertaining, his travels both within London and to the countryside and seaside resorts, and frequent trips abroad left him continually pressed for money. His financial insecurity is exacerbated by his ambivalence about writing as a profession:

> The one thing is to know whether one has done good work. And how can we ever tell? At times I feel elated, and I say to myself "Well, I have done something worth doing!" And then I feel horribly depressed, and envy every person who isn't myself, and nothing seems worth doing any more. But of course, I go on writing just what "the spirit moves one" to write, and setting against the indifference of Smith or Brown something that Pater has said or Meredith has written me. These are the consolations! (*Letters* 76)

While writing is romanticized as a spiritual endeavor, an activity shared with and nurtured by one's friends and mentors, the indifference of booksellers and a resistant public and the lack of financial reward and security undermine Symons's confidence in his work and its status as a manly or masculine enterprise. Another letter, to his friend and contemporary, Ernest Rhys, reveals Symons's sense of irony about and awareness of competing fields of knowledge, of scientific inquiry and epistemological approaches to the world, to England, and to the forces of "modernity" with which the writer must contend. Describing his stay at the Willards's home in Berlin, he writes facetiously of his collaboration with Frank Willard while the family is away: "We employed much of the time in social studies, and are prepared to write a scientific work in large 8vo. on 'The Cafés of Berlin from 10:30 P.M. to 6 A.M., sociologically considered. With Portraits and Autographs'" (*Letters* 83). Here, Symons's double-edged account pokes fun at the excesses of scientific inquiry and its arbitrary uses, but, just as tellingly, suggests the vulnerability of intellectual work and the ambiguous status of leisured spaces (i.e., the Willards's domestic haven as well as Berlin's cafés) as legitimate places for this labor.

AESTHETIC VIRILITY

We had much in common; and yet with what singular differences!
—Arthur Symons, *Memoirs*

If the flâneur poet's anxiety is managed by a virile aesthetic that feminizes the city, it is also tempered through his observations as a discriminating biographer of his peers. Symons's self-fashioning includes his evaluations of other writers as men, i.e., their ability to manage themselves and their artistic visions within a decidedly urban context. Symons distinguishes himself from colleagues such as Ernest Dowson, John Addington Symonds, and Oscar Wilde, who he believes often fail to successfully convert life into art, to aestheticize the specificity and materiality of everyday life that threaten to engulf them. As Symons writes of Dowson, "neither the stage nor the stage-door had any attraction for him; he came to the tavern because it was a tavern . . . I never could get him to see the charm in coloured and harmonious movement, like brilliant shadows seen through the flashing gauze of the music" (*Memoirs*, 83).

He tends to represent other writers' inability to successfully manage a decadent aesthetic vision in terms of physical degeneration and emasculation. While Symons and Dowson both portray the city through dreamlike imagery, the former emphasizes the gendered differences in their artistic temperaments. In another biographical sketch, "Music Halls and Ballet Girls," Symons claims that Dowson is "lacking in vitality" and suggests that the places the artist likes to go, where he chooses to live or eat, provide keys to his psyche as well as his artistic style (*Memoirs* 112). While Symons lives in the comparative bourgeois respectability of Fountain Court, Dowson, who lives in the East End and enjoys eating in cabmen's shelters, prefers "sordidness" in his surroundings (84). Despite his "exquisite sensibility," according to Symons, he is "soiled" by "gross contact" with London's East End (87). Symons's own self-fashioning as a man who can successfully navigate London "indoors and out" requires that he portray Dowson as a "dilapidated," "demoralised Keats," a figure of uncontrolled decadence whose profligate living and contact with unhealthy bodies undermine his status as a poet of the city (84). Within Symons's aesthetic, both men and women are compromised by modern city life, and can only be rescued by the more virile writer's artistic vision.

More disturbing and telling, perhaps, is Symons's description of Oscar Wilde, whose "vices were not simply intellectual perversions, they were physiological," and whose writing after the arrest and trial "had nothing virile in it" (*Memoirs* 138). Symons's treatment of Wilde's physical condition as degenerative and unmanly implies that to penetrate life, through the woman, is "virile" and masculine, while to be penetrated is to become feminine and subject to degeneration and decay. (Symons was very troubled by Toulouse-Lautrec's portrait of Wilde, especially the mouth: "no such mouth ought ever to have existed; it is a woman's that no man who is normal could ever have had" [139].) While these remembrances were likely exaggerated by age, distance, and mental illness (Symons had a breakdown in 1908 from which he never fully recovered—to which the often confused structure of his memoirs attest), they are consistent, nevertheless, with Symons's desire to feminize the city through his written observations of women and men from the 1890s. For the fin de siècle man of

letters, a well-defined masculine aesthetic and identity are essential for successful writing in a modern world that continually encroaches on and threatens the
bodily integrity of the masculine self.

MASCULINE DOMESTICITY

This Is the Realization of a Dream.
—Symons, *Selected Letters*

Symons's integrity, however, is a function of a respectable, centralized residence
that frames his sense of autonomous movement to and from the city's most heterogeneous spaces and inhabitants. After his move to London in early 1891, his
letters to friends and popular publications like the *Star* cultivate an image of
confident mobility and access. These letters continually affirm his ability to navigate himself through life and its multiplicity of spaces, an ability aggressively
tested and played out in the city. In his letter to Katherine Willard, 20 May 1891,
he cavalierly writes about his urban travels with her brother, Frank Willard:

> I don't know whether you have heard of our wanderings by night, our stud-
> ies of the ins and outs of London. They were very delightful to me, and I was
> glad of so sympathetic a companion. He and I have many curiosities in com-
> mon. Do you know, I have no interest in what is proper, regular, convention-
> ally virtuous. I am attracted by everything that is unusual, Bohemian, eccen-
> tric: I like to go to queer places, to know strange people. And I like contrast,
> variety. (*Letters* 79)

Here Symons seems to embrace the bohemian image associated with the
decadent movement, stressing his intimacy with "queer places" and "strange
people." And yet, there is something faintly suburban about this performance—
of the young man who celebrates his masculine access to seedy urban pleasures
for the benefit of his respectable female audience. His consumption of the city
as "contrast," its movement and "variety," is dependent upon the complementary
image of suburban retreat and domestic quiet that the letter's addressee represents. His long correspondence with and deep respect for Katherine Willard
reflect a traditional, if not conservative, view of proper Victorian womanhood
and its need to be protected from urban chaos and corruption. But in the context of the late nineteenth-century metropolis, the home or domestic retreat also
secures Victorian manhood, providing a reassuring haven from the city's corruption and a place to husband the male poet's impressions of modern life.

During a period when the City of London's population was shrinking, making way for commercial development, office buildings, and warehouses, as well as
trains and transportation lines, when the poorest of city residents were displaced
and the middle classes drawn to the cheaper, more comfortable suburbs, Symons's

settlement in the central location of the Temple is significant if not unusual. Though he had published considerably before moving to London in 1890, his move to the city heralded a sense of arrival and autonomy—a sense of autonomy most palpable in the description of his own four-room apartment in the respectable Fountain Court. Writing of his new home (where he would remain for ten years until his marriage in 1901), he celebrates its suburban qualities and the privacy it provides in the midst of London:

> It is the most charming locality, and also the most convenient, to my mind in London—where I have at last succeeded in getting chambers. You know the Temple is supposed to be used only by lawyers, but as a matter of fact other people do sometimes live here. It is an oasis in the heart of London—quietest spot in the great city, yet with the roar of the Strand only just out of hearing . . . there really is a fountain, and there are trees, and picturesque buildings and large stone steps, all about—a broad open space in front. My two rooms are at the top, looking down on the fountain. This is the realization of a dream. (*Letters* 70)

Shielded from the streets, shops, and commercial bustle of Fleet Street, Fountain Court became for Symons a haven from the city as well as its literary "heart"; indeed, for the next ten years it served as a quiet space for writing and a lively meeting place for a colorful stream of writers, artists, and intellectuals who decidedly shaped 1890s aesthetics. While biographers and literary critics alike have accepted Symons's self-fashioned image as urban rambler and poet, however, most have overlooked the significance of his modest, yet legitimate middle-class lodgings, or the productive spatial relationship between the professional writer's home and his centralized access to spaces for pleasure and consumption as well as writing and productivity. As Sharon Marcus has pointed out, "The absence of residential spaces seems to go without saying in accounts of modernity, which define city life as the public life that takes place in collective spaces of exchange or display and describe home life as private, concealed, and self-enclosed" (6). Indeed, Symons's homing devices (i.e., his carefully detailed and recorded movements to and from Fountain Court) reveal the flâneur poet's productive negotiation of decadent aesthetics through the controlled boundaries of a reassuring, yet fluid domestic retreat.

CONTROLLED DECADENCE

> My Life Is Like a Music-Hall.
> —Arthur Symons, *Memoirs*

In a culture seriously influenced by middle-class, evangelical ideals of work and sobriety, and an increasingly secularized world of capitalist relations that values specialization, the man of letters' claim to a wide-ranging knowledge of the world through the abstraction of art requires more ambiguous, yet ascetic regimes as well as spaces to enact them. In addition to securing privacy and respectable lodgings, middle-class men must continue to exercise ascetic regimes beyond the protective walls of the home. For the Victorian middle class, real work is performed and consolidated in its law offices, banks, and businesses, but the growth and diversification of London's economy also supports a wider range of recreational spaces, or what Peter Bailey has deemed, in his work on British music halls, "the business of pleasure." The music hall, in particular, with its diverse working-class origins and makeshift beginnings as expanded pubs, supper-rooms, and cafés would seem to represent the hybrid nature of the city that Walkowitz and Nord identify as the male spectator's undoing. However, by fashioning himself as an expert of the music hall, Symons claims a distinctive, virile relationship to the city that works to contain the fin de siècle crisis over male intellectual and artistic labor and secures his role as a figure of controlled decadence.

While the specific class origins of the music hall have been a matter of sustained debate for its historians, by the 1860s many halls were purposely built on the grand scale of the West End dramatic theaters, with amenities, venues, and fixed seating intended to cater to the city's middling classes rather than working-class patrons (Inwood 665). Despite the efforts of the more up-scale halls to gentrify, however, they remained an object of moral scrutiny for the middle class as well as its pleasure ground. Moral reformers and the London County Committee (LCC) focused on the promenade as the music hall's most promiscuous feature, which allowed men and women of indistinct classes and stations to mingle without inhibition or censure (Inwood 665). Still, if the music hall's structure, its working-class origins, and its association with excess and pleasure made it socially suspect, it also, according to Peter Bailey, provided a range of urban (and suburban) actors a relatively protected space for enjoyment:

> At its optimum, [the] music hall was a highly charged social space, a conse-quence of its genius of place and the particular dynamics of its performance. In its social logistics, the music hall combined something of the features of both pub and theater. Like the pub it was both a public and private place, where the multiple intimacies of its crowd—a more helpful designation than audience—paradoxically afforded a kind of privacy. Like the theatre it reduced the promiscuous social mix of city streets to some kind of territorial order while keeping open mutual contact of sight and sound among its different social elements. (xvii)

Of course, for Symons, the promenade's promiscuity was one of its most charming features, which he defended as an inescapable feature of modern life.

In a letter to the *Pall Mall Gazette*, he defends the Empire's promenade after a female inspector testified against the presence of prostitutes to the Licensing Committee of the London County Council.

What is fascinating about his defense is the implied vulnerability of men, rather than women, who attend the Empire, as well as the female reformer's adopted role as protector: "As to the stories of men being accosted by women in the promenade at the Empire, my own experience assures me that this is highly improbable" (*Letters* 107). But the potential threat of aggressively sexual women as well as the moral rectitude of the middle-class female inspector is eclipsed by Symons's chivalric defense of the Empire and the "excellence of its entertainment." In another letter to the *Star*, he challenges the claim that all music halls are alike. Affirming his status as "an aficionado of the music halls," and his qualifications as a "discriminating amateur," he is able to recognize each music hall's "cachet," and to distinguish and discriminate between its performers (*Letters* 85).

If other artists are compromised by the city's social ambiguity and "the disagreeable," Symons's intimate and extensive knowledge of the music halls provides a unifying thread, a means of tying together the disparate, heterogeneous aspects of London: "You will find a queer kind of unity in the midst of all this seemingly casual variety, and in time—if you think it worth the time—you will come to understand the personality of the music-halls" (*Letters* 87). His emphasis on the music hall as a totality, "its unity in the midst of all this seemingly casual variety" fosters a sense of imaginative mastery over the city's most elusive and disturbing aspects.

While London's richness and frightening complexity provide Symons and his fellow writers with the images, places, and experiences for artistic exploration, the way of life intimately associated with decadent aesthetics and urban impressionism (the movements and encounters with a seemingly endless stream of urban actors, men and women of questionable occupations and social positions, in often unclassifiable spaces), nevertheless, threatens the legitimacy of urban exploration and male artistic expression. However, while most writers associated with decadence occupy a defensive position within London culture, Symons successfully cuts a figure of controlled decadence and remains comparatively uncompromised by the city's threatening elements. If the poet's feminization of the city is not new, perhaps, the feminization of other male writers becomes an essential strategy in his ascetic, aesthetic regime. Finally, Symons successfully negotiates the two essential poles of Victorian middle-class standards of masculinity: private and public space. He secures the status that privacy affords in his lodgings at Fountain Court but also embraces the "territorial order" of the music-hall as a metonymic, nodal means of participating in London's heterogeneity while, according to Yeats, "remain[ing] himself, if I understand him rightly, quite apart from their glitter and din" (58).

NOTES

1. See Murray G. H. Pittock's *Spectrum of Decadence* for nuanced, concise definitions of late-nineteenth-century symbolism and related aesthetic movements. Refuting the perception of decadence as merely a "symptom" of Victorian culture and its degeneration, he argues that it is an active performance of symbolism that often took the form of artifice, and unconventional, exhibitionist, or illicit behaviors: "The point is that Decadence has various symptoms, but the underlying 'disease' is a consistent one, that of Symbolist thought," and therefore, Pittock implies, not a disease at all (9).

2. In *Walking the Victorian Streets*, Deborah Nord explores the trope of the male spectator, in representations of the city in nineteenth-century literature:

> In the literature of the nineteenth-century city, the figure of the observer—the rambler, the stroller, the spectator, the flâneur—is a man. As Raymond Williams rightly remarks, the entire project of representing and understanding the exhilarating and distressing new phenomenon of urban life began, in some important sense with this figure of the lone man who walked with impunity, aplomb, and a penetrating gaze. (1)

WORKS CITED

Adams, James Eli. *Dandies and Desert Saints*. Ithaca and London: Cornell UP, 1993.

Bailey, Peter. "Introduction: Making Sense of the Music Hall." In *Music Hall: The Business of Pleasure*. Peter Bailey, ed. Milton Keynes: Open UP, 1986.

Beckson, Karl. *Arthur Symons: A Life*. Oxford: Clarendon P, 1987.

———. Introduction. *The Eighteen Nineties*. By Holbrook Jackson. New York: Capricorn Books, 1966.

Gibbons, Tom. *Rooms in the Darwin Hotel: Studies in English Literary Criticism and Ideas, 1880–1920*. U of Western Australia P, 1973.

Inwood, Stephen. *A History of London*. New York: Harold and Graff, 1998.

Lynch, Kevin. *The Image of the City*. Cambridge: MIT P, 1960.

Marcus, Sharon. *Apartment Stories: City and Home in Nineteenth-Century Paris and London*. Berkeley: U of California P, 1999.

Morgan, Thaïs. "Victorian Effeminacies." In *Victorian Sexual Dissidence*. Richard Dellamora, ed. Chicago: U of Chicago P, 1999.

Nord, Deborah Epstein. *Walking the Victorian Streets: Women, Representation, and the City*. Ithaca: Cornell UP, 1995.

Pater, Walter. *Studies in the History of the Renaissance*. London: Macmillan, 1873.

Pittock, Murray G. H. *Spectrum of Decadence: The Literature of the 1890s*. London and New York: Routledge, 1993.

Symons, Arthur. *Silhouettes* and *London Nights*. Republished jointly. Oxford: Woodstock Books, 1993.

————. *Arthur Symons: Selected Letters, 1880–1935*. Karl Beckson and John M. Munro, eds. Iowa City: U of Iowa P, 1989.

————. *The Memoirs of Arthur Symons: Life and Art in the 1890's*. Karl Beckson, ed. University Park and London: Pennsylvania State UP, 1977.

Walkowitz, Judith. *City of Dreadful Delight*. Chicago: U of Chicago P, 1992.

Whittington–Egan, Richard. "Sunflower and Green Carnation." *Contemporary Review* 237.1376 (1980): 155–60.

Yeats, W. B. *W. B. Yeats: Letters to the New Island*. Eds. George Bornstein and Hugh Witemeyer. New York: Macmillan, 1989.

CHAPTER 5

The Metropole as Antipodes: Australian Women in London and Constructing National Identity

ANGELA WOOLLACOTT

*I*n the decades either side of the turn of the twentieth century, when the British Empire was at its greatest reach, London attracted imperial subjects from many of its colonies and dominions. Among the colonials resident in London in this era were a large number of white women from the Australian colonies, or, from 1901, federated dominion. Between 1870 and 1940, tens of thousands of Australian women were drawn to the imperial metropolis for reasons ranging from the social and familial, to the pursuit of education, professions, and artistic careers. At the same time, colonial agents' offices, societies, leagues, and clubs linked to the empire appeared throughout London's West End, such that the empire was visibly represented on London streets. Australian women resident in London patronized and founded some of these associations and clubs, in a real sense contributing to the mapping of empire onto the metropole itself. Through their imperial and patriotic networking, their friendships and professional circles, and their own creative productions in London, Australian women articulated their versions of Australianness, even as the meanings of that national identity were shifting along with historically changing dynamics between metropole and dominion (Woollacott, *To Try Her Fortune*). Australian women's distance from home and their status as colonials allowed them to push against gendered circumscriptions on women's movement through London's public spaces. Many of them exploited this, even

to the point of taking pride in their navigation and exploration of the great city
(Woollacott, "The Colonial Flaneuse").

There were other ways in which Australian women mapped Australia
onto London, as well. Through their complaints about the metropole, Australians either implicitly or explicitly registered their specific points of pride
in a healthful, egalitarian, and forward-looking Australia—elements of emerging definitions of nationness—thus creating a vision of London as not-Aus-
tralia, as comparatively backward and lacking. In doing so, they reversed the
dominant assumption that the metropolis represented modernity, while the
colonies were the backward periphery. Simon Gikandi has argued that colonialism was "a culture of mutual imbrication and contamination," a reciprocal process in which Britishness was invented through projection onto colonial sites, colonies reconstituted themselves in response to Englishness, and "in
inventing itself, the colonial space would also reinvent the structure and
meaning of the core terms of Englishness" (Gikandi xviii). In this chapter, I
shall examine a process in which white Australian women (and men) at once
constructed negative visions of London and self-congratulatory versions of
Australian national identity, versions that distinguished their elaborators as the
appropriate proprietors of the new nation rather than either metropolitan
Britons or Australian Aborigines. Clearly, national identities are ever-shifting
cultural constructions, fictions created through multiple processes of articulation and recognition. Anything but immanent or essential, far from organic,
shared definitions of national culture are mythologies that sustain meaning at
specific historical moments. As several scholars of Australian popular culture
have posited: "Culture does not grow out of the unity of a society but out of
its divisions. It has to work to *construct* any unity that it has, rather than simply celebrate an achieved or natural harmony" (Fiske, Hodge, and Turner x).
In the decades preceding and following the inauguration of Australia as a federated nation, the impetus for Australians to articulate a shared culture and its
meanings was considerable. Contrasts between the imperial metropole and
the federating colonies were too obvious a source of possible meanings to
resist. If cultural productions within Australia's shores by its denizens have
usually been the texts from which Australian national identities have been
read, the fragmentary recorded observations which Australians made in London, contrasting that city with their locations of origin, offer us another
archive to read. By projecting Australia from within the metropole, Australians sought to reshape London by drawing attention to its shortcomings,
while contributing to the articulation of a national, and modern, rather than
colonial set of identities for Australia.

A major critical theme running through Australians' accounts of their
reactions to London is their horror at the poverty, suffering, and class inequality they witnessed there, in comparison to Australia's relative egalitarianism,

comfortable living standards, and social welfare measures. In terms of class relations and social equity, Australians almost unanimously considered Britain to be historically lagging behind Australia, to be riddled with an anachronistic class structure and system of social deference many Australians found offensive. Australia, in contrast, they viewed as a more democratic and egalitarian culture. They saw Australia as socially and politically progressive, a turn of the imperial relationship such that the colonies were showing the metropole the path towards modernity. In the mid-1880s, a Miss Richie accompanied her father, Agent-General for Victoria, to London for several years. To her surprise, she found that she could not enjoy London as she had hoped: "The poverty in London overwhelmed my spirits; I was haunted by the faces I saw in the streets. It was the misery of London—much greater than anything we could conceive in the Colonies—which led me to serious study." Indeed, she went on to earn a B.A. in political economy and logic at the University of London (Dolman 1119).

In 1912 Australian travel writer Mary Gaunt, who made her name through her travels and accounts of West Africa, spoke out about the conditions of life for London's poor. She drew an explicit comparison between the poorer areas of London and those of Melbourne, calling the former "slums" and the latter, in contrast, "back streets." In Australia, she reported, she had called those areas of Melbourne "slums"; she consciously changed her terminology because, having seen London, she learned "what slums really are" (*The British-Australasian* 30 May 1912: 18). Historian and education scholar Barbara Falk recalled her own powerful first reaction to poverty in England when she arrived there in 1933 to continue her studies. When her uncle and aunt picked her up at the Tilbury docks, and they drove through the slums of the East End on their way to Hampstead, she was so horrified she had to cover her eyes. In retrospect she admitted that her aunt and uncle must have found her behavior somewhat strange, but, she noted, for her, poverty had been largely theoretical until then (Falk). Australians sometimes commented on what they clearly saw as the irony of the fact that benevolent organizations in Australia would raise money to send back to relieve the suffering of the English poor. An Australian writer commented in 1915 on what she saw as possible evidence that the British Empire was collapsing at the center: "Little Tasmania has to send money to our English poor, because England cannot find work or food for them herself. . . . England cannot even pay her soldiers enough to ensure their wives and children proper food" ("Decline and Fall" 2).

Australian women often commented as well on the class structure in England, on what they perceived as gross, embedded inequalities. Poet and writer Lindsay Russell commented in 1913 that London was both a wonderful and a terrible place, because "in London meet the two great extremes, and the poverty is like to none other in the world." A few Australians in London sought to redress class inequalities through their own small acts of philanthropy. Russell, for example, happened to notice "three of the raggedest little urchins you ever saw" gazing at the dresses in a shop window one day, just after she had been cabled some money by her publishers in Melbourne. On the spur of the moment she took the three girls into the shop and had them "all fitted up and dressed properly" (Prichard, "Lindsay Russell" 395). To some Australians, such as celebrated writer Henry Lawson in 1902, the class divisions in London produced a situation of imminent class warfare:

> They can't hear in West o' London, where the worst dine with the best—
> Deaf to all save lies and laughter, they can't hear in London West—
> Tailored brutes and splendid harlots, and the parasites that be—
> They can't hear the warning thunder of the Drums of Battersea.
> More drums! War drums! Drums of misery—
> Beating from the hearts of men—the Drums of Battersea. (Cronin 124)

If neither individual acts of philanthropy nor odes to working-class militancy by Australians had a great deal of impact on class relations in Britain, observing and condemning metropolitan socioeconomic injustice was a key if indirect component in their construction of national identity. Convict transportation from Britain to Australia had ended only in the 1860s. For eighty years, the Australian colonies had functioned as a dumping ground for British prisoners, a central part of the British criminal justice system that happened to be conveniently located on the other side of the globe. By the end of the nineteenth century, what had earlier been the shame and social stigma attached to the status of convicts became transmuted into cultural resentment at both the harshness of the British treatment of individual prisoners, and the relatively lengthy exploitation by Britain of its Australian colonies for this notorious purpose.

The federated Australian nation, which came into being in 1901, had its roots in the social and economic inequalities in Britain that had produced many of the convicts. Australian awareness of those historical ties, the inherited resentments passed on by Irish convicts sent out for political transgressions, and the harsh exigencies of life in the bush that fostered a masculinist mythology of mateship, all contributed to a cultural emphasis on egalitarianism. What Australians perceived as Britain's perpetuation of its hierarchical class system and gross social inequalities were thus obvious targets for critical commentary, and the corollary self-congratulations became part of their national self-definition. Australian claims to egalitarianism served, of course, to mask the very real differences in wealth and living standards, and the palpable existence of hierarchical class identities and interests in the burgeoning dominion. Yet the bases for Australians' sense of their own progressiveness were identifiable.

The process of the birth of a new nation generated excitement and optimism among its citizens as well as other observers. The idealistic title of Commonwealth of Australia represented the hopes that attended it, the sense of possibility that this white-settler nation would prove a brave new world in the southern hemisphere. For those concerned about the rights and interests of workers, one especially hopeful indicator was the rapid rise to power of the Australian Labor Party. Compared to socialist and labor organizations in Europe that stretched back to the mid-nineteenth century, the Australian Labor Party, representative of working-class people and trade-union organization, came to power in its infancy. The first-ever elected Labor government came to power in Queensland in 1899; in 1904 a Labor government came to brief federal office; and in 1910 a federal Labor government was elected with a mandate to rule, and enjoyed a full term in which to institute its platform. Prior to 1914, every Australian state experienced an elected Labor government. The agenda of these early Labor governments included the establishment of minimum wages, industrial arbitration courts and wages boards, old-age pensions, the rights of workers to organize and, in 1912, a maternity allowance. Australian governments in the decades either side of the turn of the twentieth century introduced public works projects when employment was short, land settlement schemes intended to equalize land distribution (among whites), public enterprises, and government banks.

There were other aspects of Australian politics that could similarly be seen as progressive. Suffrage was one important area: white women were given the franchise in two Australian states in the 1890s, and the federal vote in 1902, well before the attainment of women's suffrage in Britain (granted partially in 1918 and not fully until 1928). Manhood suffrage had been in place for the lower houses of parliament in Australian colonies prior to federation, and was instituted for both federal houses of parliament from the first election in 1901. In marked contrast to the British parliament, both houses of the Australian federal parliament were democratically elected.

For all of this progressiveness, there was one crucial area of exclusion upon which white Australians seemed unanimous. The White Australia policy, which had its roots in colonial legislation from the 1880s and was quickly entrenched by the new federal government, was framed explicitly to prohibit Asian immigration. At the behest of the imperial government, in practice in its federal form it consisted of a fifty-word dictation test that could be administered in any European language, so that the emphasis was displaced from race itself. But the point of the policy was racial exclusion, and one of its main effects was to underscore the exclusion of Aboriginal people from Australian citizenship. For white Australians in Britain around the turn of the century, this policy was accepted without question, and certainly was not to be considered a national failing (Macintyre, chs. 3, 4, and 5).

Australians concurred on other points of comparison detrimental to London, beside its gross exhibition of poverty and social inequality. A common complaint was the lack of bathrooms in lodgings, the difficulty and expense of obtaining adequate baths, and the seeming (or relative) aversion of Britons to bathing. In 1902 Louise Mack declared, in her novel *An Australian Girl in London*, that "the great Bath Question . . . makes all Australians mad. To come to London, the world's centre, and find big houses full of highly-civilised people and no bathroom gives one an unpleasant shock." The English must dislike cold water, Mack theorized, "or London would not endure what seems to us a misery beyond words—the absence of bathrooms" (Mack 208). Then in 1910, "Peggy," a regular columnist in the weekly newspaper for Antipodeans in Britain, complained that the population of London was "one of the most unwashed of the civilised nations." Visiting Australians, Peggy claimed, were "struck by the scarcity of bathrooms, the dearness of baths, and the disfavour shown to water both for washing and drinking purposes by the working class in general," although she qualified her class-based criticism by duly noting that for people whose houses were "well staffed with servants, of course, the extra trouble entailed by the 'bath-in-the-bedroom' system is not felt" (Peggy 24). Describing the gymnastics and discomfort she and her fictionalized roommates endured in order to take a bath from a container like "a large frying-pan" in their London lodgings circa 1910, Australian actress and writer Mary Marlowe winds up by commenting: "Bathing in London is a hobby, and often an expensive one. That the English are a clean nation is the first illusion the visitor loses" (Marlowe 36–37). Given the fundamental cultural equation between civilization and cleanliness, Australians, priding themselves on their demand for baths, were representing themselves as the ones who were truly civilized. This complaint about Londoners thus worked to refute their own position as vulgar colonials. In fact, in Peggy's view at least, this was one clear area in which "Colonials" were pushing the metropole slowly in the direction of modernity. Demanding colonials were "even influencing the London landlady to the extent of including the bath in her tariff, instead of making it the most expensive 'extra' on the list," as well as being among the most frequent customers at the "greater number of reasonably-priced Turkish baths that [were] . . . appearing recently" (Peggy 24).

The lack of bathrooms was not the only point of Australian complaint about English lodgings. Australians—used to dwellings that spread out horizontally more than they rose vertically—found the flights of stairs in London lodging houses an unwarranted hardship. The rooms in the lodgings themselves they found, in contrast, problematically restricted. Photographer Stuart Gore complained of the rooms that he and his wife rented in Hampstead in the 1950s: "In the living-room you could stand in the middle of the floor, clean your teeth at the sink in one corner, fry your breakfast at the 'cooking facilities' in the second, and eat it at the table in the third, in economical motions of three paces back, forward or sideways. The fourth corner wasn't there. It was a door" (Gore 15–16). The lack of space in English dwellings, Australians seemed to suggest, was yet another indicator of the low general standard of living.

Not surprisingly, given the climatic differences, Australians complained vociferously about inadequate heating. Marlowe, describing her and her room-mates' settling into their lodgings, reported that: "we gathered round the fire-place—I will not say the fire. One of us could have covered that in a narrow skirt" (Marlowe 37). For activist and writer Miles Franklin, author of the 1901 cause célèbre novel *My Brilliant Career*, the shortcomings of English lodgings were not only in comparison to Australian housing, but to that in America where she had lived for nearly ten years before moving to London in late 1915. Endlessly recording in her diary her unhappiness about the lack of light and warmth in her rented Chelsea rooms, and the terrible draughts, one January day in 1917 Franklin's grumbling culminated in the pithy condemnation: "Desperately cold in the holes which the English call homes" (Franklin).

If English housing was uncomfortable and not conducive to health, the English themselves, moreover, were often painted as cold and inhospitable, lacking Australians' spontaneity and generosity. Even London was at times described as inhospitable and inaccessible to the colonial stranger, and as difficult to navigate. In 1885 Australian writer Rosa Praed sympathetically reported helping a compatriote bushman lost near Belgrave Square, who complained: "'I get quite bushed in these streets. London is an awful place. It's all the same. I'd give a good deal to be able to blaze [mark] the houses as we do the iron-bark trees. In fact, I'd rather any day be lost in Never Never Country'"(Praed 29–30). In this and other representations by Australians, London was positioned as the frontier, the unknown place of difficulty and exploration requiring endurance, skill, and perseverance, in opposition to a familiar, predictable, and hence domesticated Australia.

Most pervasive of all were complaints about the English climate and land-scape, and its patent inferiority to Australia's natural environment. Australians complained loudly about the cold, English winters, and the London smoke and fog, between which they admitted (in historical retrospect, for apparently good reasons) they often could not distinguish. "Australians frequently complain that there is little colour in England," one correspondent reported (*The British-Australasian* 25 Oct. 1917: 18). Tied to their complaints were lyrical evocations of Australia. Writer Henrietta Leslie's reaction in 1920 was typical: "The London climate? I hate it, and long for the moonlit beaches, the deep Austral blue skies, and the fragrant wildflowers of Australia" (*The British-Australasian* 20 May 1920: 14). Australian singers complained about the effects of the London climate on their throats; conversely, it was widely believed (not only by Australians) that the Australian climate was a primary reason for all of the good Australian

voices—of professional singers—in London. Even British singers such as
Dame Clara Butt "spoke about the delightful voices which the Australian sunshine and azure skies produce" (Boanas 16). Successful Australian oratorio
singer Madame Mary Conly told an acquaintance that "the London fog, and
London with its wet, dreary days made her long to return to the land where
she could again smell the fragrance of the gum trees, and see the wattle in all
its beauty wavering and being so softly caressed by the spring time zephyr
breeze" (Boanas 16). The sun itself and the inadequacy of sunshine in London
serve as a leitmotif through Australians' descriptions of the metropole, a touch-
stone for the contrast between the Australian and English climates. Marlowe
included this trope too in her fictionalized description of her group's first day
in London:

> Presently Betty jumped up and went to the open window. . . .
> "Girls," she cried, "There's the sun." Belle and I dashed to the other win-
> dow, looked up and down the street and then at Betty.
> "Where?" we said both together.
> "Look between those two houses to the right."
> We looked skywards and, lo! a pale ray of sunshine crept out of the grey-
> ness, stole half-way down to earth and then grew timid. (Marlowe 37–38)

Some Australians sought to transplant a piece of their homeland by planting
and nurturing Australian flora in their London gardens, even if it meant having
to coddle them through the English winters. In 1908 concert singer Ada Crossley was extremely proud of the Western Australian boronia in her hothouse, and
the four Gippsland bluegums (eucalyptus trees) whose leaves, she claimed, her
homesick Australian friends regularly came to sniff (Pritchard [sic] 709).[1] Creating a ritual of smelling gum leaves was one way in which Australians convinced themselves and each other of the special beauty of the Australian natural environment compared to that of England.

The favorable comparison of the harsh and dramatic Australian bush to
England's tamer landscape became a staple of Australian cultural expression. It
was made famous in Dorothea Mackellar's poem, "My Country," rhetorically
addressed to an English person:

> The love of field and coppice,
> Of green and shaded lanes,
> Of ordered woods and gardens
> Is running in your veins. . . .
> I know but cannot share it,
> My love is otherwise.
> I love a sunburnt country,
> A land of sweeping plains,
> Of ragged mountain ranges,
> Of droughts and flooding rains.

> I love her far horizons,
> I love her jewel-sea,
> Her beauty and her terror—
> The wide brown land for me! (in Lever 59)

Louise Mack went so far as to commit a kind of colonial heresy by suggesting that the English painter J. M. W. Turner "ought to have been born an Australian." Contending that the English landscape had been unsuited to "his craving for great distances" she imagines instead "Turner in the Blue Mountains looking away up the Kanimbla Valley one winter sunset!" In Australia, she thought, Turner "would have satisfied himself" instead of having "to draw on his imagination, and go[ing] to the classics for something large enough to give his soul full play" (Mack 133). The Australian landscape, Mack implies, has greater potential than the English landscape to inspire powerful art.

Australian national identity, tied to the natural environment, was partly produced through Australians' complaints about London. But the meanings of constructing Australia as "the land of sunshine and gold" went beyond its natural attributes (*The British-Australasian* 3 Mar. 1898: 501). Australians came to link their climate, in opposition to the English climate and by extension the English social system, with health, vigor, progress, and modernity. Journalist Beatrix Tracy had great hopes for London when she first traveled there, but her disillusionment finally led her to argue that "You cannot feel in London as you felt at home. . . . London has killed some faculty of joyousness in you. You can't love as you used, nor quarrel, nor laugh, nor even cry as passionately. The fog and the cold have thinned your blood; your heart is hardened in the battle for a living, or for success." She challenged the other Australians in London to contrast their current circumstances with their recollections of "home":

> Do you think of it often? Of Australia, with its clean, spruce cities, its naïve, bright women in clear-coloured dresses, its cheerful, sunburnt men? . . . And the beaches, washed by a bluer sea than England ever saw, and of pure gold and silver—the warm-tinted cliffs, the sapphire skies? And the children—those straight-limbed, bold-eyed brownies, compound of fire and grace—that Australia has bred from Englishmen? . . . [Y]ou know, and I know, that Australia is the one place where an Australian can live perfectly—and that the Australian is the one human being who knows how to live perfectly. (Tracy 43).

Tracy and other Australians suggested that the Australian climate and environment produced an optimism that, while seemingly unsophisticated, led to an idealism and preparedness to try new methods and approaches that were directly connected to Australia's egalitarianism and modernity.

In the field of Australian cultural studies, it has been suggested that the national mythology constructed around the Australian bush as a place of stark natural beauty and idealized community has been a way of resolving the nature versus culture dilemma. Under pressure to construct Australianness in the decades spanning the turn of the twentieth century, writers, poets, and painters, who were themselves thoroughly urbanized, created a romanticized legend of the Australian bush. Through it, they registered the power of the Australian landscape and satisfied their own desires for community, social familiarity, and mutual obligation. Graeme Turner has suggested, moreover, that narratives of the harsh and demanding Australian bush shared central features with narratives of early Australia as a penal colony. Both of these "provide us with the alibi that we need to accept the status quo in a society where there are strong physical, social and hegemonic reasons for doing so. Within both the pioneering myth of the land, and the submissive myth of the convict system, the difficulty of survival becomes the justification for failing to do more than that" (Turner 52). Inasfar as Turner construes the joint effect of the bush myth and the convict myth to be "an ideology which depends upon the necessity of accepting personal and socioeconomic limitations, and of settling for survival as the highest good" (37), the evidence of observations by Australians in London is contradictory. Here too there is a confluence between the narratives of structural social injustice and natural environment, but that confluence serves to praise Australia at London's expense: in Australia there was little of the poverty and suffering rampant on London's streets, and the Australian climate was beneficent with the very warmth and light that London so badly lacked. The authors of these nationalist narratives, Australian visitors to the metropolis, included some of the writers and artists who produced representations of Australian culture. But the emotional valence is far from defeatist or passive. In the context of England itself, confronted with metropolitan definitions of their colonial status and differences from true Englishness, Antipodean authors responded by identifying the advantages and the potential of the Australian natural environment, society, and polity.

Linking the salubrious aspects of Australia's natural environment to what they saw as the colonies' or dominion's social progressiveness and relative economic egalitarianism, these commentators cast the new nation as a country with a prosperous future, a young nation with a full and rich life ahead. One implication of these visions of Australia as a new creation was the erasure of the continent's past and with it the existence of its indigenous inhabitants. Simon Ryan has laid out some of the ways in which Australia has been constructed historically as a tabula rasa, a blankness awaiting European "exploration," identification, and recording. He analyzes the cartographic process in which non-European social and physical formations have been denied existence and the continent has been constructed Eurocentrically as empty, to be possessed and developed. This process of European "worlding" occurred in the maps that showed Australia for centuries prior to British invasion in 1788, was a central feature of the maps and journals recorded by the early post–invasion "explorers," and persisted in Australian writing and self-description. Australian writers recirculated the assertion that Australia was a continent of vast open spaces bearing no traces of history, that it was a silent and blank land awaiting cultural inscription (Ryan, esp. 127–29). Similarly, Australians in London, through their representations of Australia as a thriving offshoot of Britain, a new country gaining its independence of the motherland and already outstripping it in important measures, obliterated the continent's past and the claims to recognition of the peoples who had long inhabited it, many of whom had in fact survived the murderous processes of white conquest.

It is especially significant that the critical trope that dominated all others was that of the natural environment: London's (according to Australians) cold and wet climate, the lack of sunshine, and the absence of particular vegetation, such as gum and wattle (acacia) trees. Prior to World War I, an Australia-wide movement had established the wattle as Australia's national floral emblem, marked by the annual celebration of Wattle Day. The pale golden wattle blossom became an icon of Australianness and a means of mutual recognition for Australians in London. For example, during World War I, Wattle Day was marked by the public selling of badges, and even sprigs of the related mimosa from France, to raise money for Australian troops. Katharine Susannah Prichard recorded in her autobiography that, during her years in London as a young aspiring journalist, she received a letter from home containing a piece of wattle blossom as a memento (*Child* 129). Wattle had come to signify, for Australians, the Australian climate and bush as a whole. Peter Read has recently written about non-indigenous Australians' relationships to the land, their feelings about the Australian landscape, their sense of place and belonging. In the last quarter-century, he suggests, at least some urban, middle-class, and well-educated white Australians have come to adopt the burden of guilt about British dispossession of the Aborigines of their land, to such an extent as to feel "self-doubt and potential paralysis" about their own position in Australia, their claims to belonging. In his exploration of the feelings about the land held by non-indigenous people, he considers specific individuals' relationships to specific Australian landscapes (Read). The constructions of Australianness put forward in London either side of federation did not often focus on particular parts of landscape, although no doubt at least some white Australians of the period felt such attachments. Rather, colonials in the metropole melded together the flora and fauna, the climate and the landscape, creating a pantheon of Australian icons from which they could draw, a pantheon that included elements of Aboriginal culture such that Australians might refer to gum trees, kangaroos, and boomerangs in the same fashion.

In part this pastiche of plant, animal, and indigenous cultural referents reflected the fact that Australia was increasingly and dominantly an urban society, and for many the bush was more mythological construct than vivid reality. But this pantheon of nationalist icons was also central to Australians' set of shared referents in the metropole, the signifiers they employed to carry the meanings of Australianness. In a way, these icons functioned as a kind of shorthand for Australians abroad. Lyn Spillman has argued that, historically, the land has become increasingly central in the Australian process of nation formation. In her comparative study of the centennial and bicentennial celebrations in the United States and Australia, Spillman found that the United States maintained an emphasis on its political culture. From the centennial of the British invasion of Australia in 1888 to the bicentennial in 1988, however, Australians' definitions moved away from political values and increasingly centered on the landscape as the most distinctive feature of the nation (Spillman 137–39).

The set of icons invoked by Australians in the turn-of-the-century metropole contributed to this longer-term nationalist articulation. But both processes—that which sought to distinguish Australia from London, and the larger discourse of shared national referents—had the effect of positioning nonindigenous Australians as proprietors and interpreters of the land, and of Aboriginal culture along with it. The representational appropriation by white Australians of the very foundations of Aboriginal cultures was yet one more stage in the process of indigenous dispossession.

Recently, concern has been aired that Australians are singularly lacking in knowledge of their national history. A 1997 government-commissioned survey established that only 18 percent of Australians could name the nation's first prime minister (Vangelova). It may well be that, due in good part to an imperially-slanted rather than nationally-slanted school curriculum, and in marked contrast to the American educational system, for example, Australians simply have not been steeped in the political narratives of their national history. It is possible to speculate even further that such an absence of national knowledge may have been a factor in the failure of the 1999 referendum to abolish the remaining constitutional links to Britain and to establish Australia as an independent republic. Perhaps Australians, relatively lacking in national political icons and formative narratives, simply did not have a sufficiently strong sense of their political past to endorse a bid for independence. But if Australians need to know more of their shared political past, it is important to consider what kind of histories they ought to study. Inga Clendinnen has suggested that what Australians need are "true stories" of their history, discrete and complex stories such as of recorded encounters between black and white, stories that will provoke reflection and the moral imagination, and perhaps be conducive to civic virtue. Too often, she argues, nations have settled for "bad history," for "one simple and therefore necessarily false [story]: a story about how fine and great we are, how fine and great we have always been" (Clendinnen 6–9). Evidence abounds that, historically, Australians have indeed engaged in national myths and cultural self-constructions, at least some of which have been of the self-congratulatory ilk.

Australians in London either side of the turn of the twentieth century chose to find fault with their imperial metropolis, in ways that could seem like a laundry-list of complaints but that in fact were interconnected and presented a coherent message. Britain's anachronistic class system was directly related to the poverty and suffering easily observed on London's streets, and the inadequate, poorly heated lodgings available to the average colonial visitor were indicative of the country's low standard of living. The imperial metropole was physically uncomfortable and inhospitable, partly because of its cold, damp, and grey climate, but also because of its clinging to traditional class structures and modes of life. Australia, on the other hand, joined its climate of warmth and sunshine to an egalitarian culture that was prepared to forge new social and economic paths, and the combination represented both a brash new nation and social and political modernity. White Australians thus projected negative visions of London through which could be seen the outlines of a far more promising young dominion. In the process they established themselves, with what they saw as their patriotic appreciation for the Australian climate and vegetation, and their political responsibility for the new nation, as the unquestioned custodians of the land on which this new society was being built, in the stead of its former custodians. In doing so, in an inversion of the venerable imperial process of constructing the colonized as odd and incomplete others, they represented the metropole itself as Australia's Antipodes.

NOTE

1. Similarly, singer Essie Ackland took back to her Edgware garden "all sorts of Australian plants from many places" (*West Australian*).

WORKS CITED

Ackland, Essie. Papers. Ackland MSS, Box 2, National Library of Australia.

Boanas, Clifton. "Cameo Studies of Famous Celebrities It Has Been My Pleasure to Meet." *Australian Musical News* 1 May 1930: 16.

British-Australasian 3 Mar. 1898: 501.

British-Australasian 20 May 1920: 14.

British-Australasian 30 May 1912: 18.

British-Australasian 25 Oct. 1917: 18.

Clendinnen, Inga. *True Stories.* Sydney: ABC Books, 1999.

Cronin, Leonard, ed. *A Fantasy of Man: Henry Lawson Complete Works 1901–1922.* Sydney: Lansdowne, 1984.

"Decline and Fall of the British Empire?" *The Woman Voter* [Australia] 5 January 1915: 2.

Dolman, Frederick. "Ladies of Melbourne." *The Woman at Home* 7 (1899): 1119.

Falk, Barbara. Personal interview. 10 April 1995.

Fiske, John, Bob Hodge, and Graeme Turner. *Myths of Oz: Reading Australian Popular Culture.* Boston: Allen and Unwin, 1987.

Franklin, Miles. Papers, CY Reel 766, ML MSS. 364/2. Mitchell Library, State Library of New South Wales. 364/2, item 10, diary entry for Wed. 24 Jan. 1917.

Gikandi, Simon. *Maps of Englishness: Writing Identity in the Culture of Colonialism.* New York: Columbia UP, 1996.

Gore, Stuart. *Australians, Go Home!* London: Robert Hale, 1958.

Lever, Susan, ed. *The Oxford Book of Australian Women's Verse.* Melbourne: Oxford UP, 1995.

Macintyre, Stuart. *The Oxford History of Australia: The Succeeding Age 1901–1942.* Melbourne: Oxford UP, 1993.

Mack, Louise. *An Australian Girl in London.* London: T. Fisher Unwin, 1902.

Marlowe, Mary. *Kangaroos in King's Land: Being the Adventures of Four Australian Girls in England.* London: Simpkin, Marshall, Hamilton, Kent, 1917.

Peggy. "In the Looking Glass." *British-Australasian* 24 Feb. 1910: 24.

Praed, Rosa [Mrs. Campbell]. *Australian Life: Black and White.* London: Chapman and Hall, 1885.

Prichard, Katharine S. "Lindsay Russell in London." *Everylady's Journal* 6 July 1913: 395.

———. *Child of the Hurricane: An Autobiography.* London: Angus and Robertson, 1964.

Pritchard [*sic*], Katharine S. "Ada Crossley at Home: A Visit from an Australian Journalist." *New Idea* 6 October 1908: 709–11.

Read, Peter. *Belonging: Australians, Place and Aboriginal Ownership.* Cambridge: Cambridge UP, 2000.

Ryan, Simon. "Inscribing the Emptiness: Cartography, Exploration and the Construction of Australia." In *De-Scribing Empire.* Chris Tiffin and Alan Dawson, eds. London: Routledge, 1994. 115–30.

Spillman, Lyn. *Nation and Commemoration: Creating National Identities in the United States and Australia.* Cambridge: Cambridge UP, 1997.

Tracy, Beatrix. "London." *British-Australasian* 30 June 1910: 43.

Turner, Graeme. *National Fictions: Literature, Film and the Construction of Australian Narrative.* St. Leonards, NSW: Allen and Unwin, 1993.

Vangelova, Luba. "100 Years Down Under." *San Francisco Chronicle* 31 Dec. 2000: A18.

West Australian. Clippings, Box 2, Ackland MSS, National Library of Australia, 27 May 1937.

Woollacott, Angela. "The Colonial Flaneuse: Australian Women Negotiating Turn-of-the-Century London." *Signs* 25.3 (Spring 2000): 761–87.

————. *To Try Her Fortune in London: Australian Women, Colonialism, and Modernity.* New York: Oxford UP, 2001.

CHAPTER 6

Modernist Space and the Transformation of Underground London

DAVID L. PIKE

> . . . so with a kind of madness growing upon me, I flung myself into futurity.
>
> —H. G. Wells, *The Time Machine*

*T*he eminent historian Eric Hobsbawm recently characterized Harry Beck's schematic map of the London Underground as "the most original work of avant-garde art in Britain between the wars" (38–39) (see fig. 6.1). It certainly represents a perfect marriage of abstract design and practical utility. By simplifying the complex network of urban railway lines into a visually pleasing and easily legible map bearing little or no relation to either the experiential or the physical metropolis of London, Beck codified a particularly modernist conception of space. Unchanged in its basic design since first sketched in 1931, the tube map is arguably the predominant summary image of London worldwide today. Hobsbawm's polemical assertion is partially based on this phenomenal popularity, suggesting that the map is the only visual artifact out of *entre-deux-guerres* England capable of competing with the enduring cultural icons that emerged from Paris and Berlin during the same decades.

In this chapter, I discuss some reasons for the popularity of Beck's tube diagram, and sketch out some of the ramifications of that popularity for the

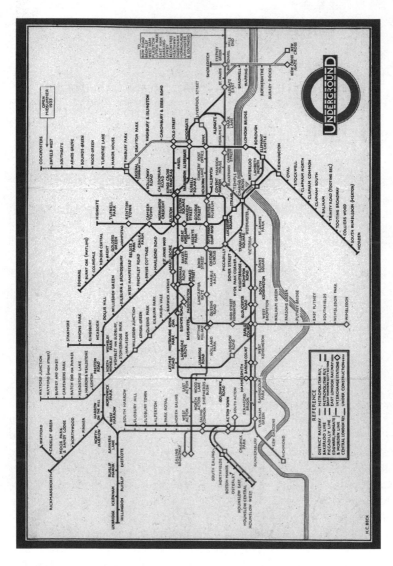

FIGURE 6.1. Modernist Space. Details of lines and colors have changed, but concept and design remain the same today. Harry Beck, first topological Underground map, 1933. Courtesy of London's Transport Museum.

imagination of London over the past seventy years. I link its design to architectural modernism, primarily on the Continent, using the theory and history of urbanism to suggest some possible connections between movements in visual arts, film, and literature of the time which have often been studied in isolation since. In particular, I argue that they can fruitfully be compared under the rubric of modernist space, a mode of conceptualizing the experience of the city whose marks can be seen in most of the canonical products of modernism; this was, after all, a moment of experimentation in dissolving the boundaries between artistic media. At the same time that I establish a shared attitude toward a specific abstraction of urban space, I also suggest that the diverse manifestations of that attitude have made it difficult for us to notice the coexistence of other spatial attitudes during the same period. Just as Beck's map has codified a dominant image of London as a whole, so have fixed ideas about modernism occluded alternate approaches to London's urban spaces, including those made available by, but remaining unrecognized within, the tube map itself. By virtue of the very qualities that have led it consistently to be regarded as suffering from a dearth of the quintessentially modernist, London pointedly questions the boundaries of the term.

THE CONCEPTUAL CITY

Beck's design responded to a practical problem of representation with a novel solution. Assuaging the eye and the mind through its symbolization of a vast network extending at least twenty miles in all directions from Charing Cross, his color-coded map also provided an enduring resolution to a crisis of perception. Consider, for example, Ford Madox Ford's assertion in 1905, at the height of London's growth, that, "One may easily sail round England, or circumnavigate the globe. But not the most enthusiastic geographer . . . ever memorised a map of London. Certainly no one ever walks round it. For England is a small island, the world is infinitesimal amongst the planets. But London is illimitable" (16). Beck's map displaced the daunting challenge of "memorizing" the modern city into the plausible if unlikely daydream of riding each line of the Underground through every one of its stations: the maroon Metropolitan from Verney Junction or Brill to New Cross; the green District from Richmond or Wimbledon to Upminster, the black Northern from Highgate or Edgware to Morden; the brown Bakerloo from Watford Junction to Elephant and Castle; the dark blue Piccadilly from Cockfosters to Hounslow West; the red Central from Ealing Broadway to Liverpool Street, and later Ongar; and the yellow Circle in an infinite loop around London.

The geographical identity of London has been defined both traditionally and officially as the space delimited by the extent of the Underground. For example, in 1938, the Chamberlain's Royal Commission on the Geographical Distribution of the Industrial Population followed Underground Director Frank Pick in presuming that, "If London grew beyond the magic 12 to 15-mile limit set by the economics of the tube, it 'must cease to be instrinsically London'" (Hall 85). Consequently, the ways in which the transport system is represented have significant repercussions for the ways in which the metropolis as a whole is imagined. Unlike earlier Underground maps, or those of other cities such as Paris, Beck's map eschewed any direct correlation with the layout of the city it conceptualized.[1] Even the signature curves of the river Thames, the only surface feature retained, were straightened out. In addition to plotting the cityscape onto a grid of horizontals, verticals, and diagonals, the map's abstraction codified several abiding distortions. The space of central London is significantly enlarged, dominating the highly compressed outlying areas; of those areas, west and northwest London occupy some two-thirds of the map's volume, while the East End is represented beyond Liverpool Street Station only by the truncated extensions of the District and Metropolitan lines. The equally vast expanse of South London is represented only by the Northern line and quite a bit of empty, white space, conveniently occupied by the London Underground insignia and, later on, by explanatory text and keys to the symbols. A complete transport map, including bus and surface railway routes in the south and east, would show a different picture of the city entirely. As it stands, the reverie of the map-gazing passenger is limited by a set of social boundaries that define his or her tastes and desires as middle to upper-middle class; the remainder are rendered invisible both on and off of the Underground.

It is in the control it exerts over the space it abstracts that Beck's map fits into a genealogy of modernist space that originated in the mid-nineteenth century and lingers on today. One starting-point of this genealogy might be the map presented by the Emperor Napoleon III in 1853 to the Prefect of Paris, Baron Haussmann, a map "on which one saw traced in blue, in red, in yellow and in green, according to their degree of urgency, the different new routes he proposed to take" (Jordan 170–76; also Pinkney 25–31). While this map shares its color-coding with Beck, what defines the space both maps develop is suggested by Le Corbusier's comment in 1925 on the prefect's execution of the imperial plan: "The avenues he cut were entirely arbitrary: they were not based on strict deductions of the science of town planning. The measures he took were of a financial and military character (*surgery*)" (259). It was in terms of urbanistic rigor that Le Corbusier conceived his landmark contribution to modernist space and improvement on Haussmann's urban surgery, the Voisin Plan, presented in the Pavilion of the New Spirit at the 1925 Exposition of Decorative Arts in Paris (275–89). Le Corbusier's scheme called for the demolition of the historic center of Paris from the Marais in the east to the Champs Élysées in the west, and from the Seine in the south to the Grands Boulevards in the north. In its place would be erected sixty high-rise office buildings, low-rise apartments, divided highways, subways, and green spaces according to a grid system. Like the street-cuttings of the Second Empire before it, Le Corbusier's plan responded to a real crisis in housing and a wide-spread concern over the living conditions of the urban poor by eliminating the entire site of the problem. Such projects undertook, in the physical space of Paris, to control the chaotic, ungraspable reality of the modern city through color-coding, straight lines, and diagonal cuts. Beck's map achieved the same goal, but it is symptomatic of the different histories of the two cities that his, like most London schemes, directly affected only the representational space of London.

Perhaps what is most emblematic about Beck's map is the way it flattened out the supremely verticalized space of the nineteenth-century city, where the growing segregation of London had been conceptualized as a divide between high and low, aboveground and underground (Pike, "Underground London" 121–25; Williams 151–53). Underground London in the nineteenth century was primarily represented as a negative, organic space, a space of cellars and rookeries, of disease and filth, of prostitution and crime (Wilson 26–46; Walkowitz 15–39). Peter Hall has argued that "twentieth-century city planning, as an intellectual and professional movement, essentially represents a reaction to the evils of the nineteenth-century city" (7). Nowhere is this reaction more in evidence than in the modernist transformation of the conception of subterranean space. In the modernist scheme, the underground was no longer just another level excavated under the layered map of the metropolis above; it was a conceptual replacement of that reality. Le Corbusier did in fact preserve a layered structure in his design for a rational Paris, but it was a planned hierarchy of levels of distinct use, rather than the confused jumble of high and low characteristic of the previous century. The new spatial hierarchy was in part a response to new technology: the sharp contrasts of electric light replaced diffuse gaslight (Schivelbusch 50–78; Schlör 66–70); steel and concrete emerged on their own as the essence of modernism (Giedion 162). As Giedion, architectural historian and theorist of the Bauhaus, wrote in 1928 about Le Corbusier's designs, "Neither space nor plastic form counts, only RELATION and INTERPENETRATION. There is only a single, indivisible space. The shell falls away between interior and exterior" (169). Out of the many layers of Victorian multiplicity, of abundant detail and ornament, was to emerge a "single, indivisible space," the essential distillation of what was truly modern in the modern city. In an anecdote reported by him as "authentic," Le Corbusier responded to the criticism that, "You trace out straight lines, fill up the holes and level up the ground, and the result is nihilism," with the straight-faced assertion that, "that, properly speaking, is just what our work should be" (273).

This willfully "nihilistic" space manifested itself in many forms in the first decades of the twentieth century. There was the Italian futurists' call to blow

up that catch-all nineteenth-century invention, the museum; the London vor-
ticists' dismissal of narrative and structure in favor of image and velocity; the
Paris surrealists' revolutionary demand to live one's life as if one inhabited a
glass house (as André Breton phrased it, "It's as if suddenly the profound night
of human existence were punctured . . . as if all things were liberated into total
transparency, strung in a glass chain whose every link was visible" [60]). There
were Piet Mondrian's colored rectangles enclosed by black-lined grids and his
colored abstraction of London and Manhattan. There were the cityscapes of
science fiction films of the '20s and '30s, of Fritz Lang's *Metropolis* (1926, reput-
edly inspired by the director's first glimpse of the Manhattan skyline from the
deck of the oceanliner, *Deutschland*), and of the English *Things to Come* (1936)
and *Transatlantic Tunnel* (1935). A staunch booster of modernist architecture, the
London-based *Architectural Review* greeted the Franco-American design of Vin-
cent Korda's sets for *Things to Come* as a leap forward from *Metropolis* in the area
of "film functionalism," and included a still of Everytown—the film's futuristic
vision of London—in a spread on Le Corbusier (Frayling 68).

The pair of English films adapted the forward-looking architecture of New
York and of Le Corbusier to the space of London. *Transatlantic Tunnel* posited a
subaqueous thoroughfare between London and New York City as necessary for
the assurance of world peace. The allegory of Anglo-American cooperation
was filmed on studio sets that rendered the tunnel and its construction as
amplified versions of the London tube, while the futuristic New York at one
tunnel entrance was once again based on the modernist concepts of Le Corbusier. The plot pitted heroic engineering against the forces of nature (an
underground volcano that erupts, killing the British engineer's son) and femininity (the same engineer must sacrifice his wife's eyesight as well as her love
in order to accomplish his task). In this vision, the antiseptic, streamlined, masculinist underground of the transatlantic tunnel could not coexist with the
organic, uncontrollable, feminine underground it was seen to be replacing.

Things to Come expounded a more complex and ambitious narrative than
that of *Transatlantic Tunnel*, but it too posited the construction of the future out
of the chaotic rubble of present-day London. Following a cataclysmic world
war in which the familiar city is destroyed by a new plague, the "Wandering
Sickness," England passes through an atavistic, cave- and ruin-dwelling epoch.
Then a technocratic legion of airmen take over, carving the new metropolis
out of the great abandoned hills of Kent: "They'd no light inside their cities as
we have," recalls the Old Man in Everytown, 2036; "They never seemed to
realise that we could light the interiors of our houses with sunshine of our
own, so there was no need to stick them up ever so high in the air" (Stover
270). The outmoded, filthy underground of mining and slums gives way to the
inorganic, ordered space of modernism. Everytown is the epitome of Le Cor-
busian ideas, eminently rational and flooded with light and clean, white lines.

The goal of this town is not the construction of a tunnel for world peace—world peace has already been achieved through the creation of the new city. The goal is to build a space gun to launch a projectile into the unknown sky, an equally fitting image for the technological conquest of irrational space.

MODERNIST SPACE

Modernist space can be defined as a totalizing vision of what French sociologist Henri Lefebvre has termed "abstract space," the conception of space as a coherent, homogeneous whole that can consequently be bought and exchanged in the same manner as any other commodity. Abstract space is a planned and organized space, thought rather than lived, and known conceptually rather than directly experienced. In its practice, modernist architecture had no more place for the individual, everyday contingency of the city dweller than Mondrian's paintings have place for human figures or any trace of their activity. This exclusion of the individual from the scale of the new space is especially visible in the speculative form of the movies mentioned above, where it manifested itself as the specter of irrationality that continued to haunt the utopian city of the future: the natural threat of an underwater volcano and the human threat of sabotage in *Transatlantic Tunnel*; Theotocopulos, the artist-revolutionary enemy of progress in *Things to Come*; the flood, conflagration, and rioting of the underground workers in *Metropolis*.

Modernist architecture and art posited a radical and utopian solution to the problems inherited from the nineteenth-century metropolis. In addition to the pressing issues of waste, disorder, and overcrowding, they also tackled new problems created by the growing dominance of abstract space over the space in which the city's inhabitants actually lived. As Lefebvre notes, the period between the wars marked not only the rise of abstract space, but the first moment of awareness of space and its production as such (18–21). The radical modernism of the Bauhaus, for example, was grounded in a global conception of space, a conviction that "things can not be created independently of each other in space" (124). For the Bauhaus, as for many other theorists of modernism, the hidden interconnection of social relations, the alienation of space endemic to monopoly capitalism, could be combated only by breaking down the spatial divisions of living. As M. Christine Boyer puts it, "Aesthetic reform, as preached by the Bauhaus and by Le Corbusier, was expected to result in meaningful new social relations, following the belief that totally redesigned everyday environments . . . would liberate society from its wants and inequities" (61). Lefebvre persuasively characterizes the *entre-deux-guerres* as the time of a search for a theory that could restore awareness of the interconnectedness of social, mental, and physical space. This is the case not only

with the architectural modernists mentioned by Boyer, but with a good number of figures who have loomed large in cultural theory over the past couple
of decades. In his account, Lefebvre focuses on the strengths and drawbacks of
the aesthetics of the surrealists and the tragic philosophy of Georges Bataille.
Even more influential have been two other bodies of theory rediscovered
more recently, and received for the most part fairly uncritically: Walter Benjamin's study of the nineteenth century through the lens of the Parisian arcade
was compiled and theorized through the late '20s and '30s; Mikhail Bakhtin's
theory of carnival and the world-turned-upside-down was written during the
'30s (although not published until 1965).

A London-based unitary theory of urban experience can be found in the
work of the English filmmaker and painter, Humphrey Jennings, who spent
much of the 1930s assembling a chapbook of quotations and commentaries to
show the effect of the coming of the machine on modern life. Jennings's starting point was Milton's depiction of the building of Pandaemonium as a first
emblem of industrialization and a futuristic image of London: "Its building
began c.1660. It will never be finished—it has to be transformed into
Jerusalem. The building of Pandaemonium is the real history of Britain for the
last three hundred years" (3). The call to transform the infernal metropolis into
the new Jerusalem echoes the utopianism of so much of modernist theory, a
utopianism that expressed itself through the total reworking of the experience
of the city.

It is not difficult to view the complex structural systems of the high modernist novel in light of this conception of modernist space, from the elevated
Alpine setting of Thomas Mann's *Magic Mountain*—far above the trenches to
which its protagonist must descend at the novel's conclusion—to the carefully
plotted urban topographies of James Joyce's *Ulysses*, Virginia Woolf's *Mrs. Dalloway*, or Marcel Proust's *A la recherche du temps perdu*. These novels have traditionally been read, in various ways, as substitutions of the hermetic world of
a fiction for the material world. This mechanism of substitution replicates the
visually and concretely realized modernist spaces of art and architecture I outlined above. It is a different strategy than that, for example, of overtly critical
urban texts such as Wyndham Lewis's work in *Blast*, Andrei Biely's *Petersburg*,
Alfred Döblin's *Berlin Alexanderplatz*, or John Dos Passos's *Manhattan Transfer*,
which aimed at giving literary (and often typographic) form to the disorient-
ing, fragmented experience of the big city rather than positing an alternative
space, as the high modernists did. But both approaches were equally indebted
to the spatial experience of urban modernity. These days, we may accept intu-
itively the idea that, as Hugh Kenner put it with reference to T. S. Eliot, "Modernism, with its percussive rhythms (the rhythm of the internal combustion
engine, as he once noted) . . . c[a]me exclusively from the great capitals, the
capitals with subways, London and Paris" (28), not to mention New York and

Berlin. We have been slower, perhaps, to grasp two corollaries to this intuition: that the modernists incorporated the raw material of the second machine age in substantially different ways than the Victorians dealt with the early Industrial Revolution or the postwar West responded to the automobile and the television; and that these encounters did not take place in a vacuum but in a social space teeming with the dominant technology of the day, the outmoded remains of the previous revolution, and the forerunners of the next, and in a world most of whose inhabitants had not yet experienced even the First Machine Age. As Lefebvre has astutely remarked, space is not an exception to the rule of uneven development; it is never perfectly homogeneous (65–66 and passim; Smith 149–59).

In a critique of contemporary architecture and urban development, Boyer has argued that the current trend in nostalgia for the forms and traces of the Victorian city has skipped over the intermediary modernist metropolis altogether, wholly negating the Grand Theory, Utopias, Communism, Collectivism, and other totalizing ideologies characteristic of it. Whatever remains in the present are only the fragments most easily assimilable to the styles of present-day mass culture. Boyer is suspicious of any recycling of old forms outside of their original context, but such an attitude, I would argue, in fact perpetuates the absolutism of modernist theory in another form. It can still be suggestive to recall a different tradition of unitary modernism, that of Benjamin citing the nineteenth-century maxim of the historian Jules Michelet, that "every epoch is dreaming the next"; the characteristic feature of modernist space, as of the abstract space it addresses, and as of a theory, like Boyer's, that remains embedded in that space, is to negate the previous epoch altogether.

And yet, as Benjamin maintained about the nineteenth century, and as Jennings revealed in the British response to its new industrialism, it was in the dreams of that last epoch, in all of the ideas discarded by the march of time and the pressure of the changing market, that potentialities for change in the present were to be discovered. Similar ideas can be found, if negatively formulated, even in the theory of such a staunch supporter of architectural modernism as Giedion. About nineteenth-century iron-and-glass architecture, Giedion wrote that "New constructional possibilities were created, but at the same time they were feared. . . . Only today can the past finally be put aside, for a new way of living demands a breakthrough. This new way of living is to a large degree equivalent to the expressions anticipated by, and latent within, the contructions of the nineteenth century" (85, 153). By theorizing a global conception of space, modernists sought to escape this dialectic of novelty and familiarity by projecting themselves into a homogeneous future, a great leap forward with nothing left behind. Instead, what this willful blindness in fact accomplished was to develop a space perfectly suited to the next technological revolution: planned for a populist world of subways, cinemas, and communal housing, the

theories of modernist space found their most efficient use in the postwar world
of the automobile, the television, and the housing project, the tower blocks that
came to blight outer London.

ONEIRIC SPACE

As current scholarship on modernism has begun demonstrating, there was a lot
more to it than the disparate members of the canon that, I have argued above,
can in fact be assembled under the rubric of modernist space.[2] To cite one
example of a different moment within modernism: Rose Macaulay's novel, *Told
by an Idiot* (1923), describes the opportunity of endless amusement offered by
the perpetual motion of the Circle line—the abstract reverie made real. While
most passengers would probably view such a possibility as nothing short of
infernal, for Imogen and Tony, Macaulay's pair of young teenagers, it constitutes
a liberation of the imagination:

> They knew what they meant to do. They were going to have their money's
> worth, and far more than their money's worth, of underground travelling.
> Round and round and round and all for a penny fare. . . . This was a favourite
> occupation of theirs, a secret, morbid vice. They indulged it at least twice
> every holidays. The whole family had used to do it, but all but these two had
> outgrown it. . . . Sloane Square. Two penny fares. Down the stairs into the
> delicious, romantic, cool valley. The train thundered in, Inner Circle its style.
> A half empty compartment; there was small run on the underground this
> lovely August Sunday. . . .
>
> And so on, past King's Cross and Farringdon Street, towards the wild,
> romantic stations of the east: Liverpool Street, Aldgate, and so round the bend,
> sweeping west like the sun. Blackfriars, Temple, Charing Cross, Westminster,
> St James's Park, Victoria, SLOANE SQUARE. O joy! Sing for the circle com-
> pleted, the new circle begun.
>
> > "Where great whales come sailing by,
> > Sail and sail with unshut eye,
> > Round the world for ever and aye.
> > ROUND THE WORLD FOR EVER AND AYE. . . ."
>
> Round the merry world again. Put a girdle round the earth in forty minutes.
> Round and round and round. What a pennyworth! You can't buy much on an
> English Sunday, but if you can buy eternal travel, Sunday is justified. (200–202)

Ignoring protocol, treating the Underground as a dreamscape rather than a
utility, Macaulay's youthful siblings uncover the childlike underpinnings of
the Underground's putatively rationalistic space, finding in the process what
can surely be called a specifically London and specifically modernist form of
urban pleasure.

And, indeed, this vision is modernist down to its historical limits. Macaulay sets this journey in 1901, and implies that in earlier years, when the Inner Circle was more novel (it had been completed in 1884), the circuit appealed to the entire family. By 1901, the now mature Phyllis, for example, prefers the Central line, "the twopenny tube": "It's cleaner. . . . It takes you where you want to get to; that's the object of a train" (200). Not if you are young, however; John Betjeman claimed that during every summer holiday between 1916 and 1921 he explored the system so thoroughly that, "the Underground map is firmly imprinted in my mind" ("Coffee" 117). It is apparent from *Summoned by Bells* (1960), his verse memoir, that this private map diverged in significant ways from the one Beck was soon to produce:

> Great was our joy, Ronald Hughes Wright's and mine,
> To travel by the Underground all day
> Between the rush hours, so that very soon
> There was no station, north to Finsbury Park,
> To Barking eastwards, Clapham Common south,
> No temporary platform in the west
> Among the Actons and the Ealings, where
> We had not once alighted. Metroland
> Beckoned us out to lanes in beechy Bucks—
> Goldschmidt and Howland (in a wooden hut
> Beside the station): "Most attractive sites
> Ripe for development"; Charrington's for coal;
> And not far off the neo-Tudor shops.
> We knew the different railways by their smells.
> The City and South reeked like a changing room;
> Its orange engines and old rolling-stock,
> Its narrow platforms, undulating tracks,
> Seemed even then historic. Next in age,
> The Central London, with its cut-glass shades
> On draughty stations, had an ozone smell—
> Not seaweed-scented ozone from the sea
> But something chemical from Birmingham.
> When, in a pause between the stations, quiet
> Descended on the carriage we would talk
> Loud gibberish in angry argument,
> Pretending to be foreign. (50–51)

Betjeman's reverie suggests a retrospective reminiscence of Beck's color-coding in the orange engines of the City and South London line, but he pushes the color into synaesthesia: the smells of each line, the sounds of the foreign tongues the boys mock to keep the carriage lively. Like those recounted in Macaulay's novel, Betjeman's experience is time-bound, as the memoir context makes clear, and as the echoes of Proustian sense-triggered memory also suggest.

The legacy of Beck's map has been both to constrain the limits of the reverie and to perpetuate its possibility: a colleague's son recently went through a phase where the only thing he wanted to do in London was what he called the "Tu-ba-loo," a game in which the goal was to travel through the Underground's ten different lines without once exiting the system. While it makes the tube into a closed system, the map also retains the possibility of such an infinite journey through an alternate London space. Beck's map is unusual, especially in London examples of modernist space, in that it permits us to glimpse the emergence of another type of space within modernism, and another way of understanding what has happened to modernist space after the epoch of modernism proper. After all, Beck's map has not only endured, it has flourished to the point where it now constitutes perhaps the single most recognizable image of London in the world, and to the point where the tube is far better loved from afar than by those who must daily suffer the progressive deterioration of an infrastructure now either approaching or well into its second century of existence. As a material space, the tube is not unified at all; it is quite literally Victorian, modernist, and postwar, all at the same time.

In the fortuitous combination of the *entre-deux-guerres* modernism of its representation and the Victorian condition of its infrastructure, the tube epitomizes a current turn-of-the-century attitude toward underground space. Aboveground, its colors and lines continue to exude the utopian modernism of an abstract, controlled, and rationally organized space; below, its cramped conditions and tiny tunnels recall not the utopian Underground, but the subterranean space from which it has always striven so strenuously to escape—the same organic space that has made its disused stations into cultish tourist attractions and settings for music videos, the arcades of Brixton into a multicultural market, and the labyrinthine arches of Camden Town into a center of countercultural consumerism, and that has made the sewers and catacombs among the most visited tourist sites in Paris.

Yet the endurance of Beck's map cannot be explained merely by the efficiency with which its conceptualization of space masks the simultaneity of epochs out of which the Underground is composed. I ascribe the success rather to the color-coding of its different lines. They are, after all, what attracts the eye no matter how many times one has seen it; they are what inspires the reverie that makes the tedious minutiae of each ride bearable; they are, in the end, what remains utopian about this space, just as it is the primary colors in Mondrian's grids that make the space of his paintings mystical as well as rationalizing, and just as, conversely, it was the grayness of postwar urban architecture that came to epitomize the intolerability of its architectural uniformity (not to mention the black-and-white of this chapter's reproductions that reinforce the point by failing to make the argument!). The thing is, the colored lines are in fact the primary feature that Beck borrowed from the failed attempts of his predecessors to conceptualize the Underground as a modernist space, the only remnants of a previous spatial organization with which he otherwise dispensed, a Victorian trace in his modernist art.

What has come to be seen in retrospect as the quintessentially modernist space should have no need for such color, only for proper order and rigorous morphology.³ Color, as Arthur Rimbaud established back in 1871 with his famous sonnet "Voyelles," where he matched colors synaesthetically with vowels, is an essential element not of rational, but of oneiric space. Viewed in this light, Louis Napoleon's map of Paris presents a daydream of power at the same time as it actualizes that power; after all, it is the childish aspect of the colored lines on that map that makes the anecdote both appealing and chilling. There was another space newly theorized during the first half of this century, the space of the dream, and this, too, was an urban space, from Freud's Vienna to the surrealists' Paris. It is not a space traditionally associated with London, however, although traces of it appear in Eliot's poetry, in figures such as Septimus Smith in Woolf's *Mrs. Dalloway*, and in the mystico-Christian novels of Charles Williams. It could also be imported, as in the phantasmagoric London of Louis-Ferdinand Céline's novel, *Guignol's Band* (Pike, *Passage through Hell* 42–48).

ALTERNATE LONDONS

This oneiric space is as much with us today as is the modernist space; indeed, it is perhaps even less self-consciously present than the other, for neither its influences nor its ideology has ever been interrogated to the degree of the totalitarian spaces engendered by the latter. But then, we are less likely to identify the oneiric as quintessentially modernist than we are the architecture and art I have briefly described above, or the high modernism which shared its conception of space. More accurate than speaking of modernist space and oneiric space would be to speak of the abstract and the oneiric spaces of modernism. One way to approach modernism differently is to observe ways in which, rather than opposing one another, these two aspects of modernist space have been fundamentally intertwined.

Such an attitude has increasingly been taken up in recent years. Take the psychogeographic maps published by the Situationist International in Paris during the '50s and '60s. These maps challenge us both to revisit all that we take for granted about the abstract space of a modern urban map, and to find within the oneiric space of that same map a set of urban experiences we had otherwise only dreamed of.⁴ To be sure, it is a tradition much more associated with irrational Paris than with business-like London, yet this same space has been claimed by novelist and essayist Iain Sinclair as constituting a secret, subterranean history of the city, its proper psychogeography. In *Lights Out for the*

Territory (1997), Sinclair documents a series of London *dérives* through the very zones of the city, the east and south, effaced from Beck's map. Similar to Jennings's recourse to Milton, Sinclair grounds his hidden London in the mythic and occult spaces of pre-Roman London and the lines of power linking up the Baroque churches of Nicholas Hawksmoor. As he recalls in an anecdote about the space of another canonical, if rather less oneirically concise, representation of London: "(A girl I know tears the pages relevant to her day's excursion out of the *A-Z*, throwing them away as she advances into fresh territory. The serial city is a manageable concept. She's in control, never tempted to go back to where she has been before)" (44). Or as he describes another "curious conceit" of psychogeography, "[T]he physical movements of the characters across their territory might spell out the letters of a secret alphabet. . . . Railway to pub to hospital: trace the line on the map. These botched runes, burnt into the script in the heat of creation, offer an alternative reading—a subterranean preconscious text capable of divination and prophecy" (1). As with the Situationists's maps, and as is proper to a dream, it is never clear whether Sinclair is serious or not, nor what, if anything, these walks are supposed to reveal. They are lyric—describing a state of mind, imparting a mood—and defined negatively—*not* a map, *not* rational—although paradoxically their planning always appears excessively super-rational.

Such planned/unplanned activities have multiplied in art over the past few decades, seeking modes of expressing a changing awareness of the multifarious experience of space. One example is the *Tate Thames Dig* organized by Mark Dion, which combined different historical spaces into a vertiginous present. Over the summer of 1999, Dion and a group of local volunteers conducted a traditionally organized archaeological dig along the Thames beaches at Millbank, in front of the Tate, and at Bankside, in front of the site of the newly opened Tate Modern. The second part of the project involved the artist organizing and cataloguing the objects uncovered, which were displayed primarily in an enormous, double-sided, mahogany *Wunderkammer*, modeled on Victorian museum cabinets. Finds ranged in age from the prehistoric (a fifty-million-year-old fossil) to the brand-new and already lost, and from the banal (rusted metal, broken ceramic, bottle tops) to those with recognizable human traces (lost toys, credit cards) to the mythic (two messages in bottles, one in Arabic, one in Italian). They are all united by two qualities: the London space in which they were buried, and their status as waste. Dug out of the shore, they not only became valuable as art, they became aesthetic in the repeated morphology of their display arrangement and in their newly visible shapes and colors, and they became newly narrativized, reincorporated into the history of the metropolis through the countless permutations and combinations of it which they allow to be assembled.

Simon Patterson uncovered another sort of hidden London in his 1992 painting, *The Great Bear*, which is nothing other than a doctored-up version of Beck's

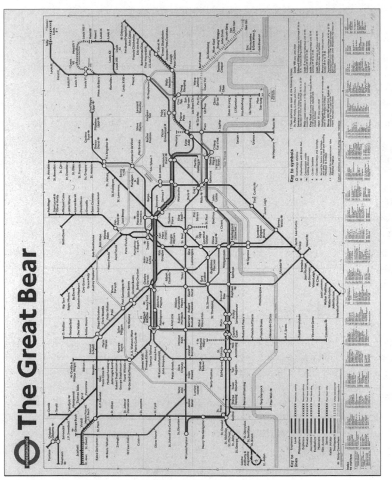

FIGURE 6.2. Oneiric Space. Simon Patterson, *The Great Bear*, 1992. Courtesy of the artist and London's Transport Museum.

Underground diagram (fig. 6.2). Patterson's brilliantly simple insight was to elucidate the dreamlike mechanism behind the map's success by transforming the
abstract daydreamer's ride through London into a single daydreamer's journey
through his cultural baggage, from high to low, journalists to philosophers, ancient
to modern, West to East. An intricate memory walk, *The Great Bear* eschews easy
London connections—the Footballers line never stops at any of the city's many
stadiums; St. Paul occupies the place of Aldwych rather than its own—in favor of
whatever dream-logic would put Chico Marx next to Bronzino and Vasari in
Brixton, or make Oliver Reed the traditional center of London, the transfer point
at Charing Cross between the Footballers, Film Actors, and Engineers lines. I
wouldn't really call this anything like a "post-modernist" space—after all, it would-
n't work if the modernist space on which it is based were not still powerfully present—; rather, I would say that Patterson, like Sinclair and Dion, discovered the
dreams of modernism within the world of the 1990s in the same way that he
found the dreams of the present lurking within the modernist space of Harry
Beck's Underground map. Rather than simply absorbing the viewer into its perfect scheme, Patterson's map challenges him or her to investigate the principles of
its organization, to search for any gaps, mistakes, or inside jokes, and to decide
whether or not it bears any concrete relationship to the tube map it mimics, or is
merely an elaborate distortion. If Beck's map found the perfect form for modernist
space in a postwar London, then Sinclair, Dion, and Patterson use verbal, physical,
and visual means to pass through the looking glass of that perfect urban image and
discover what its efficiency has occluded.

NOTES

1. The office responsible for the London Underground has published two
extremely useful volumes for studying the development of its maps: Garland, and Leboff
and Demuth. Rose provides an excellent visual summary of the development of the system. There have been myriad volumes devoted to every aspect of the Underground,
from individual histories of every line, to coffee-table books on its art and architecture,
to anthologies of Underground writing such as Meade and Wolff, to Kelly's travelogue.
Early accounts can be found in Banton and throughout Meade and Wolff, early theatrical depictions in Pike (1999). The breathless wonder at technology in Passingham (c.
1936) and Stevens (1939) gives a good sense of the dominant interwar representation.
Barker and Robbins remains the definitive general history; see also White and Howson.
Bobrick studies the Underground in terms of world subways and their myths; Trench
and Hillman places it in the context of London's other subterranean spaces.

2. Witness the annual New Modernisms conference inaugurated in 1999 by the
Modernist Studies Association, as well as the recent *Cambridge Companion to Modernism*.

3. The quintessentially modernist gesture in this light would have to be that of the
preeminent theorist of postwar American art, Clement Greenberg, when he was

appointed an executor of sculptor David Smith's estate. Convinced that color was not one of the integral features of modern sculpture, Greenberg removed the primer coats from the enormous painted steel pieces made by Smith in his last years, and left them exposed to the Vermont winter to wear away. For a summary of the relationship between Greenberg and Smith, and a measured treatment of the controversy surrounding his treatment of the painted sculptures, see Rubenfeld (21–30). On chromophobia in modern culture and the equation of lack of color with purity, see Batchelor.

4. The London Psychogeographical Association (LPA) was present at the inauguration of the Situationist International in July 1957 in Italy, apparently represented by its single member, Ralph Rumney (Sadler 4, 165–66 n. 7). In another example of the contemporary exploration of the alternate spaces of London, it was relaunched in 1992, according to Sadler.

WORKS CITED

Bakhtin, Mikhail. *Rabelais and His World.* 1965. Trans. Hélène Iswolsky. 1968. Bloomington: Indiana UP, 1984.

Banton, Eric. "Underground Travelling London." In *Living London.* George Sims, ed. 4 vols. London, 1901. 4.60–63.

Barker, T. C., and Michael Robbins. *A History of London Transport.* 2 vols. Rev. ed. London: George Allen and Unwin, 1975.

Batchelor, David. *Chromophobia.* London: Reaktion, 2000.

Benjamin, Walter. *The Arcades Project.* Trans. Howard Eiland and Kevin McLaughlin. Cambridge: Belknap P, 1999.

Betjeman, John. "Coffee, Port and Cigars on the Inner Circle." *Times* 24 May 1963. Rpt. in *Betjeman's London.* Pennie Denton, ed. London: John Murray, 1988. 117–20.

———. *Summoned by Bells.* Cambridge, MA: Riverside P, 1960.

Bobrick, Benson. *Labyrinths of Iron.* 1981. New York: Henry Holt, 1994.

Boyer, M. Christine. *The City of Collective Memory. Its Historical Imagery and Architectural Entertainments.* Cambridge: MIT P, 1994.

Breton, André. *L'amour fou.* 1937. Paris: Gallimard, 1976.

Dion, Mark. *Archaeology.* Alex Coles and Mark Dion, eds. [London]: Black Dog, 1999.

Ford, Ford Madox. *The Soul of London.* 1905. Alan G. Hill, ed. London: Everyman, 1995.

Frayling, Christopher. *Things to Come.* BFI Film Classics. London: British Film Institute, 1995.

Garland, Ken. *Mr. Beck's Underground Map.* Harrow Weald, Middlesex: Capital Transport Publishing, 1994.

Giedion, Siegfried. *Building in France, Building in Iron, Building in Ferro-Concrete.* 1928. Trans. J. Duncan Berry. Santa Monica, CA: Getty Center for the History of Art and the Humanities, 1995.

Hall, Peter. *Cities of Tomorrow*. London: Blackwell, 1988.

Hobsbawm, E. J. *Behind the Times: The Decline and Fall of the Twentieth-Century Avant-Gardes*. New York: Thames and Hudson, 1999.

Howson, H. F. *London's Underground*. 1951. 4th ed. London: Ian Allan, 1967.

Jennings, Humphrey. *Pandaemonium 1660–1886: The Coming of the Machine As Seen by Contemporary Observers*. Mary-Lou Jennings and Charles Madge, eds. 1985. London: Picador, 1987.

Jordan, David P. *Transforming Paris: The Life and Labor of Baron Haussmann*. New York: Free P, 1995.

Kelly, Michael. *London Lines: The Capital by Underground*. Edinburgh: Mainstream, 1996.

Kenner, Hugh. *The Mechanic Muse*. New York: Oxford UP, 1987.

Leboff, David, and Tim Demuth. *No Need to Ask! Early Maps of London's Underground Railways*. Harrow Weald, Middlesex: Capital Transport Publishing, 1999.

Le Corbusier, *The City of To-morrow and Its Planning*. Trans. Frederick Etchells. 1929. Cambridge, MA: MIT P, 1971. Trans. of *Urbanisme*. G. Crès, ed. Paris: Collection de "L'Esprit Nouveau," [1925].

Lefebvre, Henri. *The Production of Space*. 1974. Trans. Donald Nicholson-Smith. Oxford: Blackwell, 1991.

Levenson, Michael. *The Cambridge Companion to Modernism*. New York: Cambridge UP, 1999.

Macaulay, Rose. *Told by an Idiot*. 1923. Garden City, NY: Doubleday, 1983.

Meade, Dorothy, and Tatiana Wolff, eds. *Lines on the Underground: An Anthology for Underground London Travellers*. London: Cassell, 1994.

Passingham, W. J. *Romance of London's Underground*. London: Samson, Low, Marston, [1936].

Pike, David L. *Passage through Hell: Modernist Descents, Medieval Underworlds*. Ithaca: Cornell UP, 1997.

———. "Underground London: Subterranean Spaces on the London Stage." *Nineteenth Century Studies* 13 (1999): 103–38.

Pinkney, David H. *Napoleon III and the Rebuilding of Paris*. Princeton: Princeton UP, 1958.

Rimbaud, Arthur. *Oeuvres complètes*. Antoine Adam, ed. Bibliothèque de la Pléiade. Paris: Gallimard, 1996.

Rose, Douglas. *The London Underground: A Diagrammatic History*. London: Douglas Rose, n.d.

Rubenfeld, Florence. *Clement Greenberg: A Life*. New York: Scribner, 1998.

Sadler, Simon. *The Situationist City*. Cambridge, MA: MIT P, 1998.

Schivelbusch, Wolfgang. *Disenchanted Night: The Industrialisation of Light in the Nineteenth Century*. 1983. Trans. Angela Davies. Oxford: Berg, 1988.

Schlör, Joachim. *Nights in the Big City: Paris—Berlin—London 1840–1930*. 1991. Trans. Pierre Gottfried Imhof and Dafydd Rees Roberts. London: Reaktion Books, 1998.

Sinclair, Iain. *Lights Out for the Territory: Nine Excursions in the Secret History of London*. London: Granta Books, 1997.

Smith, Neil. *Uneven Development: Nature, Capital and the Production of Space*. Oxford: Basil Blackwell, 1984.

Stevens, F. L. *Under London: A Chronicle of London's Underground Life-Lines and Relics*. London: J. M. Dent, 1939.

Stover, Leon. *The Prophetic Soul: A Reading of H. G. Wells's* Things to Come *Together with His Film Treatment,* Whither Mankind? *and the Postproduction Script (Both Never Before Published)*. Jefferson, NC: McFarland, 1987.

Trench, Richard, and Ellis Hillman. *London under London: A Subterranean Guide*. New ed. London: John Murray, 1993.

Walkowitz, Judith R. *City of Dreadful Delight: Narratives of Sexual Danger in Late-Victorian London*. Chicago: U of Chicago P, 1992.

Wells, H. G. *The Definitive Time Machine: A Critical Edition of H. G. Wells's Scientific Romance*. Harry M. Geduld, ed. Bloomington: Indiana UP, 1987.

White, H. P. *Greater London*. Vol. 3 of *A Regional History of the Railways of Great Britain*. 1963. New ed. Newton Abbot: David and Charles, 1971.

Williams, Rosalind. *Notes on the Underground: An Essay on Technology, Society, and the Imagination*. Cambridge, MA: MIT P, 1990.

Wilson, Elizabeth. *The Sphinx in the City: Urban Life, the Control of Disorder, and Women*. 1991. Berkeley: U of California P, 1992.

CHAPTER 7

London and the Tourist Imagination

DAVID GILBERT AND FIONA HENDERSON

London is at once the centre of liberty, the seat of a great imperial government, and the metropolis of that great race whose industry and practical application of the arts of peace are felt in every clime, while they exert an almost boundless influence over the moral and political destinies of the world.

—John Weale, *London and Vicinity Exhibited in 1851*

London is enjoying a great boom in popularity these days, and indeed is often styled "The Capital of Europe." With the amazing ethnic diversity—the end result of centuries of empire-building and ocean-crossing—it could just as easily be called "The Capital of the World." African, American, Arab, Australian, Caribbean, Chinese, Filipino, Indian, Thai—there are neighborhoods for all nationalities, and all nationalities in every neighborhood. And most happily, they remembered to bring the recipes from the old country.

—*Berlitz London Pocket Guide* 2000

*T*hese openings to two tourist guidebooks, separated by a century and a half, reflect London's changing character as a global city. They can, at one level, be taken as superficial reflections of a deeper, more complex, history of the city's path from imperial capital to post-imperial metropolis. At another level, when brought together with other guidebook descriptions from the intervening years, they can be seen as more active and nuanced urban representations, with the potential to inform about changing popular understandings of the nature of the city. On first impression, however, the tourist guidebook seems an unremarkable representational form, rarely, if ever, celebrated for its literary worth. Indeed, in this collection it seems a little out of place to give close attention to a form so singularly lacking in imagination. From their inception, with the nineteenth-century handbooks of John Murray and Karl Baedeker, modern systematic guidebooks have been castigated as obvious, plagiarizing, formulaic, even cannibalistic (for many years the main source for Baedeker's guide to London appeared to be earlier editions of the same guide—choice phrases from earlier editions would be reused in quite different contexts).

Until recently, guidebooks and tourist literature more generally were marginalized in discussions of the representation of place. Where they were considered, as in Roland Barthes's famous deconstruction of the Guide Bleu in *Mythologies*, they were more often than not dismissed as empty clichés, at best hollow and derivative of more creative and innovative representations, and at worst naïve or conservative obfuscations of complex "reality." Instead of advising and informing the visitor, the guidebook was "the very opposite of what it advertises, an agent of blindness" (Barthes 76). In a conventional hierarchy of traveling cultures and their texts, the guidebook ranks far behind the accounts of exploration and ethnography (making sense of the undiscovered and the unknown), or literary travel writing (a creative and personalized engagement with geographical and cultural difference). The guidebook appears to be part of the commodification of the experience of the modern world, reducing the "aura" of places to preordained and preinterpreted trails through a shopping list of sites and sights.

Recent years have seen a shift from this position, and a move towards taking the guidebook more seriously, as part of a broader reconsideration of the cultures and practices of tourism. One of the starting places for this change has been precisely those characteristics of the guidebook that have traditionally been singled out for criticism. Following Dean MacCannell's provocative description of tourism as nothing less than an "ethnography of modernity" (MacCannell 1), the clichés of guidebook itineraries and descriptions take on new significance. The processes of making and marking attractions are a way of understanding how the modern world makes sense of itself (13). Tourist guidebooks therefore become more than practical instructions for visitors—a successful guide divides the world into visible attractions and invisible spaces between them, and in so doing identifies what in the past and present is held to be significant. Guidebook descriptions may often be artless and ordinary, but are rarely empty; indeed, their very "artlessness and ordinariness" may make them "the most transparent signs of all" (Taylor 135).

The London of the tourist guidebook has been marked by striking changes in its apparently obvious and taken-for-granted tourist landscape, which can provide a distinctive perspective on the nature of the city. While the key historic sites have provided lasting fixed points for itineraries around the city, they have been set in a changing matrix of other places and activities. These changes reflect the creative destruction of the modern city as both a physical and a cultural landscape. To contemporaries, the descriptions and organization of guidebooks appeared shallow and superficial (an ordinary list of things that must be seen or done), but when combined to form a vertical transect through the history of the city, attention turns to discontinuities, to periods when the taken-for-granted understanding of the city needed to be changed.

For this reason, this chapter concentrates on general guides to the city rather than those that present themselves as niche guides for particular activities or identities within the city. This is not to say that such guides were insignificant or marginal in the overall development of the tourist landscapes of London. Indeed, many were instrumental in changing the dominant understandings of the tourist landscape presented in mass-market guides. For example, many of the places and activities identified in self-consciously "alternative" guides published in the 1960s and 1970s were incorporated into guides aimed at a much more general audience in the 1980s and 1990s. This process changed more than just the understanding of London in the wider tourist imagination; it also fundamentally changed the nature of those places taken from the margins to the center of the tourist experience of the city.

The guidebook has also been taken more seriously in recent years because of its influence on popular knowledge. At one level this is a simple recognition of the mass readership of guidebooks. Guidebooks from Baedeker's *London and Its Environs* to the *Time Out Guide to London* have sold tens of thousands of copies. While much of the information and interpretation in guidebooks has been second-hand and derivative, they have been the primary sources of information and direction for millions. This straightforward recognition of the scale of influence of the guidebook as a form of popular culture has been complemented by changes in the understanding of the relationship between reader and text, stressing the complexity of the process of reading, and the active role of the reader (Koshar 5). In this context the guidebook is a very particular form of text because the act of reading it is so closely bound up with various other practices: looking, walking, eating, drinking, sleeping, and so on. Guidebooks are read more critically and strategically than has usually been acknowledged. While the style and form of guidebooks often imply an active author/text and a passive reader (in the terminology of early Baedekers, literally "directions for travellers"), their practical use entails an engaged dialogue between written text and personal experience.

This again points to the significance of the seemingly superficial accounts of the guidebook. If, as MacCannell suggests, guidebooks act as "markers" for the tourist landscape, making sites intelligible, then they have to do so in ways which are convincing and plausible (110). This is not simply to suggest that the descriptions and interpretations have to be consistent with the conditions experienced in situ (although, of course, guidebooks that fail this test rapidly lose the confidence of their readership). It also points more generally to the circular relationship between the expectations of their readers and the accounts of place found within them. In the case of London, where the great majority of guides sold have been produced by local publishing companies, the interpretation of the city has often had to be negotiated between a desire to promote the capital to visitors, expressions of current local anxieties about its nature, and an anticipation of what visitors expect to see. This negotiation has been most often apparent in the introductions to guidebooks, where it is the city as a whole, rather than individual places within it, that is being made intelligible.

This complicated negotiation between the changing city and the cultural expectations of insiders and outsiders points to the significance of the "lowly tourist guidebook" in cultural contact and exchange (Koshar 7). The tourist city serves as what Pratt describes as an "interculture" or "contact zone," and the guidebook acts as a "transcultural text," mediating between cultures (1–11). Some of the uneasiness and anxiety of guidebook accounts of London come from the changing position of the city in the cultural geographies of the imperial and post-imperial world. The idea that those places colonized by the European powers were seen through "imperial eyes" in travel literature and guidebooks is familiar, but London too was interpreted in terms of its imperial position (Gilbert 279). As in the quotation from John Weale's guide, one expression of this was an assertion (perhaps over-assertion) of the world supremacy and centrality of the city. But just as European travel accounts and guidebooks to the colonized world sometimes told of the complexities, anxieties, and uncertainties of the imperial project, accounts of London also betrayed worries about the city's fitness as the "Heart of Empire." The post-imperial geometry of political and cultural power also provided challenges for the interpretation of the city found in its guides. Particularly for those guides written and produced in London—part of what James Buzard has described as the "auto ethnography" of the modern tourist industry (106)—the challenge was to find ways of representing the city that were convincing for a range of different visitors, particularly Americans and Europeans, as well as for tourists from Britain itself. In this longer term context, the representation of London in the postwar period can be seen as an ongoing search for a new and stable understanding of the city in the tourist imagination.

London has experienced at least a hundred and fifty years of what might be described as "modern" tourism. Indeed, the city has some claim to being a birthplace of tourism in its organized and commodified form (Burkhart and Medlik 15). The Great Exhibition of 1851 in particular transformed the tourist industry in London. Over six million people visited the exhibition, providing the initial impetus for Thomas Cook's travel business, and concentrating the minds and efforts of the publishers of tourist literature. More than forty guides were published in English during the exhibition, and at least sixteen in foreign languages (Webb 210). In the time since the Great Exhibition, the representation of London in guidebooks has tended to use one of two tropic structures to introduce, organize, and interpret the city for tourists. First, the tourist geographies of the city have been underpinned by a strong sense of an ancient city with its roots deep in the past. Guidebooks have struggled to find ways of accommodating distinctively modern dimensions of the urban experience into this structure. The second tropic structure has been one of global centrality, frequently reinterpreted and redefined.

FROM OLD LONDON TOWN TO STYLE CAPITAL OF EUROPE

Suggested itineraries for visitors to London have developed through time as new attractions have been built, other sights "discovered" or reinterpreted as places of touristic significance, and as still other places have lost their status as attractions. (Perhaps the best example of this latter process is the London docks, promoted by nineteenth-century guides as an unmissable spectacle of trade and industry, but largely absent in guides written after 1918.) Nonetheless, the main historic sites—the Tower, St. Paul's, Westminster Abbey—provided the spine for routes around the so-called "essential" tourists' London. However, beyond this rather obvious geography of major historic buildings, were other more subtle ways in which the city was read as a venerable landscape. One of these drew attention to the cluttered and irrational patterning of streets. Even where all traces of the medieval city above ground had been swept away, the shape of the modern metropolis still bore the traces of its ancestry. As with so many other elements of the developing tourist geography of London, this feature was used as a contrast with its cross-channel rival, where "Hausmannization" had created a new, rational, and spectacular cityscape by erasing such morphological continuities with the past. Another way in which the city's rootedness in the past was emphasized was through the often repeated cliché that London was best understood not as the largest and most striking city of the modern age, but as a collection of villages. "Village London" provided the structure for many twentieth-century guides to the city, suggesting that somehow the modern metropolis was a shallow covering of an older, unspoilt landscape, and reflecting long-standing ambivalence about the metropolis in English culture.

An imagined past was also woven into tourist geographies of the city by specific tours that sought out the London of literature. For example, *The Blue Guide* (first published in English in 1918) read London as a site of history, art, and architecture, but above all, of literature. The initial sixty-five pages of the guide were given over to lengthy essays on these subjects. The only formal itineraries in the guide were a series of "literary walks," taking the visitor through the Londons of Dickens, Thackeray, Dr. Johnston, and Charles Lamb. Although literary references had long been a common feature of London guides, *The Blue Guide*'s emphasis on literature as a way of exploring the city anticipated the concerns of many late-twentieth-century guides (particularly those produced for the American market), in which heritage and literary associations displaced an overt emphasis on London's power and significance as the primary understanding of the city's essential character.

Consideration of Dickens's influence on popular understandings of London has usually concentrated on the development of literary and cinematic traditions of representation—the ways in which the dark, foggy, labyrinthine city also became a standard imagining of the city both past and present. Colin McArthur has commented on the development of a mid-twentieth-century "composite discourse" of London in cinema, deriving primarily from Dickens, but also from the Sherlock Holmes stories of Conan Doyle, from the sensational mythologizing of the Jack the Ripper murders of the late 1880s, and from Victorian sociology and travel writing on the city (McArthur 34). As well as direct representations of the Victorian metropolis, such as director David Lean's *Great Expectations* (1946) and *Oliver Twist* (1948), this "composite discourse" also shaped more ostensibly contemporary films such as Thorold Dickinson's *Gaslight* (1940) and even the Fred Astaire musical *Ziegfeld Follies* (1946). What has often been missed is how this understanding of the city became an active element of its consumption as a tourist destination. The touristic imagination, with its reliance on the familiar and usable cliché, drew upon literary and cinematic representations to turn "Old London Town" into the central element of many guidebook accounts of the city.

For much of the twentieth century, this focus on the old effectively displaced attention to the new in touristic representations of London. MacCannell argues that by 1900 the workings of the modern city itself had become part of the tourist landscape. In the Baedeker guides to fin de siécle Paris, the sewers, the morgue, a slaughterhouse, a tobacco factory, and the government printing office had been added to the expected list of historic attractions (MacCannell 57–76). Yet from 1900 onwards, the tourist geography of London seemed to be in a state of denial about the city's modern character. Unlike the early and mid-nineteenth century, when part of the attraction of the city for visitors was the sight of a modern world in the making (Potts 28), by the early twentieth century many "modern" sights were being dropped from tourist itineraries. In part this reflected changes in the economic and geographic structure of the city. The central districts of the city were increasingly dominated by service work and anonymous offices, while more obvious displays of work were being moved to the suburbs and beyond.

The most successful new tourist sight of the late nineteenth century provided a perfect expression of the London tourist industry's hesitations about modernity. Tower Bridge was opened in 1894, a giant steel lifting bridge powered by state-of-the art hydraulic machinery, yet clothed in a Gothic shell-suit of stone. Immediate reactions to the bridge were mixed: the editor of *The Builder* described it as a "pretentious piece of bad medievalism" and "a gigantic sham" (Statham 602). Yet Tower Bridge rapidly became a powerful symbol, signifying London throughout the world. It also became an essential sight in tourist itineraries, and was quickly assimilated into representations of "Old London Town," ably assisted by the mists and fogs of the river.

It was not until the postwar period that the "modern" reappeared as a major feature in general guides to the city. The period immediately after the war was relatively quiet, although some new guides did create a spectacle of bomb damage and reconstruction. In the *Spearhead London Guide*, bomb sites were given their own category as "Places to See," alongside "historic buildings, monuments, churches and parks." A more usual treatment of the bombed city wove together narratives of survival, with the expectation of the emergence of a new city. However, even in the invocation of the potential of the city of the future, references were frequently made to the past. Hervey's *Everybody's London*, for example, looked to the seventeenth century as a model of what the new London might become: "phoenix-like, the new city, the glorious metropolis as envisaged by Wren, will rise from the ashes—a thing of beauty and a source of inspiration to all men" (4).

The clearest and most confident expression of modernity in the tourist landscapes of postwar Britain came with the Festival of Britain in 1951. While not having the transformative effect on the London tourist industry of the Great Exhibition a century earlier, the festival did reveal the potential for creating successful new tourist sights within the city. Dominating the festival site were the spectacular structures of the Skylon and the Dome of Discovery, which were quickly accommodated into tourist itineraries of the city. However, the opening up of the South Bank of the Thames was just as significant as a development in directing the "tourist gaze" back towards the historic sights of the north bank of the river (Urry 1). The cover illustration for the Geographia *All in One Guide* to the festival and London combines old and new elements of the tourist landscape in a way that explicitly uses the festival exhibits to frame the established sights of the city (see fig. 7.1). Other guides went so far as to suggest that the new vistas opened up from the South Bank left the visitor feeling that "one has never seen them properly before" (Lambert 80).

Although the view from the South Bank remained, the removal of the festival's most prominent structures left the London skyline without clear symbols of modernity. The Festival Hall, and later the National Theatre, Hayward Gallery, and Queen Elizabeth Hall, significant *sites* in tourist geographies of the

128

FIGURE 7.1. *"All in One" Map Guide: Festival London* (London: Geographia, 1951). The conventional tourist landscape is framed by the spectacular—and temporary—modernity of the 1951 Festival of Britain. Courtesy of The Bishopsgate Institute.

cultural life of the city, failed to become significant tourist *sights* in and of them-selves. In the period between 1951 and the late 1990s, London was without sig-nificant modern attractions, strengthening the grip of "Old London Town" on standard sightseeing tours. Guidebooks often contrasted this with the develop-ing tourist geographies of other major cities, particularly Paris, with its *grand projets* at Beauborg, the Louvre, and elsewhere. Towards the end of the 1980s, the new landscape of Docklands became a possible excursion on tours of Lon-don (often interpreted as "Thatcher's London"), but it was not until London's own millennial burst of grand projects that new sights were firmly established as part of the essential core of the tourist city. Despite the troubled histories of the Millennium Dome and the Millennium Bridge, these projects taken together have already produced the first substantial re-evaluation of London's built form as a spectacle for the tourist, destabilizing the central understandings of London presented in its guidebooks. The most popular of these attractions, the London Eye and the Tate Modern, are effectively new additions to the tourist geography of the city, but the millennial period also saw the reinvention of established sights, particularly at the Royal Opera House, the Great Court of the British Museum, and the extension to the National Portrait Gallery.

Earlier understandings of the city as modern interpreted London in more functional terms, pointing to the activity of a vital modern city, albeit within a physical landscape that was usually noted for its historic connections. In Victo-rian and early-twentieth-century guides, Bank Junction in the heart of the city was frequently included in sightseeing tours. This was in part because of the architectural significance of John Nash's Bank of England and the Royal Exchange, rebuilt by William Tite in 1844 as a neoclassical forum. But it was also an opportunity to experience the crush and crowds of the city itself. This was presented as a revelatory moment in the visit to London: the frenetic activ-ity on the streets told the tourist of London's centrality in world capitalism. This was a space where decisions were being made that had immediate effects on the world beyond.

In the second half of the twentieth century this perspective of the city as a site of modern activities moved beyond the more passive geographies of sightseeing. Instead there was a developing sense of the city as the place where fashions and taste were being defined. Shopping, eating, drinking, and visiting theaters and concert halls have always played an important role in the visitor's experience of the city, yet the representation of London in the 1960s reveals a dramatic shift towards a younger, more dynamic, and in some ways more demo-cratic consumer culture. In words from *Time's* famous description of "swinging London" (in itself a kind of abbreviated guide), this was a city "steeped in tra-dition, seized by change, liberated by affluence" (Halasz, "London" 32). While the great shops of London had long been attractions in their own right, from the 1960s onwards it was the experience of participating in a certain kind of fashion culture that was being promoted and directed for the tourist. The transformations of Carnaby Street and the King's Road in Chelsea were dependent on their role as performative spaces—these were not simply collections of boutiques but places where fashion was displayed, watched, imitated, and transformed. Guidebooks like Piri Halasz's *A Swinger's Guide to London* (1967) rapidly recognized this, providing instruction on the right places to shop and the right clothes to wear to be a part of this "city in motion" (Halasz, *Guide* 13). Indeed, the quest for the authentic or "essential" experience of London shifted from lists of sights towards certain consumer practices—lists of essential things to see in the city were increasingly displaced by lists of things to do and how to do them.

By the 1990s, when London was again promoted as "style capital," the networks of consumption on the tourist's shopping agenda had become much more diverse and elaborate. Just as "swinging London" had been represented as something new and dynamic enacted on the stage of Olde London Town, so the rise of the city as a center of international design emphasized the links between the innovation of young British designers and the grainy authenticity of some parts of the city. Andrew Tucker's guide to the fashion spaces of the city makes this connection quite explicitly: "What would Chloé's Stella McCartney do without the markets of Portobello Road, where she rummages for antique trims with which to embellish her simple slip dresses?" (Tucker 17). Some guidebooks still treat the street markets of London ethnographically, as spectacles of authentic London or "microcosms of London life" (Williams 89). Increasingly, however, markets like those at Portobello and Camden Lock are interpreted as spaces of fusion between old and new Londons, where the tourist is an active and necessary part of the drama.

FROM THE HEART OF EMPIRE TO THE QUEEN OF HEARTS

Some of the 1990s boosterism associated with the promotion of London as a fashion capital drew upon the second major tropic structure used to explain and organize the city in the tourist imagination. Claims to be the fashion capital of Europe (or even the world) drew upon established representations of London as a global city. Of course, London's position as capital of the British empire, and subsequent struggles to establish a coherent reading of the post-imperial city, provide the main examples of this approach. In 1900, London was seemingly at its imperial zenith, the largest city of the world, the center of world trade and finance, and the political capital of the greatest empire the world had known. The descriptions and itineraries of guidebooks of the time struggled to turn the fact of London's world pre-eminence into something that could be readily seen and experienced by the visitor, a spectacle of centrality and power. Guidebook descriptions of the city in the mid–Victorian period had been suffused with a promotional zeal that was unequivocal about its place in the world. Even by the standards of the time, *Routledge's Popular Guide to London and Its Suburbs* (1862) offered an extreme example of the self-confidence of the Victorian world-view: "London is the political, moral, physical, intellectual, artistic, literary, commercial and social centre of the world" (1). Yet by the beginning of the twentieth century, representations of the city were more ambivalent, betraying a certain anxiety that the London seen and experienced by the visitor was an inadequate expression of its global significance.

In part this more hesitant representation of the city was a response to the development of other European capitals, in which the international Beaux-Arts style of architecture and grandiose expressions of "rational" urban planning had become markers of the position of Paris, Brussels, Berlin, and Vienna in the world order. The implicit or explicit model for these developments was that of the first great European imperial city, and it was hard to represent London's physical reality as a new Rome. Guidebooks would take great care to explain that the British empire was very different from other empires, and that both the importance of commerce and trade, and the absence of an autocratic central state meant that its capital was unlikely to be a closely integrated landscape of grand boulevards and ceremonial squares. Nonetheless, it is possible to detect a consistent defensive subtext in guides to London, responding to a sense that the metropolis's undoubted importance was not adequately reflected in its cityscape.

One response to this, which was strengthened in the interwar years, emphasized that London was a different kind of imperial city, the center of a new kind of empire. This was the central city of an Empire divided on racial lines, between the white dominions and the non-white colonies. In this context it was possible to present the empire as a kind of family of sibling and children peoples, and the imperial city as home space within the empire. From the time of the Great War onwards, guidebooks began to present London as a site of imperial unity, rather than as the crucible of power. In Staines Manders's *The Colonials' Guide to London*, published primarily for visiting soldiers during the war, there was a strongly romantic appeal to this sense of belonging: "The Tower, the Abbey, Westminster Hall, and St. Paul's appeal to the imagination of the peoples of the Dominions as no novelty however brilliant can appeal. For these are theirs and ours, and in the shadow of the Abbey or the White Tower, we are Londoners all" (Staines Manders 20). By the 1930s, this translation of the imperial city into the familiar, domestic home of empire had developed. In his 1937 guide to Britain, tellingly entitled *The Empire Comes Home*, W. S. Percy portrayed London as a kind of imperial front parlor, simultaneously a familiar part of the family home, but also the place where special occasions took place (fig. 7.2). In earlier guides Trafalgar Square was conventionally described as the

"Heart of Empire"; in *The Empire Comes Home* the heart was shifted to the Strand, where many of the dominions and colonies had their offices, and where men and women from the empire were a familiar sight on the street.

This reinterpretation of imperial centrality only worked for certain audiences. In those guides intended for the American market, the idea of the city as a central site of authority developed in other ways, which often emphasized tradition and ceremony rather than overt displays of imperial power. One of the key elements of the reinvention of the monarchy that took place in the late nineteenth century was a recasting of the relationship between the crown and the streets of London (Corfield 12). The monarchy became increasingly involved in highly managed public spectacles, such as the main processions held for jubilees and coronations, and more regular events such as the annual trooping of the color and the daily changing of the guard. Tourism became an essential element of these developments (indeed, so successfully that one of the justifications often made for retaining the monarchy has been its economic importance to the British tourist industry). Just as major exhibitions and festivals often created a significant boost for the London tourist industry, major royal events usually saw an increase in tourist numbers and the publication of new guides or special editions of old guides.

In these guides, royal London was increasingly understood not as the heart of empire, but as the site for supposedly "ancient" pageantry (mostly invented or reinvented by the Victorian palace and state). Particularly in guides for American tourists, the connections between Britain's imperial power and the visible pageantry of the British state were played down. For example, *London the Wonder City*, targeted at wealthy Americans and published to coincide with the coronation of George VI in 1937, eagerly awaited the "most gorgeous of processions." Set in a city which had become a "treasure house of tradition and retrospect," the coronation procession was no longer a symbol of imperial and world centrality but had become "a fairy story rather than an event in modern life" (Pullman 21).

The transformation from display of power to fairy story (or perhaps to soap opera) was completed by the second reinvention of the monarchy undertaken by the House of Windsor from the 1970s onwards. As the members of the royal family increasingly presented themselves as familiar celebrities rather than distant authority figures, so the ways in which they were treated by the tourist industry shifted towards a pattern more familiar in Beverley Hills than Westminster. What was on display was less the trappings of the head of state, and more just a different kind of tour round the homes of the rich and famous. This process reached some kind of apotheosis in the cult of Diana in the period immediately after her death. The guidebook *A Walk through Princess Diana's London* invited tourists to explore "the public and private sides of Diana's life" (Garner 1). This tour managed to combine Westminster Abbey,

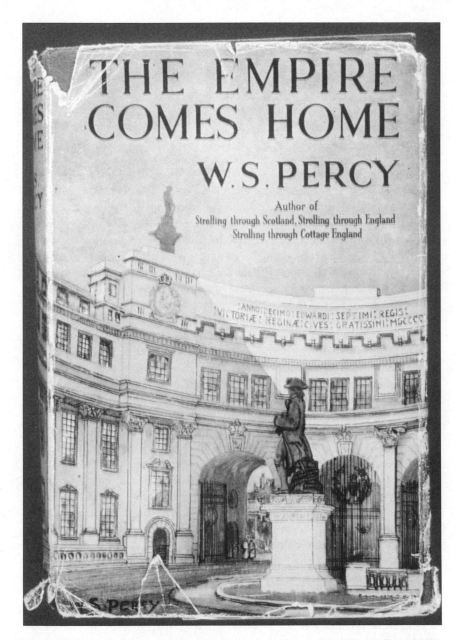

FIGURE 7.2. Cover of W. S. Percy's *The Empire Comes Home* (London: Collins, 1937). Interwar tourism increasingly reinterpreted London as the familiar home for the imperial "family," rather than as the center of power and authority. Courtesy of David Gilbert.

Buckingham Palace, Harvey Nichols (the fashion department store), Annabel's club, and Nicky Clark's Hairdressing Salon into a single route around the West End of the city.

FRAGMENTING LONDON:
POST-IMPERIAL STORIES IN THE TOURIST CITY

In late twentieth-century London a new generation of guides, aimed at young independent travelers from Europe, the United States, and some parts of the old empire, celebrated London's post-imperial diversity. The idea of the city as a diverse social landscape, the result of "empire-building and ocean-crossing" is fast becoming one of the new clichés of the tourist geography of London. As well as reflecting changes in London's social and cultural geography, this development has been driven by changes in the nature of urban tourism more generally. In many ways post-imperial London has followed the path set by mid-century New York, where the spectacle of ethnic diversity was developed into a touristic experience of transcultural consumption. Guides to New York from the 1930s onwards invited tourists to eat their way round the world in the Lower East Side, a claim now echoed in modern London guides.

In broadening the tourist gaze on modern London, guidebooks point to the diversity of the post-imperial city through representations and descriptions of Londoners themselves. Although some guides to imperial London singled out Whitechapel in the East End as a kind of domestic orient—"the motley crew speaking and shouting almost every human language, the diversity of the costume, the curious jumble of the goods for sale" (Hodder 63)— the ethnographic content of most earlier guides was extremely one-dimensional. Londoners were reduced to a rehearsed sequence of stereotypes: the London Bobby, the Beefeater, the Cockney barrow boy. Guides to the city now routinely play these stereotypes off against the evident diversity created by the "implosion of empire" and an increasingly globalized urban culture. The *Insight Guide to London*, for example, explicitly acknowledges the hybridization of London culture and the transformation of the older staples of the expected social geography of the city: "Cockneys no longer need to be white and Anglo-Saxon; there are Italian, West Indian, Jewish and Pakistani cockneys" (Williams 65).

Cultural diversity has become one way in which guidebooks have attempted to produce a coherent understanding of London at the end of the twentieth century. But in a broader sense, it is not so much diversity as incoherence that has become the way of presenting London to the tourist. Given the changing nature of consumer society in general, and urban tourism in particular, it is unsurprising that the last twenty years have seen an explosion in niche guides to particular Londons for particular identities. What is more remarkable is that singular, mass-market guides have also started to present the tourist city as a fragmentary experience. In the 1980s and early 1990s, this sense of London was often tied to an account of its political problems: "a city of spiralling extremes, ostentatious private affluence and increasing public squalor" marked by political neglect and crumbling infrastructure (Humphreys ix). These anxieties about the city remain, but they have been joined by understandings of the city that celebrate its fragmentation of the city, and point to the enabling potential for the tourist of a city that resists a single over-arching narrative of itself. The 2000 edition of *Frommer's* describes London as a "mass of contradictions . . . ancient and modern, sprawling and compact, stolidly English and increasingly multicultural," but points to this ambiguity as a source of pleasure and possibility (Porter and Prince 4). The opening of the *Cadogan London* guide describes London as "chaos," but then argues that "out of the chaos you produce a personalised sense of order, your own map of the city" (Gumbel xi). Where once the taken-for-granted clichés of the guide-book commodified the triumphalism of the imperial capital or the historical depth of the ancient city, now even middlebrow, mass-market guides try to sell London as a postmodern experience.

WORKS CITED

"All in One" Map Guide: Festival London. London: Geographia, 1951.

Barthes, Roland. "The Blue Guide." *Mythologies.* London: Granada, 1972. 74–77.

Berlitz London Pocket Guide. Princeton: Berlitz, 2000.

Burkhart, A. J., and S. Medlik. *Tourism: Past, Present and Future.* London: Heinemann, 1979.

Buzard, James. "Culture for Export: Tourism and Autoethnography in Postwar Britain." *Studies in Travel Writing* 2 (spring 1998): 106–27.

Corfield, Penelope. "London and the Modern Monarchy." *History Today* 49.2 (1999): 6–13.

Garner, Paul. *A Walk through Princess Diana's London.* London: Louis' London Walks, 1998.

Gilbert, David. "London and All Its Glory—Or How to Enjoy London. Representations of Imperial London in Its Guidebooks." *Journal of Historical Geography* 25 (1999): 279–97.

Gumbel, Andrew. *Cadogan London.* London: Cadogan Guides, 2000.

Halasz, Piri. "London—The Swinging City." *Time Magazine* 16 Apr. 1966: 32–40.

———. *A Swinger's Guide to London.* New York: Coward-McCann Inc., 1967.

Hervey, M. *Everybody's London. A Complete Guide to London.* London: Everybody's Books, 1947.

Hodder, C. *Through London by Omnibus, A Chatty Guide to the Principal Sights of London.* London: Hodder, 1900.

Humphreys, R. *London: The Rough Guide.* London: Penguin Books Ltd., 1997.

Koshar, Rudy. *German Travel Cultures: Leisure, Consumption and Culture.* Oxford: Berg Publishers, 2000.

Lambert, Sam. *London Night and Day: A Guide to Where the Other Books Don't Take You.* London: Architectural P, 1951.

MacCannell, Dean. *The Tourist: A New Theory of the Leisure Class.* Berkeley, CA: U of California P, 1999.

McArthur, Colin. "Chinese Boxes and Russian Dolls: Tracking the Elusive Cinematic City." In *The Cinematic City.* David Clarke, ed. London: Routledge, 1997: 19–45.

Percy, W. S. *The Empire Comes Home.* London: Collins, 1937.

Porter, Darwin, and Danforth Prince. *Frommer's 2000 London.* New York: MacMillan, 2000.

Potts, Alex. "Picturing the Modern Metropolis: Images of London in the Nineteenth Century." *History Workshop Journal* 26 (1988): 28.

Pratt, Mary L. *Imperial Eyes: Travel Writing and Transculturation.* London: Routledge, 1992.

Pullman Car Company. *London the Wonder City.* N.P.: Pullman Car Company, 1937.

Routledge's Popular Guide to London and Its Suburbs. London: Routledge, 1862.

Spearhead London Guide. London: Spearhead Publications, 1947.

Staines Manders, A. *The Colonials' Guide to London.* London: Staines Manders, 1917.

Statham, H. "London as a Jubilee City." *National Review* 29 (1897): 594–603.

Taylor, John. *A Dream of England: Landscape, Photography and the Tourist's Imagination.* Manchester: Manchester UP, 1994.

Tucker, Andrew. *The London Fashion Book.* London: Thames and Hudson, 1998.

Urry, John. *The Tourist Gaze: Leisure and Travel in Contemporary Societies.* London: Sage, 1990.

Weale, John. *London and Vicinity Exhibited in 1851.* London: John Weale, 1851.

Webb, David. "For Inns a Hint, for Routes a Chart: The Nineteenth-Century London Guidebook." *London Journal* 6 (1980): 207–14.

Williams, Roger. *Insight Guide to London.* Singapore: APA Publications, 1999.

CHAPTER 8

Bread and (Rock) Circuses:
Sites of Sonic Conflict in London

ALEXEI MONROE

> Anywhere I go in the world, if I look at a travel brochure about London, I know what I'm going to see: Buckingham Palace and red buses. But there's always another story—the untold story.
> —Jungle DJ Jumpin' Jack Frost, quoted in *Altered State*

*L*ondon in the 1990s was the site of a series of struggles to define the image of the city, both in relation to the rest of the world and to its dynamic and proliferating musical subcultures. To illustrate the tensions between the image and reality in London, this chapter will contrast two differing (but politically and economically related) trends. The first section will examine the incorporation of London's rock mythology into the so-called "heritage industry" and its appropriation by a series of commercial and political interests with a shared stake in the commodification and consequent political neutralization of countercultural symbols. This process finds expression in the de facto spatial-conceptual ordering of London's popular music geography, creating increasingly defined spatial hierarchies of "canonical" sites. Having described this "museumization" process, the focus shifts to the ongoing London tradition of appropriating marginal and illegal spaces by "underground" subcultures from the 1960s to the present.

Finally, there is a more detailed account of two such locations and the subgenres they have hosted. Ulf Poschardt has described how during the 1970s disco craze, clubs could serve as sanctuaries or refuges, initially for the black and gay communities, but later for white working-class youth alienated by repetitive or humiliating jobs (132). In London of the year 2000, those seeking refuge in underground clubs find sanctuary in dystopic and decaying surroundings, pushed there by the extreme cultural-political forces of the post-Thatcherite inner city: unemployment, violence, and spiritual, cultural, and educational deprivation. What should become clear is the tension between London as rock (heritage) city and "London Acid City," the city of marginalized but dynamic styles and sounds, engaged in a constant process of codification and re-codification.

LIVE FROM THE MUSEUM

Since the late '60s, rock culture has slowly made ever deeper inroads into the way in which London presents itself to the outside world. "Rock tours" of London are now an integral part of the officially promoted tourist industry. This trend accelerated under the New Labour government's early attempts to appropriate and promote the notion of "Cool Britannia," an ideological gambit that sought to glamorize a policy package containing many socially reactionary and authoritarian elements. In his ambivalently titled book *Labour Camp*, the design consultant Stephen Bayley[1] describes rock as the new people's art of "Cool Britannia" (45). The backward-looking stylistic conservativism of groups such as Oasis, a Brit-pop group of the 1990s, is seen as ideally suited to the populist and, in Bayley's view, essentially philistine cultural politics of the present day. The government's flirtation with fashion designers, actors, and rock stars is part of a controversial but ongoing attempt to "rebrand" Britain as a multi-ethnic, youth-culture dominated, globalization-friendly country in which ideological divisions have been erased. On the streets of London activities and groupings that challenge this narrative find themselves under constant pressure.

As Bayley and others have noted, official attempts to appropriate or to "encourage" cultural creativity are often embarrassing in practice and sinister in motivation. Tellingly, New Labour's attempt to appropriate the "coolness" of bands such as Oasis has coincided with two trends that doom it to failure in advance. On the one hand, the centers of creative energy within popular music are increasingly perceived to lie within dance music, and rap/hip-hop now far outsells "rock" (which itself is now mutating in an attempt to escape the stagnant limitations of its basic ideology). Due to its hard-line antidrugs stance (now ironically less liberal than the Conservative opposition) and its preference for the middlebrow, the government is (for now at least) unable to associate itself with the dance sector as fully as it has with rock. More seriously for rock and for the government's attempt to exploit its (now primarily historical) hip-ness: the genre has fallen victim to the globalizing socio-cultural trends of which New Labour is such a devoted advocate. Tourism is a globalized indus-try par excellence and attracting younger and more affluent tourists to Britain has been one of the motivations for the attempted "rebranding" of Britain. These tourists are as likely to be drawn to sites associated with Jimi Hendrix or the Sex Pistols as to Buckingham Palace, and yet, paradoxically, rock is becom-ing as much a part of "heritage" as royalty. In practice, the incorporation of rock into the tourist marketing of Britain has necessarily taken the form of the "museumization" of rock and other aspects of popular culture. The logic of the (new tourist) market demands the creation of "attractions"—family-oriented centers—which fatally undermine the very "coolness" that the government and the tourist industry wish to exploit in their marketing strategies.[2]

Despite the fact that, in appropriating the residually rebellious or counter-cultural auras of pantheonic rock stars, the heritage industry destroys what it wishes to possess, the process has been largely beneficial in reviving traditional modes of tourism. Waxworks, for instance, were once institutions primarily oriented to the depiction of official historical narratives. However, in an insti-tution such as the Rock Circus (located by Piccadilly Circus), the waxwork paradigm has been remodeled with the use of "animatronic" technologies to present performing synthetic substitutes for stars both living and dead. The star-substitutes chosen to perform here present the heroes of media-shaped popular common sense and illustrate the links between the dominant sonic and political ideologies in Britain. The "mannequinization" of rock (a process iron-ically predicted by the German group Kraftwerk in the late 1970s) symbolizes the deadening effects of the extension of the official tourist pantheon. Omi-nously, for those who still hold a romantic view of the potential of counter-culture, the Sex Pistols' Johnny Rotten is among these mannequins. The ease with which punk has been assimilated into the tourist industry should also concern those selling "Cool Britannia," as it illustrates the danger of counter-cultural glamor becoming kitsch, and therefore losing the very coolness that makes it marketable.

In the present, stylistic context sites such as the Rock Circus and the longer-established Hard Rock Café, both of which mythologize the '60s and '70s in par-ticular, are seen by many as being no less kitsch manifestations of the "olde worlde" than the rebuilt Shakespeare's Globe Theatre. For the generation of Lon-doners raised on acid house and its successor dance genres, and for the newest tourists drawn by London club culture, these sites are either irrelevant or embar-rassing. A contemporary youth-oriented tourist itinerary may now incorporate mainstream dance music sites such as the Ministry of Sound or the new "super-clubs" such as Fabric and Home, but there is an entire category of events and locations unknown even to many Londoners and rarely featured in any listings.

THE WRITING ON THE WALL:
DOMINANT IDEOLOGY AND SPATIAL HIERARCHY

Museumization also finds expression in the "blue plaque" system, which marks the birthplaces and residences of the famous with commemorative plaques, inscribing their officially approved status into the fabric of the city. Although the quaint design of the plaques is (so far) unchanged, the commercial logic of tourism has seen them expand to include addresses associated with rock-tourist icons such as Jimi Hendrix, (retrospectively) extending the pantheon of "the great and the good." Whilst on the surface liberal, this process is inextricably connected to commercial interests, and the plaques serve as markers of colonized space, marking the predominance of marketability in the historical curation of "London." It should be noted that the process is not centralized and that the selection of personalities to be commemorated in this way is marked by differing and competing agendas. Nevertheless, at the symbolic level, the plaques (as expressions of the tourist industry) function as the territorial insignia of the dominant socioeconomic order which seeks as soon as possible to assimilate subcultural forces and which typifies what Marcuse termed "repressive tolerance."

Other resonant locations, such as Abbey Road, also feature prominently in mainstream tourism, again serving to construct a narrative that reinterprets the originally insurgent properties of popular culture as symbols and guarantors of benign capitalist continuity. Beyond the best-known sites included in the general tourist market, there are a host of venues and sites that constitute a mythology of popular music in London—venues such as the 100 Club, site of early Sex Pistols shows, or the Astoria on Charing Cross Road. Such locations are often presented in the mainstream media with the prefix "the legendary," and while they are of little significance to the casual tourist, many music fans do visit precisely such sites in a manner akin to pilgrimage, notwithstanding the fact that in many cases these "sacred" sites are actually still in use, hosting new generations of performers.

Museumization produces a de facto hierarchy of dominant musical sites in London. These first-order sites include all the major historic and working performance venues (for example, Wembley Stadium and Hammersmith Odeon), as well as otherwise less conspicuous sites that have become associated with iconic moments in the history of popular music in London. These venues and locations are associated not just with radio stations, major record companies, and the brewers that own many of the venues, but increasingly with the tourist industry. Radio plays a part in this process by reinforcing "common sense" ideology and excluding threatening sounds (subgenres which, I will argue, code acute socio-political struggles which cannot be allowed to hinder radio's reproduction of ideological reality) as far as possible. "Oldies" or "gold" stations serve to reinforce the ideological bases of the rock-heritage industry, encouraging the regression of popular taste. In contrast, there is a severe under-representation of underground dance and experimental sounds on London's airwaves, and it is generally acknowledged that the most innovative sounds are audible on the numerous but harshly policed pirate stations. (It is in the interest of the official and commercial interests behind the marginalization of certain styles to promote museumization, which seeks to freeze or to exclude the disruptive speed of un-policed stylistic change, which produces rarely heard mutant dance sub-genres such as happy hardcore and gabber.[3] The creation of a pantheonic "golden age" of popular music perfectly suits the interests of reissue-dependent major record companies unable wholly to adjust to or to exploit the pace and stylistic proliferation of more contemporary styles.)

Mainstream rock culture is now integral to the way in which London is marketed to tourists. Tours and itineraries are organized to portray the capital in terms of its rock "heritage" up to and including punk[4] (if not, as yet, much beyond). Using the concepts proposed by Attali, this spatial curation of London's musical life and its reinforcement by nostalgia-biased media can be read as part of the dominant socioeconomic "noise" that is intended to drown out and pre-empt the sound and style of dissent. The seamless absorption of sites formerly associated with notions of rebellion or nonconformity does not represent a relaxation of London's official self-image so much as a colonizing extension of its corporate persona or global brand.

The assimilation of rock into heritage history is, then, a natural ideological and commercial process, partly reflective of the fact that since the explosion of dance music at the end of the '80s, the very notion of rock now seems to many irredeemably quaint and archaic. From the perspective of electronic dance music, the museumization of rock is not necessarily a cause for regret. From outside, rock is often seen as an archaic form indelibly associated with a reactionary cultural political reality, and its museumization provides a clear point of distinction and support for the dance scene's claims of radicalism and progressivness (museumization usefully destroys rock's "aura" of contemporaneity by attempting to mythologize it).

The majority of the major stylistic innovations and new trends of the past decade have emerged from outside of this static but expanding hierarchy and have taken place in second-order sites at which subcultural innovation takes place. Many of these styles heard in such underground locations are explicit forms of reaction against the culturo-political status quo and are even stylistically shaped by the politics of their locations. Some of the new forms attempt at least implicitly to contest the corporate colonization of London and its popular culture, invoking "other" Londons stylistically or even politically opposed to "rock-heritage London" and the economic and political forces that support it.

It is important to be aware that museumization does not represent the constitution of an alternative pantheon (or in rockspeak, "hall of fame"), but an
extension of the official national pantheonic paradigm. The process inevitably
extends the regime of ideological common sense (the politico-economic-sym-
bolic status quo) into spheres formerly seen as sites of stylistic or ideological
revolt against the mainstream. The media, the government's Department of
Culture, Media and Sport (DCMS), local authorities, radio stations, and record
companies are not acting according to any explicit or even expressible agenda,
but according to the natural dynamics of market-mediated culture and
"national branding." The reactionary political and cultural effects of this process
are not always the aim of those consciously and unconsciously involved in
museumization, but are side effects which certainly tend to benefit dominant
political and economic interests. In itself, this appropriation-commercialization
is typical of the postmodern culture industry and not particularly surprising.

In contrast, iconic tracks from the dance underground such as Lochi's
"London Acid City"[5] represent attempts to claim a specific underground sound
(in this case acid techno) as the sound of London and, at least symbolically, to
claim the city for the sound and the community or value-system surrounding
it.[6] Jungle, in particular, has often been presented as the sound of the city.[7]
However, sometimes such moments are a precursor to a step into a mainstream
and a new form of commercialization. Perhaps the best known example of this
process is the Speed Garage track "It's a London Thing," the anthem of a style
that is infrastructurally underground, but which in practice values materialism
and snobbery. Yet however commodified the genre becomes, it does represent
a stylistic challenge to the freezing of London into rock-heritage city, even if,
in fact, its consumerist hedonism presents far less of a challenge to the process
than the other sounds that proliferate outside the tourist zones.

THE SECOND ORDER—SITES OF ABJECTION

Beyond these first-order sites are a series of both fixed and occasional sites that
are spatially and aesthetically peripheral. A tradition of using derelict former
industrial sites for experimental and marginal events can be traced at least to the
late '60s and on through the politicized industrial music of the '80s to the illegal "free party" rave scene of the '90s. London has a series of sites strongly associated with sonic and/or political dissent and experimentation. Mapping these
sites (often un-remarked by all but specialist media and the small numbers who
frequent them) reveals a series of what are sometimes explicitly self-denoted
"temporary autonomous zones," or TAZs (see Bey; Reynolds 143). Such zones
challenge or deconstruct official narratives of sonic consumption and production in London, attempting to suspend what is experienced by some as the

repressive rule of everyday life. As in other de-industrialized metropolises such as Berlin, sub- and countercultural events naturally gravitate towards derelict and dystopic sites of social or economic abjection. These play host to a series of marginal or despised subgenres (industrial, gabber, acid techno, happy hardcore) that for economic, stylistic, or political reasons are rarely tolerated in more stable locations. The tonal characteristics and ideologies of the darker and more confrontational of these subgenres can be related to the types of space they are forced to inhabit (the dystopic imaginary of the sounds being symbiotic with the spaces they are forced to occupy). The derelict or abandoned cinemas, bingo halls, offices, hospitals, factories, warehouses, and other transitory bases these subcultures and subgenres inhabit will never feature on the mass-market tourist itineraries (though in some cases this may be so only because such sites will be shut down and redeveloped long before the styles they host can be wholly assimilated). For these reasons, it is important to explore not just the location but the fabric of the often dilapidated buildings colonized by these subcultures.

DERELICT TRADITION

The advent of brutal monetarist policies under the Thatcher governments accelerated the collapse of traditional industries and the spread of public dereliction in newly redundant inner-city areas. Just as in other postindustrial metropolises, such as Detroit, New York or Berlin, the decay of such areas produced subcultural responses. The first countercultural appropriations of postindustrial spaces and the inner city date back at least to the late '60s when the Roundhouse, a long-obsolete railway installation, played host to all-night happenings, including what was then called a rave by Pink Floyd (see Reynolds 64).[8] During the economic shocks of the '70s, the collapse of traditional industries accelerated, associated businesses and property prices collapsed, and whole areas were abandoned to dereliction. Areas such as Brixton became "front lines" between the police and the urban underclasses, many first- or second-generation British of West Indian origin. As such areas go into freefall, vacant properties are often squatted and abandoned spaces colonized by various subcultures.

These zones of inner-city London experienced increasing desolation and political polarization in the '80s, suffering from further economic collapse, benefit cuts, increases in crime, and overzealous policing. In this atmosphere, ambitious hybrid groups emerged to appropriate inner-city spaces—precursors of the rave scenes. One such group was the Mutoid Waste Company, a collective living under motorway flyovers and staging events featuring hybrid mechanical sculptures fashioned from the debris of dereliction (see Reynolds 57). The most politicized use of space in this period was by Test Department, an industrial group whose members came from South London and Glasgow, both areas in the front line of de-industrialization. Test Department expressed militant resistance to Thatcherism in their music, lyrics, collaborations with striking miners and others, and in their use of space. In 1986, in the most polarized phase of the brutal ideological struggle between the Thatcher government and its opponents, Test Department staged a spectacular event in the derelict areas around Paddington Station. These events were intended as a defiant challenge to violent de-industrialization and conservative nationalism, but could only temporarily reclaim ex-industrial space for the principles of collective struggle and solidarity.[9]

POST-DANCE FLUX

Since the explosion of dance music at the end of the '80s, the inadequate or hostile response of the established entertainment infrastructure plus the ever-proliferating amount of new subgenres has intensified the trend towards the use of marginal and abject spaces. The proliferation of autonomously organized parties and, from the early '90s onwards, the proliferation of styles—each with its own clubs and promoters—has created an explosion in demand for vacant space. Many locations were taken over for single events, the organization and logistics of which were far more covert (if no less spectacular) than the large-scale countercultural events of the previous decades. The sometimes literally nomadic flux of the new styles signified a dispersal away from fixed and controlled sites. Although the sites of clubs or of illegal raves are easily and frequently mythologized or romanticized, they are not so easily assimilable into the needs of the tourist market and provide either an obstacle to or a protection from the commercialization process.

Although there is no shortage of disused spaces in London suitable for clubs, the Conservative government (with subsequent support from New Labour) came to take an increasingly hard line against free party culture. One theory states that brewing companies (often owners of rock venues) put pressure on the conservatives to crack down; they were suffering a drop in profits in their pubs as youth migrated away from traditional pub/rock culture to the new dance scenes. Further pressure from the tabloid press, outraged by drugs fatalities, combined with the bias towards authoritarianism of the Conservative party, soon led to legislative responses. The 1990 Entertainments (Increased Penalties) Bill sought to deter unlicensed parties through increased fines. However, this legislation was only partially successful, affecting mostly the largest scale parties. So whilst many parties shifted to legal residencies in fixed locations, the appetite for underground parties was undiminished. In 1994, the Criminal Justice Bill was introduced, containing controversial powers to prevent large-scale free parties and restrict the right to free assembly.[10]

Although the legislation contains Draconian penalties and the possibility of criminal charges even for those suspected of attending illegal events, the struggle to maintain underground events in London and elsewhere continues. The law was designed specifically to criminalize the autonomous organization of events based on music "mainly or wholly characterised by a succession of repetitive beats" (dance music). The police tend to tolerate smaller discreet raves, but organizers of larger parties are forced to play a game of cat and mouse with the authorities. Organizers now risk arrest, fines, confiscation of equipment, or imprisonment.

These pressures worsen a situation in which the supply of available licensed venues is insufficient for the number of DJs, sound systems, and subgenres needing spaces to play. London club venues also tend to duplicate the most successful commercial forms repeatedly, meaning that currently favored genres tend to squeeze out those which are no longer (techno), or never were (gabber, happy hardcore), in the media spotlight. Marginalized styles that will never be profitable in most venues struggle to retain a foothold in fixed locations and as many are forced to play illegally as choose to do so. Second-order sites play host to styles and groups with nowhere else to run, those either forced into or choosing to inhabit abject spaces as far from surveillance, control, and commodification as possible. Even within the dance music media, some styles are kept at arm's length, for both social or aesthetic reasons, and those events which are not featured even in the specialist media and so rely on word-of-mouth and small autonomous networks for promotion are forced into any space available. These scenes can also be the victims of economic-stylistic censorship, which dictates in which spaces or on which frequencies they are permitted or forbidden to be heard and denies them exposure. The abject status of such styles, in particular happy hardcore, also finds expression in their pirate status in radio terms. For reasons already discussed, radio resists the incursion of new subgenres for as long as possible. Whilst there is some limited airplay on legal stations, those involved in the scenes tend to prefer pirate stations. These stations offer direct access to callers and do not have to make concessions to a non-initiated audience and compromise the underground inter-referentiality of the scene.

Some party organizers have no wish to "go legit" and to settle, or they enjoy the danger of running illegal parties. Others, descendants of Spiral Tribe and other hardcore sound systems, refuse for ideological reasons to submit to what is perceived as unjust legislation based on ideological prejudice and vested interests. In terms of spatial politics, the links between the free party scene and squatting are crucial. Even in the present boom conditions, London has numerous surplus industrial and office spaces, lying empty and unused until recuperated back into the loop of property speculation and gentrification. In these circumstances, the temporary occupation of such a space to create a Temporary

Autonomous Zone (TAZ)—within which the rules of everyday economic and political norms that create dereliction are suspended—is seen as a point of principle. The Weltanschauung of the free party movements is based on chemical, sexual, and (by default) political nonconformism, and, through links with anticapitalist and green direct action groups, represents a visible form of dissidence that at least intermittently extends beyond mere stylistic revolt.

Whether necessary or not, the spatial and political marginalization of many events reflects and is audible in the nature of the affected musics—the so-called "sounds of the underground." This facilitates an analysis that attempts to relate the marginal status of the styles and groups involved to the aesthetic qualities of the sounds, which are influenced by the locations in which they are heard and produced.

SOUNDS OF THE UNDERGROUND, SITES OF THE UNDERGROUND

It is clear that underground spaces in London are frequently strongly associated with particular subgenres, and a very close connection can be detected between the sites, their audiences, and the sounds. It is also clear why, in the post-Criminal Justice Bill context, some subcultures have to and others choose to inhabit such spaces. It is a general principle that the most marginal styles inhabit marginal cultural, economic, and physical spaces. What remains unexplored is what happens when fugitive genres do find permanent bases in marginal spaces and what effect their locations have on them. In practice, the category of locations inhabited by both the transient illegal events and the fixed but marginal events overlap. Both transient and fixed sites are venues for musical, stylistic, legal, economic, and political conflicts. These include the literal struggles between police and organizers of illegal events; the internecine struggles between the various small scenes; and the cleavages within such scenes between those hoping for eventual "crossover" into the mainstream and those hoping to "keep it real" in the underground.

Though it can have acute risks and drawbacks, the location of clubs and scenes in semi-derelict and bleak environments does carry some stylistic advantages. The location or the condition of the venue can add subcultural glamor or romance, adding a bohemian ambience. This factor can also serve to boost the credibility of a club or a party, acting as a guarantor that the experience offered will be more "real" and closer to the edge of abandon or experiment than anything offered in more conventional club spaces. In the gabber/speedcore networks in particular, it is almost a truism that stylistic and personal freedoms are only possible in such marginal zones. Katie Milestone's discussion of the northern soul movement suggests that the movement was an attempt to compensate for the lack of cultural infrastructure in some urban

FIGURE 8.1. Labrynth 1. Courtesy of Alexei Monroe.

FIGURE 8.2. Labrynth 2. Courtesy of Alexei Monroe.

FIGURE 8.3. Labrynth 3. Courtesy of Alexei Monroe.

areas—a condition particularly applicable to the areas of inner-city London that tend to host second-order sites. Dance scenes have emerged in locations of almost dystopian bleakness and neglect as an attempt to create a context within which it is possible to escape the spiritual, economic, and cultural poverty of the surroundings.

The spatial and stylistic conflicts of the past decade and the links between spatial, cultural, and economic marginality are most apparent in two of the most spectacular fixed second-order sites in North and South London—the Labrynth in Dalston and the now closed 121 Centre in Brixton—and the particular stylistic practices associated with the locations. The conflicts associated with the two venues illustrate a wider struggle for the legitimation and re-legitimation of modes of "hearing London": the full range of sonic diversity as opposed to the more restricted canon that the dominant sonic ideologies of London attempt to enforce and present as the definitive representation of the city and its musical life.

LABRYNTH

Labrynth (figs. 8.1–8.3) is situated in a spectacularly abject location inside a crumbling, dystopic former cinema painted entirely black. It is located in Dalston, a blighted inner-city area so far resistant to regeneration. It overlooks a bomb site and derelict houses. The music associated with Labrynth is happy hardcore—a sub-genre that brings alternative and mainstream media together to condemn its defiant proletarian tastelessness. The centers of popularity for the genre and most of the large-scale raves that take place are in provincial England and Scotland, and within London it is often seen as unsophisticated and provincial, even within the dance scene. A crude characterization might be of a genre no-one else wants inhabiting a space no-one else would wish to.

Although hugely popular, the subgenre is shunned by all but its fanatical devotees, and the "apartness" of the venue symbolizes the apartness of the style and its fans. Nothing marks the site but its apartness, and it has an inherently "unreal" status as a site of stylistic exile and hardcore hedonism. The building absorbs all light and clubbers seem literally to disappear into its interior, dropping out of the visibility of the everyday and into another reality. The building plays up the music's untouchable status; it could be seen as a contemporary Dickensian den, a warren filled with the stereotypical underclass urchins that terrorize the imagination of bourgeois London. The bleak exterior usefully deters the uninitiated and sets the party taking place within into stark contrast with the world outside. Happy hardcore represents a type of defiant hedonism, absolutely decoupled from any political or moral framework and anything but the here and now.

Reynolds alludes to the links between the tone of the genre and the desire to obliterate daily experience of the economic forces that create the abject spaces in which it shelters:

> Amidst the socio-economic deterioration of a Britain well into the second decade of one-party rule, where alternatives seem unimaginable, horizons grow ever narrower, and there's no constructive outlet for anger, what is there left but to zone out, to go with the flow, to *disappear?* There's also an inchoate fury in the music that comes out in an urge for total release from constraints, a lust for explosive exhilaration. "Ardkore frenzy is where the somnambulist youth of Britain snap out of the living death of the nineties to grasp at a few moments of fugitive bliss. . . . It's a quest to reach escape velocity." (quoted in Collin and Godfrey 252)

The paradox is that the gateway to escaping the reality of inner-city life is a building in an area that seems to epitomize decay and despair. The happy hardcore played at Labrynth is typified by high tempos, high-pitched vocals, histrionic piano lines, and a kitschy, militantly euphoric atmosphere—all designed to prolong the escapist gratification of early rave. Stylistic innovation is an extremely low priority, and because of the speed at which dance sub-genres form and deform, the Labrynth strangely echoes tourist London's rock museums, showcasing a style deliberately kept in a state of arrested development—albeit one that would not welcome conventional tourists.

DEAD BY DAWN: THE 121 CENTRE

Brixton, a tense area south of the Thames, has been the site of some of Britain's worst riots; it has also offered a home to several marginal subcultures. For fourteen years a squatted house at 121 Railton Road housed the 121 Centre—an anarchist squat and information center that from 1993 hosted regular industrial and speedcore/gabber techno events (figs. 8.4 and 8.5). While Labrynth was desolate but spectacular, the 121 was a more covert, incongruous venue located at the domestic end of Coldharbour Lane in a neglected but inconspicuous two-story house with a basement. The building occupied by Labrynth was the passive host for a refugee subgenre with no other home, but 121 served as a center of creative and protest networks, complete with a library of conspiracy-theory literature, legal advice on drugs and squatting, and exposés of abuses of power. Despite the potentially incendiary nature of some of the information and the sounds performed there, the venue kept a surprisingly low profile. That, together with the relatively small numbers involved, enabled it to survive.

Whilst the local authorities would certainly have been uneasy about some of the literature and events associated with the venue, what finally led to the repossession of the venue was a rise in housing prices that made it both

FIGURE 8.4. 121–1. Courtesy of Alexei Monroe.

FIGURE 8.5. 121–2. Courtesy of Alexei Monroe.

profitable and politically convenient for the local council to extinguish this particular TAZ. Further along the same road, a former employment office also saw regular use as a rave venue during the '90s. The symbolism of illegal events in a former official building, however, perhaps proved too provocative, and the space was reclaimed more rapidly than that at 121. The only remaining "underground" venue on Coldharbour Lane (as of 2000) is a house at number 414. Converted haphazardly into a club, it does almost nothing to disguise its status as a bare shell of a former domestic property. The "chill out" area is the upstairs front room overlooking the street, decorated only by cheap lighting and self-consciously trippy decorations. The building at 414 hosts regular acid techno and other subgenre nights that attract many who also attend illegal raves. It does not, however, have any associated ideology in the sense of 121, or an agenda that extends far beyond the hedonistic.

Across Europe, particularly in Italy and Germany, squatted or reclaimed venues have a tradition of hosting newly emerging and more established but still marginal ultra-experimental scenes and subgenres. The 121 Centre offered a haven and a networking center for extremely specialized and confrontational subgenres (gabber and speedcore techno, techstep, and variants on industrial music). The most consistent musical phase at 121 commenced with the Sate industrial nights in 1993. Bands and DJs played in the ground-floor main room, watched by small but growing numbers that in almost any other context or venue would have been hopelessly unfeasible economically. The surreality of the still recognizably domestic location added to the strange atmosphere of the experimental performances at Sate.[11]

Moving into the mid-1990s, hardcore techno had mutated into gabber, an ultra-fast, ultra-severe style of linear techno that originated in Rotterdam. From the outset, gabber was treated with fear, contempt, and suspicion in the mainstream music media and club scene. As with happy hardcore, there was a fear or dislike of velocity and high tempos as such, but gabber's harsh (post)industrial bass and atonal, (apparently) nihilist textures were seen as even more threatening. The more violent and experimental subgenres are popularly associated with heavy drug consumption and characterized even by much of the music press as "mindless." Gabber never established a foothold in the conventional club system and it reveled in its outlaw status, being confined to one or two tolerated fixed sites and the twilight world of one-time illegal raves. However, these prejudices overlook the intricacy of manipulation of speed and textures in gabber and related styles, and the music is no more purely functional than house music, for instance. The paranoiac, repressive atmosphere that followed the Criminal Justice Bill was increasingly expressed in the music, which blended extreme velocity with ever darker textures and samples. By 1996, the DJs were including techstep, the darkest, coldest, and most militant variant of drum 'n bass.

As I have previously argued (Monroe), the structures of musical consumption encourage a constant diversification and splintering of genres into fratricidal subgenres and sub-subgenres. When tastes shift, some subgenres are left behind, and some are never "picked up" by the media. Partly by default, and partly as an expression of subcultural choice, these are confined to marginalized and illegal venues that serve as de facto musical ghettoes inhabited by one or two subgenres. The ever-increasing speeds of commodification and technological innovation produce styles such as happy hardcore and gabber, and the extreme velocities of the latter are expressive of this situation. Gabber and associated variants (stormcore, nordcore, hartcore, speedcore) all represent not just aesthetic extremism but a frantic search for un-colonized sonic space that will prove resistant to commodification and appropriation. All are based on the testing and surpassing of kinetic-sensory-pharmacological-sonic frontiers and a reaction against ideological, economic, and stylistic taboos.

At the center of this stylistic mayhem lay the Dead by Dawn nights at the 121[12] and the associated micro-scene centered on the Praxis label and the *Alien Underground* and *Datacide* magazines—the most comprehensive documentations of both local events and the international networks of underground parties and producers in France, Germany, the Netherlands, the Czech Republic, and beyond. The magazines are no less politicized than the information held at the 121, reporting not just on the specific repression against illegal raves but on wider civil liberties issues and threats to freedom, discussing issues such as electronic surveillance and the CIA's links to drug importation. *Datacide* in particular stresses solidarity against repression and has a loosely defined ideology based on communal values and the thought of figures such as Rosa Luxemburg and the Italian and German autonomist/squatter movements. Though not pessimistic and stressing the importance of cultural and political resistance, the tone of the reportage can be as apocalyptic as the sounds discussed on the extensive review pages. The works of Deleuze and Guattari, Hakim Bey, and others are a conspicuous presence, and the emphasis on theoretical activity and practical action stands in contrast to happy hardcore's pure escapism and distrust of complexity and innovation. The conceptual sophistication and political awareness of the writers, producers, and those attending the events does not contradict so much as complement the music's emphasis on brutal sensuality that to the outsider seems nothing more than a soundtrack to the temporary obliteration of the self.

The 121 and the Dead by Dawn parties symbolize a twin process of stylistic and musical ghettoization, some of the most extreme sounds to have been heard in London playing to an audience of one or two hundred in an almost stereotypically bleak basement space. Though at one level it was indeed a ghetto space, anyone who attended an event at 121 will remember its unique atmosphere. In the small hours, for listeners slumped in armchairs on the ground floor surrounded by the blast of dystopic noise emerging from the basement space, the 121 could seem as hyperreal as anywhere, even without chemical enhancement. The incongruity of the location could actually fuel the intensity, the awareness of being in a parallel space that was at least symbolically beyond the reach of daily commodification and oppression. The space served as a nexus of extreme sensory experience and had a unique atmosphere. When the local authorities finally moved to reclaim the site for its version of reality, the extent of support and affection for the 121 became clear. A protest campaign gained publicity even in the squatter-hostile *Evening Standard* newspaper, and the council received e-mail protests from America and elsewhere. When the venue was finally reclaimed at the end of 1998, London subculture lost one of its key focus points.

CONCLUSION: DEEPER UNDERGROUND

When marginal spaces such as the 121 are shut down, events of the type they host do not cease but move even further into invisibility, temporarily occupying and colonizing abandoned spaces produced by cycles of speculation and recession, and intermittently gaining footholds in small pubs and other venues. To a large extent, the economic and legal repression of such spaces and events has been successful, but the associated musical scene and information networks survive and continue to mutate, and it is even arguable that without a regular localized "site of infection," the viruses of stylistic and political order may find more hosts as they are dispersed across the metropolis. For now at least, the constant struggle to construct alternative spaces and experiences continues, even as the museumization of "London Rock City" gathers pace. In his eulogistic work on disco, Poschardt quotes Richard Dyer's 1979 apologia for disco in which he argued that the "stylistic anarchy" of contemporary capitalism enables oppressed minorities to create and develop their own cultures (113). Two decades later, under a more intensive form of market domination, it is unclear how "enabling" stylistic anarchy is. The spectacular genre politics of the styles clustered around happy hardcore and gabber express constant struggle against stasis and commodification in London, and the sheer *speed* of these styles (and of their mutation) can be read as a desperate attempt to create a "line of flight" away from incorporation into and exploitation by dominant market cultural practices. If nothing else, it is clear that the cultural politics of London are far more complex than the de-politicized narratives, which support and enforce the monetarist-realist idyll of free capitalist creativity, seek to claim. An uneven but still strongly fought struggle is constantly underway between the forces of ossification and the forces of dynamism.

NOTES

1. Bayley worked for six months as a design consultant for the Millenium Dome before resigning in protest at what he saw as political and bureaucratic interference in the creative process. Bayley's polemic is at times over-dramatized; however, his analysis of the ideological attitudes underpinning present government cultural policy does cast light on the processes under discussion here.

2. In its wholehearted collaboration with the museumization process and its emphasis on the mythology of rock, the "mainstream" music industry betrays no concern for the loss of "street cred." If the museumization of rock takes away the radical edge of the back catalogue and thus opens it to a wider demographic, the industry is poised to take advantage.

3. Happy hardcore is a British style that emerged roughly between 1991 and 1992. It is a relentlessly cheerful blend of high tempo beats with kitschy melodic elements and vocals. The scene is highly popular but rarely crosses over into mainstream consciousness and is derided even by much of the dance media. "Gabber" is a generic term for the darkest and fastest styles of hardcore techno which originated from Rotterdam in 1992 and has several subvariants.

4. Punk has perhaps been assimilable into the dominant tourist paradigm only because it took place "then" and "there" in a pre-globalized context that has increasingly few direct implications for the present context.

5. Included on the Routemaster Records double CD compilation, *Political Party Broadcast*, Routepile 001, London, 1997.

6. This can be seen in the promotion of compilations such as Trouble On Vinyl's *Code of The Streets*, the cover of which incorporates a street map showing an area of Battersea and Clapham, marking out a specific territory and claiming it for a specific sound.

7. Jungle (later also known as drum 'n bass) is characterized by its use of complex "breakbeat" patterns and heavy bass and appeals to a multi-cultural urban audience. Having emerged in London, it is generally recognized as the first distinctively British form of dance music.

8. The Roundhouse is still used, but for the more regulated form of art installations rather than the less commodifiable and therefore more subversive "happenings" of thirty years before.

9. It was the fact that their activities were supported by arts funding organizations and sympathetic critics in the mainstream media that enabled those events to take place. The autonomously organized raves and festivals of the nineties were far more vulnerable to suppression precisely because they did not have the shelter of institutional and media support. Autonomous events are far easier to suppress than those with at least semi-official sponsorship.

10. The law (described by lawyer Michael Mansfield as "a fascistic piece of legislation") was unopposed by the New Labour opposition, despite its stated concern for civil liberties (see Collin 230).

11. Since early 2000, a related industrial night, Hinouema, has taken place in a pub in the similarly marginal North London area of Finsbury Park.

12. See the compilation *Dead by Dawn* (Praxis Records 21, 1996), which features photos of the club nights and some of the main artists associated with the scene.

WORKS CITED

Attali, Jacques. *Noise. The Political Economy of Music*. Minneapolis: U of Minnesota P, 1996.

Bayley, Stephen. *Labour Camp: The Failure of Style over Substance*. London: Batsford, 1998.

Bey, Hakim. *T.A.Z. The Temporary Autonomous Zone, Ontological Anarchy, Poetic Terrorism*. Brooklyn, NY: Autonomedia, 1991.

Collin, Matthew, with John Godfrey. *Altered State: The Story of Ecstasy Culture and Acid House*. London: Serpent's Tail, 1998.

Marcuse, Herbert. *Eros and Civilization: A Philosophical Inquiry into Freud*. New York: Vintage Books, 1962.

Milestone, Katie. "The Love Factory: The Sites, Practices and Media Relationships of Northern Soul." In *The Clubcultures Reader*. S. Redhead, D. Wynne and J. O'Connor, eds. London: Routledge, 1997. 152–67.

Monroe, Alexei. "Thinking About Mutation: Genres in Nineties Electronica." In *Living through Pop*. Andrew Blake, ed. London: Routledge, 1999. 146–58.

Poschardt, Ulf. *DJ Culture*. London: Quartet, 1998.

Reynolds, Simon. *Energy Flash*. London: Picador, 1998.

Shields, R. *Places on the Margin: Alternative Geographies of Modernity*. London: Routledge, 1991.

CHAPTER 9

The Political Construction of Diasporic Communities in the Global City

JOHN EADE, ISABELLE FREMEAUX, AND DAVID GARBIN

INTRODUCTION

*I*n this chapter we want to explore contemporary, multi-ethnic London and the imagined communities constructed by Bangladeshis, in particular. Rather than consider those involved in artistic and aesthetic creativity we turn the spotlight on the political construction of imagined communities and the changing character of peoples and places in specific localities. This chapter contributes, therefore, to a comparison between the imperial capital of the nineteenth and early twentieth centuries and the global city of the new millennium.

The settlement across London of migrant workers from various parts of the New Commonwealth after the Second World War has led analysts to talk of the creation of "diasporic communities" (see, for example, Appadurai; Cohen; Vertovec). These communities have forged transnational links not only with their countries of origin but also with their fellow migrants around the globe. Those migrating from the Indian subcontinent to Britain, for example, may see themselves as members of imagined communities incorporating settlers in North America, the Caribbean, East Africa, Hong Kong, and the Pacific Ocean. The basis for such incorporation may be language, caste, region, religion, and/or nation. These different identities overlap and change through a process of identification defying simplistic notions of belonging to clearly demarcated (local or national) communities organized around homogeneous cultural traditions (see Hall, "New Ethnicities" and "The Question"; Albrow; Smith).

The political context of community construction has frequently been ignored in local community studies. Sociologists and anthropologists have been mainly concerned with what they regard as the social or cultural foundations of communities. The family, kinship systems, and religious institutions, for example, have been the focus of their attention, especially when South Asian migrants in Britain have been studied (see the debate involving Benson, Eade, and Werbner in Ranger, Samad, and Stuart). Yet political processes play a crucial role in the construction of communities, as lived both through the imagination and social relations. These processes operate at a number of levels—local, metropolitan, national, and transnational. In London, Bangladeshi political and community activists deal with the local state (borough council and political parties), as well as metropolitan structures (a new London assembly and a populist mayor, Ken Livingstone) and central government. They also deal increasingly with private business as services are privatized and with agencies operating transnationally between Britain and Bangladesh, as well as with Muslim-majority countries. This complex pattern of interweaving and competing allegiances produces a multiplex vision of London as a global city, both a national capital and much more.

The complex process of constructing imagined communities is vividly illustrated in the London that has emerged during the post-imperial period as a "global city" (see Sassen; Jacobs; Eade, *Living the Global City* and *Placing London*). The metropolis has been deeply involved in the development of a post-industrial social and economic order which overlays the remnants of modern industrialization. The new global order has built on the commercial institutions created during the period of empire and new social divisions overlap with older cleavages. Global flows of capital, people, information, and ideas have created a crucial boundary between (*a*) an information-rich elite and service class, employed within business and financial services, the professions, and high-tech firms, and (*b*) information-poor, lowly skilled workers in the service sector, traditional manufacturing, and the informal economy who occupy an insecure position close to the unemployed, homeless, and long-term sick. This polarization may be overdrawn, but it highlights the important ways in which the British nation-state has been changing during the post-imperial period as London engages with the economic and political exigencies of closer ties within a regional global bloc—the European Union.

LONDON AND SOUTH ASIAN SETTLEMENT

London's dominant and dynamic economic position within Britain encouraged a high proportion of "black and Asian" migrants to settle within its boundaries. Although by 1991 the percentage of South Asian residents in London was lower than the African-Caribbean population, London still attracted between two-thirds and three-quarters of Britain's South Asians (see Peach). Indian and Pakistani settlement overlapped across three main areas—(a) the western and north-western belt running from Finchley round to Wembley and down to Hounslow, (b) the northeast between Newham and Waltham Forest, and (c) the southern concentration of Tooting. Bangladeshi settlement, upon which we will focus in this chapter, was more concentrated and detached from these Indian and Pakistani strongholds. Bangladeshis were largely confined to the boroughs of Tower Hamlets, Camden, Westminster, and Newham, with the highest concentration in Tower Hamlets.

Our knowledge about these South Asian Londoners is very uneven. The more middle-class Indian settlements in western London have attracted far less attention than the Bangladeshi concentration in the East End borough of Tower Hamlets. Whatever the reasons for this disparity, a considerable body of evidence now exists about how Bangladeshis have politically and socially organized themselves in localities where the global economy has dramatically altered the local material world and people's understandings of that changing world. A focus on this particular area of the global city provides us, therefore, with rich insights into how people outside the literary and aesthetic elites, considered by many contributors to this volume, have constructed diverse imagined communities which embrace London and the transnational ties linking them to their country of origin.

BANGLADESHI SETTLEMENT IN LONDON'S EAST END

During the last twenty-five years, a first generation of migrant workers has been joined by a second and third generation, whose younger members may think of themselves as "Cockney Bengalis." Links with ancestral villages in the Sylhet district from which most Bangladeshis have come are changing in character as the future appears to be ever more shaped by the experience of living within London and Britain. A wider vision reaches beyond the villages of Sylhet and the urban villages of Tower Hamlets to the nation (Bangladesh, Britain), the metropolis (London and Dhaka), the Muslim world, and possible futures in other parts of the western world. London has become the site for imagining multiple communities extending far beyond the localities of London's East End.

During the 1980s and 1990s residents in the East End saw a dramatic social and economic change. Tower Hamlets had developed during the nineteenth century as an overwhelmingly working class area containing pockets of intense poverty. Its economy was dominated by the docks to the south, associated services such as the transport system, and small manufacturing and craft enterprises. In the early twentieth century, an emerging strong sense of class solidarity, expressed through the Labour and Communist Parties and trade union movement, was accompanied by powerful ethnic ties forged among the various overseas settlers (Irish Catholics and East European Jews in particular).

Out-migration during and immediately after the Second World War weakened this early twentieth-century social base, while the collapse of the docks in the 1960s and 1970s seriously undermined the traditional economic foundations of localities to the south of the borough. The western wards were less affected economically, since the small manufacturing businesses in the garment industry benefited from the arrival of Bangladeshi workers during the 1960s and 1970s. In Spitalfields and neighboring wards the rapid expansion of Bangladeshi residents resulted in the creation of a community structure incorporating small shops, travel agencies, welfare organizations, and sports clubs. A second generation of activists emerged in the late 1970s and 1980s to rival the elders and establish alliances with the local and central state (Labour Party, borough council, Greater London Council and the Inner London Education Authority).

Although the western wards did not radically change economically, the arrival and eventual settlement of Bangladeshis and, to a lesser extent, Somalis and white middle-class gentrifiers altered the ethnic and racial character of this part of the East End. To the south, a more drastic transformation was effected through the redevelopment of the docks. A new local identity was created—Docklands— under the central government and for the benefit of white middle-class newcomers, high-tech industries and business, and financial services competing in the global market. Docklands revealed the physical, social, and economic restructuring involved in the emergence of London as a global city—a process that largely excluded working-class residents, whether Bangladeshi or non-Bangladeshi.

Spitalfields has become the heartland of the Bangladeshi community, but the ward was not immune from the pressures dramatically revealed to the south in Docklands. City of London businesses were eager to move into an area designated by council planners as the "city fringe." The expanding numbers of tourists drawn to the ward by the internationally renowned Petticoat Lane street market were also attracted by the array of cafés, restaurants, and ethnic shops along Brick Lane and adjoining streets. Bangladeshi entrepreneurs were encouraged by external agencies to give the locality an identity, which enabled it to rival other ethnic enclaves, especially Chinatown in the West End (see Eade, *Placing London*). A new place identity—"Banglatown"—was created through a political process involving borough council officials and councillors, as well as private agencies such as Cityside Regeneration (see Jacobs).

The Bangladeshis involved in shaping this new identity were not only male entrepreneurs who ran the local cafés, restaurants, and garment trade factories and shops—they also included political and community activists. These different social actors were deeply embroiled in both local political agendas and political developments unfolding within their country of origin. As Jacobs has already pointed out, Bangladeshi entrepreneurs collaborated with white Labour Party activists in an alliance where the white activists presented themselves as:

> Paternal protectors, not of the Bengali community *per se*, but of Spitalfields itself. Bengali residents are both incorporated and displaced by this paternalism. The Left is reinstated as guardian of the inner city—not a working class inner city but a multicultural inner city. But this new Spitalfields of difference often took forms that unsettled the "pre-modern," anti-urban, communal nostalgias that gave affective drive to the Left's alliance with the Bengali community. (Jacobs 96)

BANGLADESHI SECULAR NATIONALISTS AND THE CONSTRUCTION OF IMAGINED COMMUNITIES

Bangladeshi entrepreneurs countered this construction of locality with their own essentialist and consumerist notions of Bengali identity. In turn, this entrepreneurial construction of place and person was paralleled by Bangladeshi community activists whose vision was shaped by a secular nationalist discourse emerging during and immediately after the creation of Bangladesh in 1971. Young secular nationalists had enjoyed considerable success during the 1980s in challenging the claims by older entrepreneurs to represent the Bangladeshi community within the local political arena. A number had become Labour councillors and had acquired white-collar jobs within the local state administration, community organizations, and non-government organizations.

During the 1980s, their vision was expressed in the wide variety of campaign documents that accompanied the numerous public meetings and lobbying of political and administrative bodies. These meetings did not just consider local issues. A bridge was built between community struggles in London and in Bangladesh as the secular policies of the Awami League and its leader (the founding father of Bangladesh, Sheikh Mujibur Rahman), weakened and concessions were made to Islamic organizations and discourses. The assassination of Sheikh Mujib and the policies pursued by his rivals during the late 1970s and through the 1980s and 1990s strengthened political activists espousing Islamic concerns—a process strengthened by *The Satanic Verses* controversy from the late 1980s and the emergence of Islamic groups on the national stage in Britain. Across localities such as Tower Hamlets, the political and ideological differences between secularists and Islamists were fought out through competition over urban space as community organizations vied with each other for public funding and room for their activities.

Some sense of these political and ideological struggles can be gained from different publications, as well as from interviews with specific activists. During the early 1980s the young secular activists expressed their view of Bangladesh's origins through a number of organizational reports, including this one produced by the Federation of Bangladeshi Youth Organizations (FBYO), which celebrated the national calendar and Victory Day:

> The Pakistan Army was totally defeated and people could look forward to an era of peace in which social justice could be achieved. (These hopes were shattered with the murder of Sheik Mujib at the hands of the CIA using reactionary Bengalis linked to the army.) (quoted in Eade, "Nationalism" 496)

Events unfolding in Bangladesh were linked to struggles facing Bangladeshis in Tower Hamlets as the FBYO's monthly journal, *Jubo Barta* (published with the support of state funds), explained. In its 1986 Victory Day issue it claimed:

> The people of Bangladesh, men, women, peasants, workers and students, all united for victory against oppressive forces. Today, the Bengalis in Britain can learn a lot from the struggles of their brothers and sisters. We need a united front against all oppressive elements in British Society. Once unity is achieved we will override all opposition and Victory will be ours as it was in '71. *Joi Bangla* [victory to Bangladesh]. (Eade, "Nationalism" 496)

During the late 1980s and the 1990s, public funding in Tower Hamlets for the organizations led by secularists declined, while support for mosques, madrassahs, and Islamic community organizations expanded. Public expression of this shifting balance can be seen in the opening of the borough's first purpose-built mosque, the East London Mosque, on a major thoroughfare and the visit by President Ershad in 1985 to the London Great Mosque (*Jammé Masjid*), Spitalfields, where he pledged money for its internal refurbishment. By the beginning of the new millennium, it was estimated that Tower Hamlets contained over forty places of Muslim worship and education. Yet secularists remained embedded within the local political and administrative arena, continuing to build alliances with state and private funding organizations. In Spitalfields they took advantage of the new opportunities provided by Cityside Regeneration and lobbied successfully for funds to introduce a new "invented tradition"—the Bengali New Year festival (Baishakhi Mela).

THE BENGALI NEW YEAR CELEBRATIONS: AUTHENTICITY AND THE ELABORATION OF A "MULTICULTURAL" TRADITION

The festival celebrated the Bengali seasonal calendar as distinct from the western Gregorian calendar (introduced through British colonialism) and the

Islamic calendar. Its celebration was encouraged in Dakha, the Bangladeshi capital, by secularists and other nationalists who wanted to emphasize its contribution to the independence movement. Shammim Azad, a London-based writer and journalist, for example, argued that:

> If we look into the history of the sub-continent, when Bengal was divided on the basis of religion [in 1947], it gave birth to fundamentalism and unrest. [The] majority of the population resented and protested the discrimination. During the Pakistan regime Bengali New Year acted as a political movement. It was to show their togetherness through an occasion which would simply celebrate their Bengaliness. (Azad 27)

Although the festival was only introduced to Tower Hamlets in 1998, the treasurer of the Mela Committee wanted to emphasize that the celebration was not confined to particular urban areas—it was a truly national event linking Bangladeshis in their country of origin with the Bangladeshi diaspora:

> The Baishakhi Mela is celebrated all over [Bangladesh], by cooking food, especially sweets—Indian sweets, *michti*—which are everywhere and free for everybody. Everybody is wearing clothes (red and white) etc. There are a lot of celebrations, music, dance, performances. (Interview with the treasurer of the Mela Committee, 2000)

This secularist interpretation, where nationalism is linked to an authentic Bengali cultural tradition, was even more forcefully developed in a multicultural guide for schools produced by a London Bengali community organization outside of Tower Hamlets. The guide explained that the festival was introduced by the Mughal emperor, Akbar, in 1556 to make the collection of revenue easier. The event had developed into a fair, recreating a rural Bengal:

> which is the traditional Bangladesh, its arts and crafts, games, sports, songs and dances. The "Nobi Barsha" (New Year) is more popular in the countryside, where the Bangla calendar has a firmer footing, with its traditional, Baishakhi fair (the month of Baishak), its appeal is more to the young people. . . . The celebration of the Bangla New Year reveals the Soul of Bangladesh and pronounces the truth about the people and the country. [It] is free from class and caste . . . and is in the care of the entire society. (Khan 115)

Although it was impossible to reproduce the cow or boat races held in Bangladesh, the organizers in Tower Hamlets tried to replicate the joyful, crowded, and artistic atmosphere, which they saw as the authentic mark of the *mela* in Bangladesh. Brick Lane, in the heart of Spitalfields, was turned into a pedestrian zone. This allowed the restaurants and cafés to set out tables and chairs al fresco, whilst a vast array of stalls sold homemade food and small handicrafts. The focal point of the *mela's* cultural activities were three stages where different artistic events were performed: *baul* (traditional folk music), classical (music, dance, poetry and drama), and pop/DJs.

The event was subsidized by the Cityside Regeneration Fund and, in consequence, had to abide with rules established by non-Bangladeshis that reflected multicultural and regeneration policies. The event was formally justified as a celebration for the "whole community," not just Bangladeshis. It was also supposed to advance the economic regeneration of the locality by attracting outsiders and strengthening the new place identity of Banglatown. The chair of the Mela Committee explained that:

> Brick Lane is a Banglatown. It is true for the local community but also for Bengali people outside London or outside the area. For them Brick Lane is theirs. They can identify and think: "Hang on, this is ours." Like Afro-Caribbean[s] think: "It is ours" about Brixton, even though they might live somewhere else. (Interview with the treasurer of the Mela Committee, 2000)

Yet he was quick to counter any suggestion that the *Mela* was an exclusively Bangladeshi event:

> It is a celebration of the Bengal people here. . . . At the same time we want to accommodate as many people as possible. This means that we need to consider the Bengalis themselves—and the three generations of them—but we also want other communities to be able to relate. (Interview with the treasurer of the Mela Committee, 2000)

The event brought together different interests and policies, but to secularists, such as the chair of the Mela Committee and his Bangladeshi colleagues, the celebration had a clear political purpose. It helped to sustain between Bangladeshis in Britain and their country of origin a link which showed how Bengali cultural heritage transcended religious differences. Bangladesh's Hindu minority could enjoy a festival influenced by the traces of a long-established syncretism between Hindus and Muslims in the Bengal region, while non-Bangladeshi in London could enjoy a multicultural day out. London's image as a cosmopolitan, global city was enhanced through an event that celebrated both multicultural harmony and the distinctive cultural traditions of a particular ethnic minority. Moreover the Baishakhi Mela shed light on a local—rather overlooked—phenomenon: the amount of factionalism among local community leaders. Indeed, even though there was a clear, widely shared consensus about the political purpose of the festival as a spatial and cultural marker for the Bengali community, the organization of the *mela* triggered high tensions among community leaders.

It is important to highlight that the margins of power enjoyed by local community leaders are still rather restricted. Even though there is now a fair number of Bengali local councillors—about half of the local councillors for the London Borough of Tower Hamlets (LBTH) are of Bangladeshi origin—they tend not to be at highly strategic levels of the local administration. Likewise, the board of directors of the local regeneration agency features some local

Bangladeshi members, but their role seems to be more honorific than strategic. The local political climate thus features tense struggles for limited resources, which tend to emphasize, as well as modify, the original factions that characterize the local social organization in Bangladesh. These are based on patron/client relationships and reflect the general power structure of the Bangladeshi society.

The recent availability of large sums of money for local regeneration (Cityside is now managing a 32,000,000-pound budget) has clearly encouraged local power struggles among Bangladeshi activists and their non-Bangladeshi funders and colleagues. Indeed, the current model for urban regeneration emphasizes that community involvement must be part of the delivery process. Local community organizations, therefore, have access to ever-increasing funds. The availability of monies encourages the competition between secular activists, who seek to control Bangladeshi participation in local regeneration projects and the elaboration of rituals performed in Bangladesh for a multicultural London audience (e.g., the Baishakhi Mela). Power struggles have moved from the town hall to the regeneration agency's offices (Neveu).

RECONSTRUCTING LONDON'S EAST END:
MOSQUES AND ISLAMIC REGENERATION

Islamic political parties such as the Muslim League and organizations such as Dawatul Islam had been thrown into a defensive position by the breakup of Pakistan and the creation of Bangladesh in 1971. Their support for Pakistan, and the involvement of some of their members in what their opponents described as "war crimes," left a bitter legacy. These enmities were embraced by Bangladeshis in Britain as supporters of the Pakistan regime fled to London and other British cities. Tower Hamlets' mosques, prayer rooms, and *madrassahs* (Islamic educational institutions) were inevitably influenced by the political struggles between secularists and Islamists, between the Awami League (a political party associated with Sheikh Mujibur Rahman) and its opponents.

The movement towards a more Islamic interpretation of Bangladeshi nationalism from the late 1970s onwards strengthened the position of local Islamist groups, and the East London Mosque in particular. At the same time, Bangladeshi secularists sought to control the management committees of these institutions and to maintain the campaign against certain religious and community leaders accused of war crimes or of collaboration with the pre-independence Pakistani regime. In turn, Islamists developed a critique of the corrupt dealings of their opponents, which touched an important nerve both in Bangladesh and in Britain. Many younger Bangladeshis, as well as their elders, accused political and community representatives of financial graft and "cronyism." With high rates of unemployment, poor housing conditions, growing drug addiction, and very limited prospects, young Bangladeshis in Tower Hamlets were attracted by Islamist denunciations of the immorality of secularist Bangladeshi elites and their non-Bangladeshi collaborators.

The leaders of the East London Mosque played a major role in this political struggle. They were eager to challenge secularists' claims to being the natural representatives of the Bangladeshi community and they found support among certain factions within the local political and administrative arena. During an interview with members of the mosque management committee, the *imam* emphasized the central position occupied by the mosque not only in Tower Hamlets, but across East London:

> This [mosque] is considered as the central mosque in this region. Although in London [generally, there is] a mosque [which] is called Central Mosque . . . in Regent's Park, [the East London Mosque] has a central position in the Tower Hamlets and . . . the whole East London area. (Interview with the East London Mosque Management Committee, 2000)

The mosque played a key role in fighting the increasing moral degradation of young Bangladeshis:

> Drugs, alcohol and the gang-fighting and all the other wrong things, . . . unemployment and [the] unhealthy housing situation and the cultural gap between the older generation and the younger generation. Families are suffering. Marriages are breaking. (Interview with the East London Mosque Management Committee, 2000)

These problems were tackled through counseling sessions, evening talks (especially during Ramadan), religious and language classes, and the functions provided by the Young Muslim Organization (YMO).

The *imam* was insistent on correct behavior between Muslim men and women; this was intimately associated with how they dressed and mixed in public space. Such an insistence led easily to a discussion of the forthcoming *mela* celebration, which was dismissed as an un–Islamic event encouraged by a secular minority:

> In Bangladesh they don't exercise . . . like this . . . [only a minority]. . . . It is nowadays happening in Dhaka. . . . There is a secular trend and there are people who are purely having their own understanding about community, about culture. . . . This was the culture of the Hindus. . . . Nowadays some people are getting very much influenced by some other faith—that's why those people are away from Islam. They look for something fun. Whatever it is, which culture, which religion, no matter. (Interview with the East London Mosque Management Committee, 2000)

The younger generation was especially vulnerable to the enticements of a festival that was originally observed by Hindus and Sikhs:

Like our younger generation, why are they jumping to all the wrong things, drugs and crime? Because they find ways to enjoy the life in a wrong way. We have our framework of celebrations, our cultural exercise. We have our own thing. Don't adopt this. (Interview with the East London Mosque Management Committee, 2000)

The *mela* could be transformed into an Islamic event but it would have to include:

Some kind of literature. Some kind of . . . exhibition brought from Bangladesh to let our younger generation know what is their parents' early life, how many rivers are there [in Bangladesh], how many districts there, what is the temperature there. Have a display, talk about [the] new country [Britain], your culture, your literature. Think of those [things] where we can agree and the greater community rather than making upset [for] many people. (Interview with the East London Mosque Management Committee, 2000)

The *imam* expressed a vision of a metropolitan locality where young Bangladeshis could be saved from the moral degradation of urban crime and drug dependency through the observance of correct Islamic behavior and values. According to this vision, the *mela* and its supporters (both Bangladeshi and non-Bangladeshi) only encouraged the kinds of immorality and excess to which at least some young Bangladeshis were prone. The East London Mosque's leaders sought to link its particular interests with those of British Muslims generally, and to take the lead in representing Islamic concerns within the local political and administrative arena. Consequently, when a youth rally was held at the mosque to support its campaign to gain council approval for the expansion of its premises, a YMO representative associated this particular struggle with the survival of Muslims across Britain:

My dear brothers in Islam, we are representing one of the oldest organizations in the UK. . . . We are proud to be associated with the Islamic Mosque. Historically all people who forget Islam are taking advantage and degraded all the institutions of Islam, including the mosques. . . . This is the beginning . . . of the struggle for survival as Muslim in this country. Especially the youth, you have to detect and defend your right as Muslim. We cannot no longer say that we will be old and then we will become good Muslim. We have to start now. Until then, we will be finished, basically. (Garbin 178)

Young Bangladeshis should develop into the ideal type described by other YMO leaders. The ignorant, living-for-the-moment type and the self-absorbed careerists who "see Islam as part of their culture" are distinguished from the "ideal Muslim youth" who "know the importance of learning about Islam, striving to practice it and spreading the message to the others" without condemning them (Garbin 114).

Although the East London Mosque's leaders and associated organizations claimed to represent the East End's Muslim community, their claims did not go unchallenged. Other mosques approached religious practice and community involvement from different directions and their religious leaders were supported by rival groups of lay activists. In the opinion of secularists, such as the chair of the Mela Committee, the differences between the Great Mosque in Brick Lane and the East London Mosque could be explained partly in terms of political influences linking the locality to Bangladesh and other Muslim-majority countries:

> The people who are running the Brick Lane Mosque are coming from the Bangladesh politics—a range of political parties: Awami League, BNP, others, "left" political parties, except Jamaat [i-Islami]. At the Whitechapel [East London] Mosque there is only one political party affiliation—Jamaat. Also [the East London Mosque's] funding comes from the Middle East . . . whereas the [Brick Lane] mosque was built by the community. There was not a single penny from outside the country or outside the area. (Interview conducted by Eade and Fremeaux with the treasurer of the Mela Committee, 12 Apr. 2000)

ISLAMIC FESTIVALS AND THE CONSTRUCTION OF AUTHENTICITY

We have concentrated on secular political activists and Islamic leaders, but in this section the views of Tower Hamlets' "ordinary" Bangladeshis will be considered. For many, the multicultural "syncretism" of the Baishakhi Mela contrasted with the "authenticity" of traditional religious events, in particular the two festivals of Eid. Islamically, these festivals are extremely important since they institutionalize a set of practices strictly defined by the Koran and the Hadiths (Sayings of the Prophet) and performed by the entire Muslim community (umma). On the day of Eid ul Adha, the ritual of *korbani* commemorates Abraham's willingness to sacrifice his son Isaac. An animal has to be slaughtered, divided into parts, and then equally distributed to kin, friends, and poor people as *zakat* (charity). This period coincides with Hajj, the pilgrimage to Mecca, one of the five pillars of Islam. Charity and donations (*sadqua al fitr*) also play a central role in the festival of Eid ul Fitr, which marks the end of Ramadan. Among Tower Hamlets' Bangladeshis, special Eid ceremonials are held in the local mosques where male members of the community gather in large numbers. Eid reunions contribute to socialization and the consolidation of links between families and friends. Clothes or money (*salaamis*) are given to children; food and sweets (*mishtis*) are exchanged when relatives and neighbors invite each other for the traditional greetings (Eid Mubarrak).

In Bangladesh, the same religious and social rituals are taking place, but there employees and workers can enjoy a short period of holidays, and they travel back to their native places, in villages or towns. Compared with Britain, Eid festivals have a stronger visible presence in the public sphere. In the local bazaars commercial activity reaches its annual peak. The entire village or neighborhood (*para*) assembles at an open space (*eidgah*) outside the mosque for prayer. During Eid ul Adha, the sacrifice of cows for *korbani* is also highly ritualized and conducted by religious specialists in the presence of lineage members. In East London, however, Eid customs have to be renegotiated according to constraints inherent to the use of public space for religious rituals in a non-Muslim society. For *korbani*, a suburban site in Dagenham is used, but most of the time the meat (goat) is directly ordered from specialized shops.

British restrictions concerning religious practices, on one hand, and the difficulty of maintaining the extended family structure, on the other, has led many first-generation Bengalis to emphasize their emotional attachment to Eid celebrations in Bangladesh rather than Britain. Moreover, Bangladeshi Muslims cannot distribute meat as charity in Britain, and debates often occur between local religious leaders about whether donations to mosques can replace traditional *zakat*. Families in Britain often prefer to send large sums of money to Sylhet for the purchase of several cows for sacrifice and distribution, with a third given to poor people in local villages. This practice appears to be a powerful status symbol, but it also helps to reaffirm the ties between British Bangladeshis and their country of origin while uniting divided families across the global diaspora of believers.

Both in Bangladesh and Britain, therefore, the Eid festivals are greatly awaited events which symbolize religious commitments to moral values and provide a sense of unity and identity for Muslims. Not surprisingly, then, religious leaders and "purists" in Tower Hamlets and Sylhet feel confident in contrasting the "un-Islamic" Baishakhi Mela with the sacred celebrations of Eid, which underpin the basic principles of Islamic devotion. Yet perhaps a more important element here is the festive character of the religious events. Social cohesion is expressed through collective consumption and common joy, especially during Eid ul Fitr, the day ending the one-month fast of Ramadan. In Tower Hamlets, some young Bangladeshis sometimes refer to these celebrations as "their own Christmas" within a secular British urban environment. This reinterpretation is paralleled by an appropriation of local spaces outside mosques and prayers halls. In Spitalfields, for example, they drive around in private or hired cars, listening to Asian and *bhangra* music. These practices are continually criticized by the elders, but they add a special atmosphere to a Muslim festival traditionally restricted to the observance of various rituals in private and community spaces.

A combination of commensalism and Islamic moralism defines, therefore, the notion of a "community festival" based on religious principles and observed throughout the global *umma*. Despite the adaptation and reinterpretation of traditional rituals in Tower Hamlets, religious celebrations still link Britain to other imagined communities, such as Bangladesh or the Middle East (Mecca).

In this context, the Baishakhi Mela can easily be interpreted by its critics as an inauthentic celebration lacking any essential community relevance and even reducible to an event grounded in Hindu/Sikh Otherness and the customs of Puja (festival of gods and goddesses).

ISLAMIZATION, TRANSNATIONAL LINKS, AND IMAGINED COMMUNITIES

The focus within this chapter has been on the London-end of the Bangladeshi migration process. However, as we have outlined the contestation of urban space, it has become clear that local political and ideological struggles between secularists and Islamists have been deeply informed by the continuing links with the country of origin. These links are, not surprisingly, stronger among the first generation of settlers than among their descendants, but it would be a mistake to assume that these ties will inevitably fade with the passing of the elders. If we are to understand more fully the multilayered character of the constructions of imagined communities described above, we need to consider developments in Bangladesh, especially the district of Sylhet from which most settlers migrated.

London's Sylheti population was almost exclusively recruited from the rural, small-landholding class. The first generation of these "Londonis" still retained a keen interest in their Sylheti landholdings, which they were usually able to expand through remittances (see Gardner). Their improving economic fortunes encouraged them to become more respectable as Muslims—a process of Islamization where they distanced themselves from the long-established syncretic traditions of "folk" religion and adopted a "pure," scripturally based Islam (see Gardner). Islamic respectability could also be expressed through a widening support for or the building of new mosques and *madrassahs* in both Sylhet and Tower Hamlets.

This combination of economic, social, and religious forces was further strengthened from the mid-1980s by political decentralization in Bangladesh. Leadership of the sub-district (*upazilla*) committee became fiercely contested with *probashi* (ex-patriate) "Londonis" entering the fray and using community centers in Tower Hamlets and elsewhere as a platform for these Sylheti factional conflicts. When Bangladeshi political leaders visited London they were courted by *probashi* Sylhetis, whose influence was sustained by their position as lineage leaders (*matbors*) building networks between neighborhoods (*para*), village, district, and national boundaries. A diasporic identity politics had developed where power was exercised transnationally not just between Bangladesh and Britain, but also between other countries to which Bangladeshis had migrated—the Gulf, Italy, and North America, for example.

The local communities imagined through these networks could not be explained, therefore, solely in terms of the political and administrative structures operating within Tower Hamlets, London, or Britain. Local perceptions of place were shaped by transnational flows of people, capital, goods, information, and ideas. Even more important, for our analysis, this multilayered process of community construction could not be dominated by one particular institution—the East London Mosque—or political party (Labour Party, Awami League, Bangladesh National Party). The leaders of the East London Mosque claimed a position of centrality within Tower Hamlets and the East End generally, but other groups of influential Sylhetis championed the London Great Mosque in Spitalfields as the "community mosque," while Bangladeshi residents could choose between another forty prayer rooms and mosques scattered across the borough. Expressing one's identity as a "respectable" Muslim could take subtly different forms and ensured that Islamization was far from creating a uniformity of religious practice and belief.

CONCLUSION

In this chapter we have examined the construction of imagined communities through the political and ideological struggles between Bangladeshi secular nationalists and Islamists and related them to the perceptions and practices of "ordinary" Bangladeshi residents. In the multicultural, global city that is contemporary London, Bangladeshis bring together changing and contested understandings of local places and people through imagined communities which transcend national boundaries. These communities refer to their country of origin and to the villages of the Sylhet district in particular, but they also embrace a global, supranational Muslim community (*umma*). Secularist leaders have collaborated with local public funding bodies through the discourse of multiculturalism to adapt a Bangladeshi festival—the Baishakhi Mela—to the streets and parks of Spitalfields. At the same time, the *mela* is challenged by Islamists who extend the political and social influence of mosques, prayer rooms, and *madrassahs* through alliances with local non-Muslims. They enjoy the implicit support of many Bangladeshis who seek to perform traditional Muslim festivals and rituals and enhance their credentials as "proper" Muslims.

Many features of what we have discussed above will be familiar to the other contributors within this volume. However, what may well be different in the contemporary global city is the resistance of these imagined communities to the corrosive force of national assimilation. London demonstrates, in the most vivid way, the challenge to the "melting pot" assumptions which have informed traditional models of immigration and the nation-state. More flexible and subtle understandings of the open and heterogeneous character of

Western countries have emerged, even though we must not underestimate the continuing influence of the assimilation model within political and media circles. As nation-state elites respond to transnational flows of people, capital, goods, and information, and acknowledge the force of supranational allegiances, so there is a gradual understanding of how global cities like London have changed in the aftermath of colonialism. Our particular local example involving one ethnic minority group may have thrown some light on the complex process of imagining community in contemporary globalizing conditions.

WORKS CITED

Albrow, Martin. "Travelling beyond Local Cultures: Socioscapes in a Global City." In *Living the Global City: Globalization as Local Process*. J. Eade, ed. London and New York: Routledge, 1997. 37–55.

Appadurai, Arjun. "Disjuncture and Difference in the Global Cultural Economy." In *Global Culture*. M. Featherstone, ed. London: Sage, 1990. 295–310.

Azad, Shamin. "Baishaki Mela." The *Star*, June, 2000 (no volume or page numbers used in this publication).

Benson, Sue. "Asians Have Culture, West Indians Have Problems: Discourses of Race and Ethnicity In and Out of Anthropology." In *Culture, Identity and Politics: Ethnic Minorities in Britain*. Terence Ranger, Yunas Samad, and Ossie Stuart, eds. Aldershot: Avebury, 1996. 47–56.

Cohen, Robin. *Global Diasporas: An Introduction*. London: UCL P, 1997.

Eade, John. "Ethnicity and the Politics of Cultural Difference: An Agenda for the 1990s?" In *Culture, Identity and Politics: Ethnic Minorities in Britain*. Terence Ranger, Yunas Samad, and Ossie Stuart, eds. Aldershot: Avebury, 1996. 57–66.

———. "Identity, Nation and Religion: Educated Young Bangladeshis in London's East End." In *Living the Global City: Globalization as Local Process*. J. Eade, ed. London and New York: Routledge, 1997. 252–59.

———. "Nationalism and the Quest for Authenticity: The Bangladeshis in Tower Hamlets." *New Community* 16.4 (1990): 493–503.

———. *Placing London: From Imperial Capital to Global City*. Oxford and New York: Berghahn, 2000.

Garbin, David. "Immigration, Territoires, et Identités: Enquête dans un quartier de l'East End de Londres." Diss. U of Tours, France, 1999.

Gardner, Katy. *Global Migrants, Local Lives*. Oxford: Clarendon P, 1995.

Hall, Stuart. "New Ethnicities." In *'Race,' Culture and Identity*. James Donald and Ali Rattansi, eds. London: Sage, 1992.

———. "The Question of Cultural Identity." In *Modernity and Its Futures*. David Held, Stuart Hall, and Anthony McGrew, eds. Milton Keynes: Open UP, 1992. 274–316.

Interview conducted by John Eade and Isabelle Fremeaux with the East London Mosque Management Committee (name withheld), 10 Feb. 2000.

Interview conducted by John Eade and Isabelle Fremeaux with the Treasurer of the *Mela* Committee (name withheld), 12 Apr. 2000.

Interview conducted by Eade and Fremeaux with the Treasurer of the *Mela* Committee (name withheld), 10 Feb. 2000.

Jacobs, Jane. *Edge of Empire: Postcolonialism and the City*. London and New York: Routledge, 1996.

Khan, Lila. *Bangladesh Information Handbook*. London: Inner London Education Authority, 1990.

Neveu, Catherine, ed. *Espace Public et Engagement Politique: Enjeux et Logiques de la Citoyenneté Locale*. Paris: Harmattan, 1999.

Peach, Ceri. *Ethnicity in the 1991 Census, Vol. 2: The Ethnic Minority Populations of Great Britain*. London: HMSO, 1997.

Sassen, Saskia. *The Global City*. Princeton: Princeton UP, 1991.

Smith, Michael Peter. *Transnational Urbanism: Locating Globalization*. Oxford: B. Blackwell, 2000.

Vertovec, Steven. *The Hindu Diaspora*. London and New York: Routledge, 2000.

Werbner, Pnina. "Essentialising the Other: A Critical Response." In *Culture, Identity and Politics: Ethnic Minorities in Britain*. Terence Ranger, Yunas Samad, and Ossie Stuart, eds. Aldershot: Avebury, 1996.

CHAPTER 10

Lonely Londoner:
V. S. Naipaul and
"The God of the City"

GAUTAM PREMNATH

*I*n an essay written in 1958, at an early stage in his career as a writer, V. S. Naipaul asked, "For how long can I continue to live in London and continue writing?" ("London" 9).[1] The piece explored the issue of what Naipaul called "the regional barrier," a problem confronting all non-Western writers based in Britain and perforce dependent upon a British audience for their work. Naipaul's essay begins as an indictment of metropolitan critics, complaining that "the social comedies I write can be fully appreciated only by someone who knows the region I write about" (11). Yet, as the piece proceeds, it turns inexorably into an indictment of the metropolis itself. The sterility and "privacy" of London life oppress and depress him, and seem to defeat all his writerly instincts and training. As he remarks, "I feel I can never hope to know as much about people here as I do about Trinidad Indians, people I can place almost as soon as I see them" (14–15). This inscrutability of the metropolitan populace leads him to the paradox with which the essay closes:

> I like London. For all the reasons I have given it is the best place to write in. The problem for me is that it is not a place I can write about. Not as yet. Unless I am able to refresh myself by travel—to Trinidad, to India—I fear that living here will eventually lead to my own sterility; and I may have to look for another job. (16)

Any reader familiar with Naipaul's subsequent work will be struck by the poignance of this concluding statement. After all, it comes from someone whose telling and retelling of his personal and family histories in the years to come will dwell obsessively on the vanity of writerly ambitions and the fragility of the writerly vocation (and whose customary biographical note, in boasting that "he has followed no other profession," simultaneously gestures towards the abyss always threatening to swallow up the failed writer).[2] Yet the pathos of the statement should not distract from the note of resolution it also strikes. Indeed, at this moment close to the outset of his career, Naipaul is already beginning to map out the course he will pursue in the ensuing decades, and to envisage the distinctive place he will come to occupy in twentieth-century letters. The path he will choose will require him to reimagine his vocation as a novelist— to move away from the "social comedies" with which he made his name towards a darker and more self-referential literary mode. It will also entail a careful staking out of his place in London, and of the place *of* London in his life as a writer. Almost a decade after the publication of the essay, this process will bear fruit in *The Mimic Men* (1967), the first fully realized novelistic articulation of his new self-understanding as a London-based "postcolonial mandarin."[3] With this novel, London finally becomes "a place . . . [he] can write about."[4] Departing from his own previous practice, and that of other Caribbean writers who take London as their subject, *The Mimic Men* is a pivotal moment both in Naipaul's career and in the literary history of the city.

Naipaul's novels of the 1950s, such as *The Mystic Masseur* (1957) and *The Suffrage of Elvira* (1958), are closely observed satires of Trinidad politics and society. Written prior to the moment of formal independence in 1962, they mock, more or less gently, the pretensions of decolonization and anticipate a delusory postcolonial future. In his own celebrated analysis of the metropolitan mediation of West Indian writing, George Lamming attacked him for the "castrated satire" of these works (*Pleasures of Exile* 225), in a troubling echo of Naipaul's own anxieties about "sterility." Yet, if the heroically masculinist and rigorously committed mode of writing Lamming pioneered was fundamentally antithetical to Naipaul's understanding of the writer's role, he was nevertheless able to find a way to move, on his own terms, past the limited canvas of these early works.[5] In *A House for Mr. Biswas* (1961) he achieved a humane, expansive, and penetrating social vision that elicited comparisons to the nineteenth-century masters of high realism. The novel brought him the kind of acclaim that enabled him to break past "the regional barrier" and stake a claim to being one of the major novelists working in the English language. Yet, if *A House for Mr. Biswas* is the high-water mark of Naipaul's phase as a novelistic observer of the human comedy, it is also a kind of terminus. At the time of its publication he had already embarked on a very different kind of project, one which was to set his bearings as a writer for much of the coming decade.

In 1960, Eric Williams, prime minister of Trinidad and Tobago and leader of its independence movement, commissioned Naipaul to write a nonfiction book about the Caribbean, which was eventually published as *The Middle Passage* in 1962. In his foreword to the work, Naipaul emphasized his ambivalence at Williams's proposal that he depart from his developing practice as a writer of fiction: "I hesitated. The novelist works towards conclusions of which he is often unaware; and it is right that he should. However, I decided to take the risk" (*Middle Passage* 6). He also expressed a wariness of being co-opted by the emergent postcolonial state, acknowledging the work's sponsorship by Williams and the government of Trinidad and Tobago while adding: "It is in no way, however, an 'official' book. It sells nothing" (6). These two gestures combine to define Naipaul's emerging politics of location. The "risk" he is taking—the risk of nonfiction—is precisely that the writer must submit himself to worldly constraints and determinations, rather than operating in a realm of supposedly unfettered imagination. However, this risk is rendered acceptable by his decision to explicitly renounce any "official" role for himself as a servant or booster of the postcolonial state, and thus to offer a guarantee of his legitimacy as an autonomous observer and bearer of truth. Naipaul holds in abeyance what he sees as the inevitable corruptions that accompany a representative role for the writer—to say "my book sells nothing" is also to say "I cannot be bought." These statements anticipate his many subsequent self-positionings as beyond the ideological hold of Third Worldism or any other variety of minoritarian politics (gestures abetted and endorsed by British and American champions of his work such as Paul Theroux and Irving Howe, and buttressed by his own expressions of allegiance to universal values implicitly grounded in metropolitan culture).[6]

Naipaul's words add a sense of purpose to the desire he expressed in 1958, to "refresh" himself by means of travel away from London to places like Trinidad and India. *The Middle Passage* was the first of a series of works of documentary and historical reportage which helped to establish him as a distinctive kind of postcolonial intellectual: a Third World Cassandra debunking the liberatory pretensions of decolonization, and insistently reinscribing a despairing vision of universal civilization threatened by the encroaching barbarism of "the bush."[7] Naipaul's next substantial work, *An Area of Darkness* (1964), was an excoriation of postcolonial India that extended his reach beyond his earlier focus on the New World—not incidentally, it also gave him a sizeable new audience in South Asia, and a host of new interlocutors and antagonists. Devoting himself to this new role entailed an extended hiatus from novel writing (with the exception of the 1963 novel *Mr. Stone and the Knight's Companion*[8]). Yet these writings are characterized by features that will come to also define his subsequent fictional work: a febrile and compacted prose style; the furthering of his arguments through the extensive use of dialogue with strategically chosen interlocutors;

and a narratorial persona of heightened sensibility and Orwellian fidelity to the truth of his own experience, whose visceral response serves as a measure of the reality he observes.[9] Many of these features recur in *The Mimic Men*, in which Naipaul finally finds a *fictional* mode in which to consolidate and develop his new self-understanding as a writer, while also concluding his long and productive detour and establishing London as an imaginative space that he can inhabit.

Naipaul takes the first step on this path in his declaration of autonomy at the beginning of *The Middle Passage*. Yet his anxious self-distancing from Williams, the fierce critic of colonialism, seems superfluous in light of the content of *The Middle Passage*. He opens the book with an epigraph from James Anthony Froude's notoriously racist travelogue *The English in the West Indies* (1887), and much of the book is given over to echoing and validating the claims of nineteenth-century British observers like Froude and Anthony Trollope about the fecklessness, squalor, and absence of history of the British West Indies. Naipaul is thus entering into a longstanding tradition of Caribbean dialogue with colonial observers like Froude, while attempting to reverse the terms of engagement established by precursors like the nineteenth-century Trinidadian intellectual J. J. Thomas. Thomas's *Froudacity* (1889), an eloquent and devastating rebuttal of Froude's screed, set a pattern for Caribbean literary intellectualism that is homologous with the dynamics of decolonizing nationalism. In the works of Thomas's twentieth-century successors—writers like Martin Carter, Austin Clarke, and George Lamming—Caribbean literature becomes the site of a Hegelian struggle for recognition, in which the relationship between metropole and periphery is mapped onto the relationship between master and slave. Literature works to elaborate a project of nation-building, imagined as a twofold task of engendering collective self-recognition while also claiming recognition among the comity of nations. Yet this understanding of decolonization as the struggle for recognition remains crucially predicated on an imperialist geography. To this extent, the poetics of decolonization of a writer like Lamming turns out to be a secret sharer of Naipaul's poetics of despair. Novels like Lamming's *The Emigrants* (which narrates the mass migrations from the Caribbean to Britain in the years following the Second World War) or *Of Age and Innocence* (which follows nationalist revolutionaries in the other direction) depend, like *The Middle Passage*, on stabilizing a sense of the immense distance separating imperial metropolis and colonial periphery.

Of course this sense of commonality should not be pressed too far. While for Naipaul this distance maintains the perpetual belatedness of the colonial subject, in Lamming its traversal becomes the enabling condition for the forging of a pan-Caribbean postcolonial nationalism. In this, Lamming's fictions bear out, up to a point, Edward Said's analysis in *Culture and Imperialism* of the possibilities created by "the voyage in" of anti-imperial intellectuals from the colonies to the metropolitan centers. In Lamming's *The Emigrants* (1954), the section entitled "A Voyage"—which follows a ship first as it travels from port to port in the Caribbean Sea gathering up its cargo of migrants and then as it bears them to Britain—takes up close to half the book and encompasses much of the dramatic and thematic scope of the novel as a whole. It is in this section that Lamming establishes a sense of the distance separating colony and imperial center, prompting an ideology of artistic commitment and intellectual direction that is necessary for the writer to methodically traverse this distance and discover its meaning. Over the course of "A Voyage," the narrative gradually centers itself upon the character of Collis, who in many ways serves as a surrogate for Lamming himself—and who, like Lamming, is a writer. This vocation serves to separate though not to distance him from his fellow migrants. For over the course of their voyage the ship's passengers have been transformed from a motley assortment of types (identified in terms of personality quirks, nicknames, and islands of origin) into a collectivity—a multiplicitous, differentiated, critical mass. As one of these passengers (identified only as "the Jamaican") puts it: "'Different man, different island, but de same outlook. Dat's de meanin' o' de West Indies. De wahter between dem islands doan' separate dem'" (*Emigrants* 61). The subject of "A Voyage" is the constitution of a pan-Caribbean nation-people out of a "fragmented nationalism" mired in the particularities of Barbados, Trinidad, and other Caribbean nations.[10] The voyage across the Atlantic forges this new national consciousness, albeit under the sign of metropolitan domination (the migrants are not magically transformed by their passage into politically committed actors, but remain somewhat hapless figures at the mercy of historical processes that are beyond their grasp). If Collis is individuated over the course of this section, it is as a representative figure who can voice the experiences of the collectivity. Indeed, towards the end of the section he is lectured by one of his fellow passengers on the high stakes of his vocation as a writer and the representative duties that it demands of him:

> "You're a public victim," he said. "You are articulate not only for yourself, but thousands who'll never see you in person, but who will know you because the printed page is public property. And if you betray yourself, you can betray thousands too. To be trivial, dishonest or irresponsible is criminal." (101)

Yet at the end of *The Emigrants*, Collis bitterly declares "'I have no people'" (280). Crucially, the second half of the novel does not develop and intensify the sense of a critical mass constituting itself, but rather traces its dissolution on the streets and in the bedsitters of London. Mostly in the bedsitters—one of the striking features of the London portion of the book is how much of it is set indoors, in cramped and constricted spaces, and how markedly absent is the sense of urban openness and metropolitan possibility that animates the contemporaneous London fictions of Lamming's friend, the Trinidadian writer

Sam Selvon (the two sailed to England together in 1950). The narrative of collective self-discovery initiated in "A Voyage" is forestalled upon arrival in London, to be resumed only in Lamming's later novels dealing with revolutionary nationalism upon the fictional Caribbean island of San Cristobal. The hallmark of these works is not "the voyage in," but rather "the voyage back," whether in the sense of physical return (*Of Age and Innocence*), rediscovery of the native land (*Season of Adventure*), or revival as living memory of the historical experience of colonization (*Water with Berries*). London exists in these novels as a kind of non-place, functioning primarily as a point of departure for these narratives of return.[11]

The sense, in *The Emigrants*, of London as zone of dissolution and dispersal inflects even Selvon's "London trilogy." The first of these novels, *The Lonely Londoners* (1956), is characterized by a far more open embrace of London and its possibilities than Lamming allowed for. Selvon's novel, like Lamming's, comes to center itself around a writer figure, Moses, but one who arrives at his discovery of writerly vocation as a result of his time in London, and after a rhapsodic stream-of-consciousness passage in which he both celebrates and claims possession of the city.[12] The discovery of a pan-Caribbean national consciousness, which in *The Emigrants* had taken place on the voyage across the Atlantic, begins instead upon arrival in the great city. It is instantiated in the very language used by the group of migrants in the novel, a generic Creole which cannot be identified with any specific Caribbean locale or ethnicity (unlike the far more particularized vernaculars Selvon uses in his fictions that are set in Trinidad). In the two subsequent novels of the trilogy, *Moses Ascending* (1975) and *Moses Migrating* (1983), as well as in the freestanding novel *The Housing Lark* (1965), Selvon traces the inevitable dissolution of this collectivity of migrants as a result of spatial dispersion, generational change, divergent political paths, and upward mobility and bourgeoisification. Moses the *flâneur*, poet of urban reverie in *The Lonely Londoners*, transforms into Moses Aloetta, bourgeois property-holder and memoirist, disdaining the very fellow-migrants for whom he had once functioned as sage and chronicler.

For all their manifest differences, both Selvon and Lamming concern themselves in their London writings with the relationship between the artist and a mass of migrants of which he is a part—or, to put it another way, with the often vexed relationship between aesthetic and political representation. Not so with Naipaul's *The Mimic Men*. Early in the book its protagonist and narrator, Ralph Singh, in speaking of himself and other exiled postcolonial politicians, observes with regret that "in the lower-middle-class surroundings to which we are condemned we pass for immigrants" (*Mimic Men* 8). Shortly afterwards, he primly notes of Kensington, where he lived as a student, that "it has . . . become a centre of racialist agitation, and I do not now wish to become involved in battles which are irrelevant to myself" (10). These early statements are not problematized over the course of the novel, but function more simply as boundary-markers, serving to specify and delimit its concerns. To the extent that Singh can have any representative role at all, it is not in relation to a collectivity but rather in the capacity of a mirror and surrogate for Naipaul himself. Thus London serves as an extremely private stage for Singh's drama of self-making and exclusion. His pursuit and eventual abandonment of "the god of the city" provides the dramatic structure through which Naipaul is able to stage his concomitant disillusionment with decolonization. The novel attempts to show the paradoxical complicity of these two false gods—metropolitan acceptance and postcolonial autonomy. London is both the landscape through which Singh voyages in search of these gods, and the site of his eventual "shipwreck."[13]

The novel features strong images of its narrative instant—the shabby-genteel hotel room in a London suburb from which Singh (a high-flying politician from the fictional Caribbean nation of Isabella, who has fallen from grace and now lives in exile) relates the story of his damaged and interrupted life. In this regard the novel evokes one of Naipaul's literary forebears, Joseph Conrad, who in *Heart of Darkness* also uses a location on the outskirts of the great city as the scene of storytelling—the place from which Marlow is able to look outward and backward into darkest Africa.[14] Yet Naipaul departs in crucial ways from this Conradian mode, and thus also from the literary geography to be found in his earlier works like *The Middle Passage*, and the works of contemporaries such as Lamming. If Lamming's work shows how the geography of imperialism makes it necessary for the anticolonial writer to take on the demands of a committed mode of writing, Naipaul in *The Mimic Men* abjures such a path and instead submits himself to the vagaries of Singh's memory as it moves back and forth between London and Isabella. In this way the narrative establishes a sense of the interpenetration of metropole and colony. Elements of the London landscape frequently serve for Singh as points of access to his memories of the Caribbean. At other moments distance breaks down and the distinction between the two spaces becomes difficult to maintain. Early in the novel Singh comes across "Victorian working-class tenements whose gardens, long abandoned, had for stretches been turned into Caribbean backyards" (*Mimic Men* 9). Subsequently, as he walks from his hotel to the pub where he whiles away his afternoons, "the red brick houses became interchangeable with those others in our tropical street, of corrugated iron and fretted white gables, which I had also once hoped never to see again" (154).

At moments like this, Singh's narrative recalls that of Anna Morgan, the protagonist of Jean Rhys's *Voyage in the Dark* (1934). Rhys's novel is the story of a white female immigrant from the Caribbean, adrift in 1914 London. On its opening page Anna closes her eyes and is instantly transported from her cold, grubby rented room to a marketplace near her home in the Caribbean. In making sense of this moment, she remarks, "Sometimes it was as if I were back there and as if England was a dream. At other times England was the real thing and out there was the dream, but I could never fit them together" (*Voyage in the Dark* 8).

Throughout her novel Rhys elaborates upon this theme of the simultaneous irreconcilability and interpenetration of England and the Caribbean, expressing this paradoxical relationship through the irreconcilable yet interpenetrating terms "reality" and "dream." The novel's most striking and important accomplishment is its reimagining of the place of London in a Caribbean geography. It is on these grounds that *Voyage in the Dark* needs to be seen as an important element in an alternative tradition of Caribbean literature to the line that derives from J. J. Thomas. Rhys is a product of the Creole plantocracy of Dominica, and her status as "Caribbean writer" has never been a comfortable one; critics like Edward Kamau Brathwaite have argued violently against her inclusion in the canon of Caribbean writing.[15] Yet, if Rhys's work is not amenable to canon- and nation-building gestures, it nevertheless powerfully informs the writings of canonical writers such as Derek Walcott and especially Wilson Harris. *Voyage in the Dark* crucially disrupts the discourse of "home" (in the sense of the home counties or the BBC Home Service) that is so important to the stability of the metropolis-colony relationship in high imperial discourse. Anna Morgan's narrative resonates with Roger Caillois's contemporaneous writings on "legendary psychaesthenia" in 1930s Paris, work that pre-emptively problematized all the various forms of Hegelian phenomenology that subsequently rose to prominence in France by blurring and disrupting the distinctions—between self and surroundings, subject and object—so critical for them. The cognate achievement in *Voyage in the Dark* is the use of techniques of spatial estrangement (houses slant before Anna's eyes, the pavement rises up to hit her, her bed vaults into the air) that turn London into a dreamscape. For Anna, the metropolis is a dream of "home," and in a strong sense a figment of the colonial subject's imagination, constructed out of scraps and fragments like the picture in an advertisement for biscuits (149). It is this sense of a dreamlike reality that allows Rhys to open up interfaces to the Caribbean within the very landscape of the imperial metropolis, as well as to track imaginative traffic in the other direction. Thus she disrupts the stately distancing of imperialist geography, which in her later work gets reinscribed as the "wide Sargasso Sea."[16] *Voyage in the Dark* is generally read by Rhys's critics as the narrative of a "fallen woman"; yet it should also be seen as opening up a line of flight to post-imperial geographies.

Rhys's legacy is palpable in the work of more recent writers like Wilson Harris and Merle Collins. Collins's collection of poems, *Rotten Pomerack* (1992), shuttles between Grenada and Britain, allowing for the simultaneous consideration of the defeat of nation-based decolonization in Grenada and the generation of a Caribbean diaspora in Britain. As an individual life history proceeds, its backdrop often shifts from one location to another, in the manner of a cinematic "jump cut." In poems like "Where the Scattering Began," Collins also breaks out of a reductive binarization of metropolis and periphery in her explorations of the diasporic fantasy of the return to the native land. She shows it to be a "return" to a potential space, located at the horizon of decolonization (what C. L. R. James, following Aimé Césaire, billed as "the rendezvous of victory"), reinventing poetic conventions of landscape to describe this space without imbuing it with local or memorializing detail. A different but related literary geography is elaborated in Harris's *Carnival Trilogy*. This 1980s sequence of prose fictions is organized around the interpenetration of London and the fictional Caribbean land of New Forest—characters literally step out of one space and into the other. Harris reorients the richly elaborated mythic and spatial structures of his earlier fictions in order to respond to the fading of a prior imperialist geography and the emergence of a new one. Writers like Collins, Harris, and Fred D'Aguiar (in his novel *Dear Future* and in his many works of poetry), following in the line of Rhys, have been able to develop complex imaginative resources out of their meditations upon the migrations of formerly colonized peoples to the old metropolitan centers. These works register how the "new circuits of imperialism" *recenter* the former imperial metropolis in relation not to a colonial periphery but rather a "transnational hinterland."[17] The migrants in these narratives are not drawn "home" like moths to a flame, but arrive in London as volitional agents whose actions are shaped by historical processes. These works embrace the contradictions of their situation without succumbing to the pathos of such slogans of diasporic self-understanding as "we are here because you were there."[18] Moreover, the writers themselves partake of this migrant sensibility, rather than bewailing the fact, as does Naipaul's Ralph Singh, that they are mistaken for "immigrants."

Naipaul also differs from these writers in figuring London as a more complex place than the Caribbean. Indeed, part of the initial challenge London poses for Singh is the paradox that its multifarious reality has a flattening impact on his subjectivity—the three-dimensional city generates a two-dimensional urban subject:

> In the great city, so real, so three-dimensional, so rooted in its soil, drawing its colour from such depths, only the city was real. Those of us who came to it lost some of our solidity; we were trapped into fixed, flat postures. And, in this growing dissociation between ourselves and the city in which we lived, scores of separate meetings, not linked even by ourselves, who became nothing more than perceivers: everyone reduced, reciprocally, to a succession of such meetings, so that first experience and then the personality divided bewilderingly into compartments. (*Mimic Men* 27)

Here Singh echoes and elaborates Naipaul's lament in his 1958 essay about the oppressive privacy and compartmentalization of London life, connecting these features more precisely to the unmasterable and brutalizing massiveness of the city. Unlike the heroic "ordinary practitioner" celebrated by Michel de Certeau (95), whose peripatetic movements disaggregate the urban mass and generate an anonymous urban "text" for which his subjectivity serves as an unifying principle, Singh feels defeated by London. He asks: "How, in the city, could largeness come to me? How could I fashion order out of all these unrelated adventures and encounters, myself never the same, never even the thread on which these things were hung?" (*Mimic Men* 28). His narrative is set up as a losing battle, a quest doomed to failure for a masterful comprehension of the city and his own experience of it. Yet the accompanying sense of London as the primary reality ("only the city was real") also has implications for his figuring of Isabella. The two do not exist in any kind of reciprocal relationship. While London provokes thoughts of Isabella, the landscape of Isabella cannot provide points of access to London. The colony is presented as "a function of the phantasy of the metropolitan order" (Dhareshwar 99). Unlike Rhys's Anna Morgan, whose dreams provide interfaces and connections between London and the Caribbean, Singh's narrative puts dreams to a very different purpose—they are not a means of access to other places that might help to define the reality of London, but instead a mode of negotiation and processing of the self-contained reality of the city (*Mimic Men* 91, 237).

Singh's first extended stay in London, as a student in the years immediately following the Second World War, is defined in terms of his quest for "an ideal landscape" to which he can "attach" or affiliate himself. His expectations of London encompass both the generalizable glamor of all great cities and a specifically imperial metropolitan authority. Yet in a striking passage set in the most significant of locations—Bush House, the headquarters of the BBC—such expectations are revealed as illusory, and the aura of a great metropolitan institution is replaced by a more mundane reality:

> there in the canteen of a radio service which, when picked up in remote countries, was the very voice of metropolitan authority and romance, bringing to mind images, from the cinema and magazines, of canyons of concrete, brick and glass, motorcars in streams, lines of light, busyness, crowded theatre foyers, the world where everything was possible; there now, at the heart of that metropolis we sat, at a plastic-topped table, before thick cups of cooling tea and plates with yellow crumbs. (*Mimic Men* 46)

Singh comes to London "seeking order, seeking the flowering, the extension of myself that ought to have come in a city of such miraculous light" (26), but finds "only a conglomeration of private cells" (18). He imagines London as a zone of order and stability, but comes to see it as a place of "emptiness" (8).[19] He is eventually led by his experiences to the realization that "it is the god of the city, we pursue, in vain" (18). Despite its loose structure, *The Mimic Men* can be broadly construed as a Bildungsroman, a passage from innocence to experience, and the lesson of this first phase for Singh is that the ideal landscape of London, if available at all, is not available to him. This sense of exclusion prompts a violent counterreaction: "I abolished all landscapes to which I could not attach myself and longed only for those I had known" (31), prompting Singh to flee the city and return to the familiar landscape of Isabella. There he quickly finds himself on a rapidly ascendant path to riches and political power. This new phase of his life feels like nothing more than an extension of the dandyism of his student days, when he had carefully cultivated an image as an "extravagant colonial" (20). Yet he realizes in retrospect that the shape of his career is not a function of his individual psychology, but rather closely matches a generalizable trajectory for the formation of Third World politicians, one that ends in "inevitable failure" (184). As he puts it: "From playacting to disorder: it is the pattern" (184). Singh's subsequent sabotaging of his own political future is thus presented both as inevitable and as a function of the disorder of Isabella itself. Significantly, his final disgrace comes in London, through an extended and public affair with a British heiress that irredeemably destroys his political prospects. The eventual conclusion of his life's arc in exile in London has almost the air of a homecoming, a return to reality from the benighted and unreal landscape of Isabella.

In a premonitory comment in his 1958 essay, Naipaul observed that "after eight years [in London] I find I have achieved, without effort, the Buddhist ideal of non-attachment" ("London" 15). At the time he lamented his sense of removal from the world of affairs, yet in *The Mimic Men* this ascetic ideal is one that Singh prizes. It informs the writing of his memoir in his suburban exile. Singh crucially distinguishes this work from the explicitly political articles he wrote on Isabella for a newspaper called *The Socialist*—articles that were "balanced, fair, with the final truth evaded, until at last this truth was lost." In contrast, "Writing this book has been more than a release from those articles; it has been an attempt to rediscover that truth" (189). Detachment from the worldly realm of politics provides Singh with a space for thought, reflection, and discovery. It also gives him a sense of horizontal connection to other exilic individuals:

> We are people who for one reason or another have withdrawn, from our respective countries, from the city where we find ourselves, from our families. We have withdrawn from unnecessary responsibility and attachment. We have simplified our lives. . . . It comforts me to think that in this city there must be hundreds and thousands like ourselves. (247)

Singh has replaced the vulgar and specious collectivities of politics with an anonymous and unseen fraternity, with whom he can commune in private. The privatized and interiorized life of London, which he had earlier found so oppressive, thus provides him with both comfort and a sense of location. This is a location in London, but also in the final, ascetic stage of the fourfold journey of life "prescribed by our Aryan ancestors" (251). For Singh, an "East Indian" Caribbean who all his life has struggled to sustain a cosmopolitan "creolized" self-image, has come in exile to a newfound realization of his essential identity. Searching within the interior compartments of his experience, he gains access to a deeply buried racial memory: "I have visions of Central Asian horsemen, among whom I am one, riding below a sky threatening snow to the very end of an empty world" (82). Thus, in London, he gains access to an essential truth about himself that trumps the false notions of peoplehood and national identity—the "suddenly realized concept of the people" (197)—propounded by postcolonial politics in the Caribbean.

Singh concludes his account by stating "I no longer yearn for ideal landscapes and no longer wish to know the god of the city" (250). Singh enacts here a characteristically Naipaulian gesture, in which "arrival" (at closure, resolution, a way in the world) is signified by the acceptance of failed promise and relinquished expectations. If he ultimately gives up the fantasies he had earlier sustained about both London and Isabella as "ideal landscapes" in which he might have free play, he is able to find compensation for this loss only in London—in the privatized interiority of metropolitan life, which affords him space in which to take refuge, to meditate, and from which to convey his dystopian view of the world and the possibilities for transformative human agency.

NOTES

1. First published as "The Regional Barrier" in the *Times Literary Supplement*, the essay was subsequently republished as "London" in Naipaul's collection of essays *The Overcrowded Barracoon*.

2. The theme of the writerly vocation (and its conditions of possibility) has been a constant feature of Naipaul's writing, from early works like *A House for Mr. Biswas* (1961) to more recent writings like *Finding the Centre* (1984), *The Enigma of Arrival* (1987), and *A Way in the World* (1994). A particularly striking aspect of these discussions is his recurrent attention to the unrealized literary ambitions of his father, Seepersad Naipaul. The relationship between father and son is amply and poignantly documented in their correspondence, published in V. S. Naipaul, *Between Father and Son*.

3. This fine term is borrowed from Rob Nixon, *London Calling: V. S. Naipaul, Postcolonial Mandarin*.

4. According to a Trinidad journalist who interviewed him soon after the publication of *The Mimic Men*, Naipaul took pains to emphasize that "the novel was more about London than anything else." The interview features an interesting echo of "The Regional Barrier" in Naipaul's comment: "'If a writer has to make a living in the outside world—which is concerned with the whole world and not just one part of it—to be purely regional is in fact to sink'" (see Ewart Rouse, 10).

5. Fawzia Mustafa makes the interesting and illuminating argument that "the culmination that *A House for Mr Biswas* represents . . . has been rehearsed, recast, and severally rewritten through the exercises of *The Mystic Masseur*, *The Suffrage of Elvira*, and *Miguel Street*" (see Mustafa, 33).

6. For a recent article that is is perhaps his most explicit statement of this position, see V. S. Naipaul, "Our Universal Civilization."

7. Rob Nixon makes the astute observation that "'Bush' is simply Naipaul's buzzword for barbarism; it has nothing to do with vegetation" (*London Calling*, 183 n. 58).

8. This is a brief work which has the flavor of an exercise—an attempt to write a non-"regional" narrative set in England, featuring a protagonist who is not racially marked and hence white by implication.

9. Fawzia Mustafa describes "Naipaul's use of physical discomfort—his own as well as others'—as a gauge for his reading of the functioning, or completeness, or societal health of the place in which he finds himself" (79).

10. I take the term "fragmented nationalism" from Franklin W. Knight's influential study, *The Caribbean: The Genesis of a Fragmented Nationalism*.

11. I extend this claim even to *Water with Berries* (1971), the last of these works (and the last of Lamming's published novels). While the novel is set largely in London, where the artist Teeton finds himself unable to act on his resolve to return from self-exile to the revolutionary struggle in San Cristobal, the city itself does not provide the occasion for Lamming's explorations of the submerged consciousness of colonialism.

12. In a short story published in 1957, Selvon figures London as a woman, and command of the city as sexual conquest. See "My Girl and the City" in Selvon, *Ways of Sunlight* 169–76.

13. For a reading of the metaphor of shipwreck in the novel, that usefully relates it to Naipaul's other writings, see Thieme.

14. For Naipaul's account of his debt to and departures from Conrad, see "Conrad's Darkness." For an astute analysis of this essay, see Suleri, 150–53.

15. See Brathwaite. For a more sympathetic assessment of the Caribbean dimension of Rhys's writing, which focuses on *Voyage in the Dark*, see Morris's aptly titled piece "Oh, Give the Girl a Chance: Jean Rhys and *Voyage in the Dark*."

16. *Wide Sargasso Sea* (1966) is Rhys's last novel and the one which, given its status as a "rewriting" of *Jane Eyre* and a "reappropriation" or "talking back" to the British literary canon, has been most successfully assimilated into the canon of postcolonial literature.

17. For "new circuits of imperialism," see Sivanandan. For "transnational hinterland," see Sassen, 127. For a related argument to Sassen's, which places its emphasis on the reinvention of formerly imperial circuits as newly transnational circuits, see King.

18. This sense of how the internationalization of London has transformed the meaning of Black Britain is missing from Winston James's otherwise excellent "Migration, Racism and Identity Formation: The Caribbean Experience in Britain."

19. In a recent essay, Sukhdev Sandhu discusses the pining for "order and mature certainties" of British-based Black writers since Ukawsaw Gronniosaw in 1772. His essay contrasts this lineage with the anarchic, mobile, pleasure-seeking ethos of Hanif Kureishi's London writings. See Sandhu, 152.

WORKS CITED

Brathwaite, Edward Kamau. *Roots*. Ann Arbor: U of Michigan P, 1993.

Caillois, Roger. "Mimétisme et Psychasthénie Légendaire." *Minotaure* 7 (1935): 4–10.

Collins, Merle. *Rotten Pomerack*. London: Virago, 1992.

Conrad, Joseph. *Heart of Darkness*. 1902. Harmondsworth: Penguin, 1973.

D'Aguiar, Fred. *Dear Future*. London: Chatto and Windus, 1996.

de Certeau, Michel. "Walking in the City." In *The Practice of Everyday Life*. Trans. Steven Rendall. Berkeley: U of California P, 1984.

Dhareshwar, Vivek. "Self-fashioning, Colonial Habitus, and Double Exclusion: V. S. Naipaul's *The Mimic Men*." *Criticism* 31.1 (Winter 1989): 75–102.

Froude, James Anthony. *The English in the West Indies: The Bow of Ulysses*. 1887. New York: Charles Scribner's Sons, 1897.

Harris, Wilson. *The Carnival Trilogy*. London: Faber and Faber, 1993.

James, C. L. R. *At the Rendezvous of Victory: Selected Writings*. London: Allison and Busby, 1984.

James, Winston. "Migration, Racism and Identity Formation: The Caribbean Experience in Britain." *Inside Babylon: The Caribbean Diaspora in Britain*. Winston James and Clive Harris, eds. New York and London: Verso, 1993. 231–87.

King, Anthony D. *Global Cities: Post-Imperialism and the Internationalization of London*. New York and London: Routledge, 1990.

Knight, Franklin W. *The Caribbean: The Genesis of a Fragmented Nationalism*. 2nd ed. New York and London: Oxford UP, 1990.

Lamming, George. *The Emigrants*. 1954. Ann Arbor: U of Michigan P, 1994.

———. *Of Age and Innocence*. 1958. London: Allison and Busby, 1981.

———. *The Pleasures of Exile*. 1960. Ann Arbor: U of Michigan P, 1992.

———. *Season of Adventure*. 1960. London: Allison and Busby, 1979.

———. *Water with Berries*. 1971. New York: Holt, Rinehart and Winston, 1972.

Morris, Mervyn. "Oh, Give the Girl a Chance: Jean Rhys and *Voyage in the Dark*." *Journal of West Indian Literature* 3.2 (1989): 1–8.

Mustafa, Fawzia. *V. S. Naipaul*. New York and Cambridge: Cambridge UP, 1995.

Naipaul, V. S. *An Area of Darkness*. 1964. New York: Vintage, 1981.

——— . *Between Father and Son*. Gillon Aitken, ed. New York: Alfred A. Knopf, 2000.

——— . "Conrad's Darkness." *The Return of Eva Peron with the Killings in Trinidad*. 1980. New York: Vintage, 1981. 223–45.

——— . *The Enigma of Arrival*. 1987. New York: Vintage, 1988.

——— . *Finding the Centre: Two Narratives*. 1984. New York: Vintage, 1986.

——— . *A House for Mr. Biswas*. 1961. New York: Vintage, 1984.

——— . "London." *The Overcrowded Barracoon*. New York: Vintage, 1984. 9–16. Rpt. of "The Regional Barrier." *The Times Literary Supplement* 15 Aug. 1958.

——— . *The Middle Passage: Impressions of Five Societies—British, French and Dutch—in the West Indies and South America*. 1962. Harmondsworth: Penguin, 1969.

——— . *The Mimic Men*. 1967. Harmondsworth: Penguin, 1969.

——— . *Mr. Stone and the Knight's Companion*. 1963. New York: Vintage, 1985.

——— . *The Mystic Masseur*. 1957. New York: Vintage, 1984.

——— . "Our Universal Civilization." *New York Review of Books* 39 (31 Jan. 1991): 22–25.

——— . *The Suffrage of Elvira*. 1958. New York: Vintage, 1985.

——— . *A Way in the World*. 1994. New York: Vintage, 1995.

Nixon, Rob. *London Calling: V. S. Naipaul, Postcolonial Mandarin*. New York and London: Oxford UP, 1992.

Rhys, Jean. *Voyage in the Dark*. 1934. New York: W. W. Norton, 1982.

——— . *Wide Sargasso Sea*. 1966. New York: W. W. Norton, 1982.

Rouse, Ewart. "Naipaul: An Interview with Ewart Rouse." 1968. In *Conversations with V. S. Naipaul*. Feroza Jussawalla, ed. Jackson: UP of Mississippi, 1997. 10–13.

Said, Edward. *Culture and Imperialism*. New York: Alfred A. Knopf, 1993.

Sandhu, Sukhdev. "Pop Goes the Centre: Hanif Kureishi's London." In *Postcolonial Theory and Criticism*. Laura Chrisman and Benita Parry, eds. Cambridge: D. S. Brewer, 2000. 133–54.

Sassen, Saskia. *The Global City: New York, London, Tokyo*. Princeton: Princeton UP, 1991.

Selvon, Sam. *The Housing Lark*. 1965. Washington, DC: Three Continents P, 1990.

——— . *The Lonely Londoners*. 1956. Harlow, Essex: Longman, 1985.

——— . *Moses Ascending*. 1975. Oxford: Heinemann, 1984.

——— . *Moses Migrating*. 1983. Washington, DC: Three Continents P, 1992.

——— . *Ways of Sunlight*. 1957. Harlow, Essex: Longman, 1987.

Sivanandan, A. "New Circuits of Imperialism." *Communities of Resistance: Writings on Black Struggles for Socialism.* New York and London: Verso, 1990. 169–95.

Suleri, Sara. "Naipaul's Arrival." *The Rhetoric of English India.* Chicago: U of Chicago P, 1992. 149–73.

Thieme, John. "A Hindu Castaway: Ralph Singh's Journey in *The Mimic Men.*" *Modern Fiction Studies* 30.3 (autumn 1984): 505–18.

Thomas, John Jacob. *Froudacity: West Indian Fables by James Anthony Froude.* 1889. Port-of-Spain and London: New Beacon, 1969.

CHAPTER 11

Undoing London or, Urban Haunts: The Fracturing of Representation in the 1990s

JULIAN WOLFREYS

> Kew holds even more attractions, if only bitter-sweet ones, memories of prewar lust.
> —Michael Moorcock, *Mother London*

> [. . .]—or as [if] noon and night
> Had clapped together and utterly struck out
> The intermediate, undoing themselves
> In the act. Your city poets see such things. . . .
> —Elizabeth Barrett Browning, *Aurora Leigh*

> She's certainly a great World, there are so many little worlds in Her;
> She is the great Bee-hive of Christendome. . . .
> —Donald Lupton, *London and the Countrey Carbonadoed*

When seeking to address the modalities of urban representation in much recent London textuality, myriad questions impose themselves insistently. Beyond any boundary or convention, the insistence of such queries, their frequency and resonance, announces nothing other than London's illimitable nature, and the experience of this condition. Amongst such questions raised by writers and artists through the 1990s, one

FIGURE 11.1. Stonework 1. Courtesy of Julian Wolfreys.

might consider the following: are we spectators to the empirical coercion of the individual response due to the overwhelming nature of the subject? Or are we witness to some phenomenological act of what might be called appropriately an intimate (and, perhaps, therefore partially inaccessible) psycho-topographical reconstitution? Can we tell or, even more fundamentally, separate, the one from the other? The texts, for example, of Iain Sinclair, Patrick Keiller, or Allen Fisher appear to disturb simultaneously the limits of the urban condition objectively rendered on the one hand and any purely individual, idiomatic translation on the other. Is there then in operation a certain passage between modes or locations between the external and the internal (or vice versa), in which all such boundaries either begin to be or are otherwise always already dissolved? Does the very nature of London itself put to work a complication, and concomitantly a destabilization, of modalities of the very idea of representation, within and from themselves? In an effort to comprehend what is at work, might this be termed, provisionally, urban disidentification? And is this frequently readable through a perceived anachrony of a "remembrance of things past," all the more dissonant for being ostensibly registered in an ever present tense?

Clearly, the questions which the city text foregrounds come to articulate themselves within spatial and temporal matrices, which in turn interface with engagement between topography and subjectivity. It is possible to read through the texts of Sinclair, Keiller, Michael Moorcock, Lavinia Greenlaw, and others a concern with a comprehension of urban time which differs from a purely linear, progressive historical understanding. In the works in which we are interested, there is registered a sense that the past is transformed, but has never disappeared (even though, obviously, it is never there as such). Recognizing both the psycho-topographical nature of London and, with that, understanding the experience the city imposes on us, amounts to the recognition of a materiality, distinct from any phenomenology or aesthetic intervention, which persists throughout history. Comprehending in this manner is perhaps a question of seeing "as the poets do it" (*wie die Dichter es tun*), to borrow from Kant on the material sublime (Kant 130). Such an act of seeing, "merely in terms of what manifests itself to the eye," to cite Kant once more (130), registers that striking out of the intermediate as Barrett Browning has it in *Aurora Leigh* ("Your poets see such things"). Such registration involves a chronicling and revelation of temporalities expressed through the enfolding and unfolding of material and spectral phenomena onto the present experience of both the city and the text, and, it has to be argued, in the re-marking of the text *as city*, a topography comprising and comprised of so many encrypted and overt citations. Sinclair and the other artists to which this chapter will turn explore a temporal paradox in relation to the experience of London, as this paradox is best expressed by F. W. J. Schelling: "For different times . . . are necessarily at the same time. Past time is not sublimated time.

What has past certainly cannot be as something present, but it must be as something past at the same time with the present. . . . And it is equally inconsistent to think of past being, as well as future being, as utterly without being" (76). The city, articulated through text, photography, film, and installation comes to be revealed as having a "materiality without matter," in the words of Jacques Derrida (187). This recognition of temporal and material aspects of London, in turn, makes the city available (to borrow from the liner notes from the video of Patrick Keiller's 1993 film, *London*) "as it is and, at the same time," as it can be reconstructed and reimagined. Thus, with this implicit comprehension at work, the writers and artists in question interrogate the interstices which emerge and open as the imagined coordinates of such concerns.

In such openings, other questions appear: in what sense, for many London artists, is the past always with us, never as such, never belonging to an overall homogeneous, idealized, or romanticized space? Instead, the past figures as so many haunting traces, disjointing the fields of vision and registration. In what ways do alternative chronicles and catalogues of the city come to be figured in flows through both the individual figures of writer, artist, or narrator, and technological media such as the still, cinematic, or video camera? And is it the case that we might read these fluxes or pulsions as challenging the classical efficacity of mimetic, hegemonic representations, thereby demanding in turn a response, and a responsibility, first on the part of the artist and subsequently on that of the reader, spectator, or audience, to the persistent experience of the city? Risking all, perhaps, in that knowing conjuration of nostalgia, is the call of the past where, paradoxically, one gives up the illusion of any possible possession as one gives oneself over to becoming possessed. The city becomes available as so many ungovernable events of revenance, regeneration, and affirmative resistance to the authority of, on the one hand, the city planners, and on the other, any grand narrative. Such excess, ironically appropriate to the condition of London, informs and generates this chapter in its brief consideration of novelists, essayists, film-makers, poets, sculptors, photographers, and artists of the last decade of the twentieth century. It will be impossible, in so short a space as this, to pretend to a "reading," but I hope to introduce and indicate certain shared interests and obsessions amongst current urban artists.

Let's begin with the first epigraph of this chapter. Michael Moorcock's *Mother London* is a novel in which three outpatients from a hospital for the mentally ill wander through the city, "overhearing" or otherwise being the conduits for alternative, marginalized, and forgotten London voices. At first glance, Moorcock's apparently whimsical phrase (274) might be taken as somewhat Betjemanesque: the ambivalence intrinsic to nostalgia, the encrypted resonance of personal memory (appealing *because* exclusive), the nod towards secreted impropriety, as predictable in its own way as the banal security of the suburbs.

By extension, the suburban location, Kew, furthers the passing resemblance between Moorcock and Betjeman on initial acquaintance, being one of those untimely places which persist around the peripheries of London, belonging simultaneously to London and to one of the home counties also (in Kew's case, Surrey). Kew, typically of so many of the capital's liminal sites, is recognizable architecturally: there are the mid- to late-Victorian and Edwardian houses and, less frequently, purpose-built apartment buildings which are, in Moorcock's words, "scarcely touched by the War" (273). There is just enough of the past, then, materially visible in the present to suggest the passage between external, material form and the internal, mutable structures of attempted *rememorization* (to adapt and borrow Toni Morrison's term). Moreover, Moorcock's play between material persistence and immaterial memory arguably effects the "striking out of the intermediate," to borrow Elizabeth Barrett Browning's definition of temporal confusion and the concomitant erasure of knowable specificity.

At the same time, however, in the instance of recall, and despite the "striking out," there is nonetheless the unveiled perception—perception as urban sensibility—in the act of memory as afterthought, a reconstitution which is also the trace of incommensurable identities, drifting, disinterring, within one place, yet taking place and returning from different times. Layered one over the other, that which returns in present memory undoes identity's stability through what might perhaps be called the work of that which Freud terms *Nachträglichkeit*. There is thus mapped out as the work of memory in response to a particular aspect of London, in the words of Nicola King on the Freudian concept, "an exploration and an enactment of the interplay between social structures and the structures of the psyche" (King 35).

Such exploration and enactment is at work in particularly intimate fashion in Rachel Lichtenstein's installations involving images of a room inhabited by David Rodinsky. Rodinsky lived above a synagogue in the East End of London, in Princelet Street. This area is traditionally associated with the settlement of immigrants over several centuries, whether Huguenot, Chinese, Jewish, or Bangladeshi, as well as being the place associated with dissenting religious proletarian groups. While vital to the life of London, this area has nonetheless come to be associated with an identity "somehow alien and mysterious," as Peter Ackroyd puts it (xiv; see also Palmer). It is on such identities that Lichtenstein draws, as she traces a much more personal identity, enfolding as she does fragments of her own family history (Polish Jews who fled from Poland to England in the 1930s), and centered on the fact that, Rodinsky, otherwise unknown and unremarkable, disappeared mysteriously in the mid-1960s. He left only his room and, particularly, its countless fragments of writings, books, and notebooks covered in annotations, all of which are concerned with matters of language, encryption, cabbalistic scribblings, and "strange indecipherable symbols" (Lichtenstein and Sinclair 27). Even Rodinsky's *London A to Z* had been written over with scrawled fragments, installing it simultaneously as a textual access to London *and* an implicit acknowledgement that any area of the city is traced, haunted, by an ineffable, forgotten, and frequently resurrected otherness.

As part of the preparation for the installations, and in order to place herself in a particular relationship to Rodinsky, Lichtenstein walked the streets highlighted by Rodinsky in his *A to Z* (Lichtenstein and Sinclair 286). Such acts, and the subsequent rewriting of the events as a record of Lichtenstein's processes of rememorization, arguably bring back in discontinuous moments a London past which always belongs to the imaginative reconstitution of the urban site. Thus Lichtenstein works with what Iain Sinclair has described as "[n]umerous fragments that composed an unreliable biography . . . before memories became memorial plaques" (Lichtenstein and Sinclair 4). Such fragments are put to work reassembling, as he puts it, the mementoes of a "missing text" through "sympathetic marriage," whereby the installations refigure what the room always already was: a "structure in abeyance"(5). Rodinsky's room thus becomes a "theatre of ghosts" passing "beyond reconstruction and authenticity" (9). Lichtenstein's installations take on a performative role as acts of resistant rememorization. Resisting official memorialization, situating in particular relationships personal and impersonal memories after the event, the installations maintain the fragment as that in which is focused revenance and responsibility beyond the immediate life of either David Rodinsky or Rachel Lichtenstein, to speak, in encrypted, archival fashion, of the East End's alternative histories. Arguably what comes to be maintained is the necessity to bear witness, to maintain relationships of witnessing, as if there is a recognition on Lichtenstein's part that "[w]hen there are no longer any witnesses, there is no longer any memory," as Paul Virilio has suggested (15).

In this, I would contend, we read the negotiation between the limits of the empirical, the question of ineffability, and a certain return, not *to* but *of,* the urban fragment—London as so many fragments, London in ruins, and naming the experience of an urban mnemotechnic. London is perceived and conceptualized in much recent writing as exactly *just* this recognition of fragmentary revenance, of which Moorcock's commentary and the various pieces of Rodinsky's room are exemplary, but which Lavinia Greenlaw also gives articulation to in her poem "Love from a Foreign City":"There are parts of the new *A to Z* marked simply / 'under development'. Even street names have been demolished" (Greenlaw 44). Here, the city trembles through specifically fragmentary textual-topographical traces and coordinates, already erased, momentarily suspended, awaiting inscription, the memories of a particular site no longer accessible except as the potential ebb and flow of the fragment. When Greenlaw writes, "The one-way system keeps changing direction, / I get lost a hundred

yards from home" (44), she provides access to London's ineluctable discontinuities, its bit-stream processing of constantly changing flows which render the
familiar uncanny.

There is a sense of the ineffable which the fragmentary writing of the city
perpetuates, an ineffability which is also marked as the experience of urban
iterability. Greenlaw's narrator getting lost so close to home appears to recall
those figures from Dickens's *Martin Chuzzlewit* who can never find Todgers'
boarding house. It is as though, in seeking to measure memory against place
in response to the city, one finds oneself left with "the phrase book / for yes-
terday's language" (Smith 53). Yet there is also in such writing and other textual forms a comprehension of the significance of the fragment for the resur-
rection of the other histories of London, as well as an endlessness, a sense of
Londons to come. If what we read is what is supposedly lost or disappearing,
it is also, in being read, in being remembered after the event, a sense of memory's haunting persistence. Writers such as Iain Sinclair or Aidan Andrew Dun,
and artists such as Rachel Whiteread and Rachel Lichtenstein, comprehend
the necessity of what Hans-Jost Frey calls the "depiction of several fragmentary states" (Frey 48) as appropriate to the description of the city. Instead of
reading the various fragments as objects to be defined and placed in a deter-
minate context, responding to the fragmentary states of the capital's places,
inhabitants, events, and temporalities announces an "anonymous, posthumous
endlessness" (Frey 48) to the condition of London. This is, I would suggest,
precisely the gesture of "undoing" readable in the processes of a revenant writing residing within, acting as the countersignature to, those Betjemanesque
resemblances, noticeable for example in the epigraph taken from Moorcock.
In large part, it is the work of such undoing—dislocating the organization of
the familiar through the conjuration of the forgotten or otherwise occluded—
disquietingly traced, and the play between the spectral and the material which
this implies, that touches and illuminates so much London textuality of recent
years, as already intimated, whilst also acknowledging the irreducible singularity of the experience and memory of the fragment. Reading and writing London in the instances in question *just is* the experience of the fragmentary text;
this experience does not stop at the limit of the fragment, but rather, as Frey
suggests, outlasts it (Frey 49).

Allen Fisher's poetry is very much a poetry of fragments, particularly his
sequence *Brixton Fractals*. Since the 1980s at least, Fisher has concerned himself
with alternative poetic modes for the representations of local London history.
At the same time, however, as *Brixton Fractals* shows (and as its name intimates)
phrases, "facts," details, and other fragments, they resist any coalescence into an
homogenous meaning. Instead, the lines we read amount to nothing other than
the inscribed translation effects of response to the materiality of the city, or
what Fisher calls (in the prose poem, "The Mathematics of Rimbaud") a series

formed from "generalised, unformalizable changing topologies—the poetries
of the inventive memory," otherwise called in the same poem, "the multiplicity of attentions" (Fisher 49). Clearly, in the announcement of attention and
memory there is the acknowledgement of some subject. This is, however, the
most meager of personae, opening onto and as the conduit for, the various, irreducible fluxes of the city.

Brixton Fractals compiles detail; it records and catalogues fragments of its
South London location, as the poems, in their irregularity, their unpre-
dictability of motion, rhythm, form, or focus remain resistant to analysis, maintaining themselves in their irreducible complexity. Archetypal figures—
Painter, Bellman, Informer, Photographer—appear, disappear, and reappear,
modern urban types, impossible to describe, traversing the city. Seemingly
anonymous, each "character" (if we can use this term) is less a figure than one
facet of a composite medium through which to perceive a particular aspect of
or moment in Brixton. For example, "The burglar leans out of someone's window," while the Painter "follows a path to a simple hut" (94). Each archetype
inscribes himself into, onto, the topography of Brixton, becoming the trace of
himself, which is subsequently retraced by "A reader [who] follows the marks
up the path / occasionally losing balance / . . . / stopped short by the figure
of Blake" (96). In this the reader marks one more moment in a relay, another
re-marking of the trace, which in turn is displaced onto another reader. The
loss of balance, the figural disorientation, at once announces the reading experience, which can equally be considered as gesturing towards the experience
of the city and/or the experience of our encounter with the text. The invocation of Blake provides a form of reference, though any potential meaning
which such a moment of signification might produce is inevitably poor and
limited, as the occasional enunciation of an anonymous first-person narrator
makes plain: "I respond to the stimuli realised / as alien to my nature" (96).
Atypical events disinter the reader from any formalizable relationship to both
the text and the city, for there is little here that one can connect to Brixton in
any comforting manner. We might, for instance, point out that Blake lived at
one time in adjacent Lambeth, but this gets us nowhere. We are in a "landscape of events," to borrow Paul Virilio's phrase, a landscape, which, according
to Virilio, "has no fixed meaning, no privileged vantage point," least of all in
the location or locution known as "I" (Virilio xi). To cite Virilio further, what
we encounter in reading Fisher is a sense that "it is no longer the big events
that make up the fabric of the landscape . . . but myriad incidents, minute facts
either overlooked or deliberately ignored. Here, *the landscape is a passage*" (xi,
emphasis in original).

The idea of landscape as passage rather than fixed site with determinable
coordinates is crucial in the textual imagination of London as here considered,
whether by "passage" one understands the movement through particular places

or that which returns through the temporal passage implied in the conjuration of alternative pasts. Irreducible to a technique precisely because that which haunts and returns determines the mnemotechnicity of the London text, there is nonetheless to be comprehended what Bernard Cache calls the event of seizing (82), a process of sampling wherein is acknowledged the excess which always escapes apprehension. Such apprehension or perception "places us immediately within memory" (Cache 143), where "memory" comes to name, beyond the immediately personal, acts of overfolding and unfolding the inscriptions of place, in the course of which, the "entire past [at least by implication] becomes concentrated in the present of an excessive reaction" (146).

Such excessive reaction is to be found everywhere in the writing of Iain Sinclair. So much so, in fact, that when Sinclair writes, "We're moving on now, exchanging the odd unconnected anecdote or random fact" ("All Change" 10), one could easily be forgiven for taking this as both a statement on the experience of random drifting through London on the part of the psycho-geographical tour guide, as well as being a reflexive, if not performative, commentary on the constitution of Sinclair's own texts. As one reads Sinclair, whether the early poetry (*Lud Heat*, on which we will focus below) or the most recent raging polemic against the drab excesses of New Labour (the fiasco of the Millennium Dome exploded in *Sorry Meniscus*), reading becomes the experience of exactly this: seemingly aleatory motion, fueled equally by rage, obsession, memory, and history. In short, it is the endless exchange of odd unconnected anecdotes (on Sinclair's part and on the part of those he encounters) and random facts. Simultaneously, however, this writing/reading process is also an imaginative act of alternative mapping, a mapping which undoes the very coordinates on which the presumption of knowable, finite topography relies. It relies on resistance to finite instances of comprehension or absolute accessibility, in Sinclair's constant, obsessive drive to disinter the phantom effects of the city's familiar sites.

Take, for example, an essay on New Labour's attempted sanitized reworking of a peninsula of land in Greenwich, through the building of the Millennium Dome. Such a process Sinclair reads as "[c]lap sores revamped as beauty spots . . . while the dark history of Greenwich marshes, a decayed industrial wilderness is brutally elided." However, it is Sinclair's project to return to us the proper name of that which has been erased from nineteenth-century maps, "a pre-amputation stump known as Bugsby's Marshes" (Sinclair, "All Change" 10). This resurrected name provides the potential for an alternative counter-narrative, haunting the present authorized revivification with its distinctly Dickensian sonorities; pushing against received wisdom, official histories, it provides Sinclair, and the reader, access to an alternative history of

the manufacture of ordnance, brewing, confectionary, black smoke palls and sickly sweet perfumes. The cloacal mud of low tide mingled deliriously with

sulphurous residues trapped in savage greenery. . . . Terrible ghosts were
trapped in the ground. . . . Executions and bloated bodies washed over by three
tides. ("All Change" 10)

The unconnected and the random succumb, of course, to chance gatherings
through Sinclair's edgy conjuration. This is, though, in a way, the very point:
For an other London emerges, as traces interweave in a disparate seriality of
vengeful specters through such concatenations, undoing in the process the
organized and official images of Greenwich as the location of the prime merid-
ian, erstwhile center of the British Empire, the Royal Naval College, and what
the writer names archly "[a]cceptable glories" ("All Change" 10).

Moreover, such mediation of urban revenance that traces certain returns *of*
rather than *to* other Londons resonates in memory of other instances of textual
dissidence. The "black smoke palls" echo or, at least, gesture towards William
Blake's "London," a poem which, as is well known, also invokes terrible ghosts
juxtaposed to the "charter'd Thames." Through such recognizable conjunctions,
Sinclair weaves the random and chance through relationships at once esoteric
and mythopoetic, while also factual and historical. He produces a similar effect
in the title of one of the many sections of *Lud Heat*, "From Camberwell to Golgotha." There is in this a doubleness, projecting London in the act of undoing
any finite, knowable identity. Sinclair thus engages in a paradoxical poetics of
the city, an excessive, fragmentary inscription which both speaks of the city and
speaks to the city's ineffability.

If Sinclair appears to owe more than a little to T. S. Eliot in *The Waste Land*
in his quasi-modernist bricolage drawn from the sensual experience of life and
mythological, arcane knowledge, there is also a sense in which he owes as much
to Dickens, if not Blake. The apocalyptic, idiosyncratically visionary quality of
his writing, which cuts past Eliot's studied (self-)reflection and despair over the
absence of mastery, unfolds for the reader with sensuous immediacy the spirit
of the city, a spirit at once protean, labyrinthine, and babelian. Sinclair impresses
on the reader the conditions of the metropolis in all their paradoxes, so that,
"[w]hen we understand the condition it no longer exists" (Sinclair, *Lud Heat*
69). When we believe we comprehend London it ceases to be, for perception,
sensuous communion with the city, precedes and escapes understanding.

Command of comprehension founded on representation is thus avoided,
ahead of the settling of any representation, by the very condition of London,
which Sinclair would have us know is not to be understood if we are to be true
to any thinking or writing of the city. Such a challenge to conventional epistemological frameworks with regard to the production of urban space in imaginative terms is at the heart of Sinclair's writing, while at the same time it conveys imperfectly the sense of perceiving the city. We are forced to read the city's
fragments in *Lud Heat* as we receive London itself: imperfectly, semi-consciously,

FIGURE 11.2. Brick Wall 1. Courtesy of Julian Wolfreys.

sensuously, without analytical distance, disinterested overview, or comforting sense of tradition or history. Revealing this, Sinclair's poetry fails to apprehend the city, yet its failure is not a limit so much as it is the only appropriate strategy of urban inscription. Reading *Lud Heat*, we share in the very condition of the city even as we fail to capture finally its nature. As readers, we may recognize the signs which constitute London, but translation is always left in ruins. Identifying all the figures, tropes, images employed in *Lud Heat* will do no more than offer us an entertaining intellectual jigsaw puzzle.

Lud Heat is composed of one book, "The Muck Rake," which in turn is divided into sixteen sections, including "Nicholas Hawksmoor, His Churches," "Closed Field, the Dogs of the Moon" ("Field" is within a closed field, framed by a rectangle), and "The Immigrant, The Sentimental Butcher." "The Muck Rake" is also named book one, leading you to believe, perhaps, that there might be a book two or three, although (so far, at least) this has not proved to be the case. (Though, then again, it might be argued that Ackroyd's novels, *White Chappell, Scarlet Tracings*, *Radon Daughters*, or *Downriver* are continuations of the London project.) Thus what the reader is confronted with is what seems to be an unfinished work—not that we can be sure—or, at least, a work with no ending, which is quite a different thing. The poem opens itself onto a futurity without horizon, much like the city itself. Some of the sections assume the form of rambling reflections on, amongst other things, the cabbalistic pattern allegedly mapped onto central and East London by the churches of Nicholas Hawksmoor (a conceit developed by Peter Ackroyd in his novel *Hawksmoor*). The sections break off and start up abruptly, as indeed do sentences within sections, and as do the areas of London and the streets traced therein; some seem ordered, some appear shabby. Thus the structure of *Lud Heat*, at once open-ended and willfully fragmentary, appears to be motivated or governed by no clear plan, other than that which London imposes as the structure of the city itself.

The text is marked throughout by a particular Egyptian hieroglyph, in what is apparently a form of sectional punctuation and division, while the literary, historical, sociological, cultural, and mythopoetic references are as diverse and random as the city's own histories and memories. Thus we proceed as we would according to Sinclair's proposition for passage through London: by exchanging the odd unconnected anecdote or random fact. Street names appear, as do area names, while place names can be equally contemporary/real or mythical/biblical, as with the Blakean "Camberwell to Golgotha," where the map translates itself, from one place to another, from one order of place, and also in the same place, a phantom effect or ghostly event oscillating within supposedly knowable or locatable topography.

Such work is taken further. We encounter street names which are also the names of authors, for example Ben Johnson Road (*Lud Heat* 43). Places, in

fact, nearly always serve doubled, doubling, disorganizing functions, functions
which are governed by both fact *and* mythology or textuality. Lambeth, for
instance, is not simply Lambeth but also Blake's Lambeth (17), which in turn
jostles for attention in the text with Cleopatra's Needle, situated on the
Chelsea side of the Thames across from Lambeth. Furthermore, we read a quotation taken from Pepys's diary, delivered in the passage through London, while
we are informed, elsewhere and in passing, of a location where Dickens once
stayed. De Quincey, Newton, and many others rub shoulders in this London,
regardless of the specificity of temporal location. This is a place where the
Mile End Road, Ratcliff Highway, Limehouse, and Lambeth cohabit quite
happily with Cardinal Heenan and the gods of Ancient Egypt or the Temple
of Mithras. Hawksmoor's churches occupy sites in real urban space—Blooms-
bury, Limehouse—as well as being transcribed as the structures and places
focusing metaphysical, arcane dark powers. The occult and the criminal
inhabit the same passages as the cultured and powerful. Ryvita and Greek epic
share space in the same lunch box. Why mention all this detail? The city, thus
conceived, as *objet trouvée*, as so many found objects in relation to recovered or
occluded memory, demands an activity of responsive, endless reading as a necessary task. If we don't begin by *sensing, feeling*, the teeming excess of London's
being, throughout all the discontinuous interrelations, along all the chance
diachronic and synchronic axes, we can begin nowhere legitimately in Sinclair's text. And yet, reading this text reinforces the sense that there is no
absolutely justifiable starting point as such. The city, and the poem which
responds to London, is always already an event of constant becoming, without
origin, without center, without absolute truth, except that truth which is London itself. The architectures of both *Lud Heat* and London are always on the
way to becoming, because neither can be read as complete; neither are finite
or closed systems. Instead, the text of the poem and that of the city always
remain ahead, before us, awaiting traversal and translation but, equally, never
offering any promise of completion and always re-marked through processes
of renewal, return, reiteration. To draw on Sinclair's poem again, "These are
rhythms to recognise, to accept or oppose" (68).

Sinclair also installs into his text certain prescriptions and caveats, pertinent
both to the city and his poetry:"What you suffer is the place you choose to live.
Do not remain victim to a solitary level of discourse . . . avoid the static condition" (*Lud Heat* 69). Such a direction arguably presents the conditions for imagining the provisional, open-ended reading of both Sinclair and London. As *Lud
Heat* is always composed of multiple discourses, so too is London at particular
levels. Similarly, both text and city are events, always taking place, dismantling in
the process any static condition, identity, or meaning. If we are urged to avoid
the condition of the solitary—perhaps the architectural or architectonic level of
discourse—whereby all is ordered in the projection/comprehension of unity

and uniformity, so too are we given examples of such avoidances on a textual, metropolitan, and historical/mythical scale.

To conclude with Sinclair, one brief passage, where landscape is passage, intervallic and irregularly rhythmic mapping, the program of the map interrupted by the event of replotting (taken from "The Immigrant, the Sentimental Butcher," addressing the East End):

> We all adjust: over the stadium, the missing spire, the half-circle of border ditch around Limehouse keeping out the histories of Mile End, Ratcliffe, Poplar. Laneways weighed under different glasses.
>
> > The encroaching fen. The
> > speed of time of the place
> > changes. Now I am frighted
> > in retrospect by a glimpse
> > of the original wood:
> > Hawksmoor's staircase
> > rising from the recently
> > sealed porch. Unvarnished
> > grain of parallel universe.
> > There is also Hablot Browne's
> > etching. Strong ground.
> > To be here is wide enough. (123)

We begin with incompletion, the city undone through that which is absent ("the missing spire"), that which remains to be closed or finished ("the half-circle"). Structure in ruins, in fragments, remaining to be completed, and haunted by the ghosts of structure to come, while also disturbed through the spectral possibility of that which might once have been there. The time of the city is every moment, though never present as a finished architecture, or totalizable in the present as such. Names sketch a skeletal map, the points awaiting connection, while the prose passage ends in its announcement of an alternative modality of urban spectatorship. Later in this section, we will read references to tabloid newspapers, the *Mirror* and the *Sun* (125), nylon stockings (125), and Virgil's *Aeneid* (126), along with "cheese rivita tomato Homer" (126). What we read is the gathering of ungovernable elements, having discernible taxonomic economy, randomly brought together, and this by the merest of coincidences, in text and place (as the textual fragments of place, the taking place of place). Where we are is almost as uncertain as *when* we are; memories and echoes of endless voices merge without coalescing, the seventeenth-century architect's design jostling for attention with the etching of Dickens's illustrator. Sinclair creates an experience of the landscape which is not grounded, and which, in fact, inaugurates what Ulrich Baer has called (with regard to the relation between subject position and landscape in Baudelaire's "Landscape"), the "deconstruction of position" (101). Released, as Baer has it, "from contingency, it [the landscape] is neither confined nor free" (Baer 100). Thus Sinclair's poetry situates the experience of the city as the constant event of the aporetic, as "the freedom of poetic speech" (Baer 102).

If London is thought of as a series of events, as that which is not so much a place as that which takes place, it has to be acknowledged that the apparently chance temporal and spatial conjunctions and juxtapositions which inform the urban condition, and which, subsequently, when registered in textual form, assume this uncanny force we name the experience of the aporetic in the most supposedly familiar locations, in those places where we might believe we no longer have to read. Indeed, it may be said that the textual form as urban locution is precisely that which traces the dislocation within location, unveiling invisible confluence within any given site, and thereby opening to us the necessity *and* the impossibility of reading.

Patrick Keiller's film *London* searches obsessively for the unhomely, the unfamiliar, within the recognizable, bringing back the invisible within visible form, structure, or place—whether by the "invisible," one acknowledges an alternative past, a forgotten fact, a submerged detail, or, more simply, an otherwise overlooked coincidence of disparate elements, the resurfacing, or even the imagined construction, of a memory. The film is neither simply factual nor fictional, neither wholly documentary *reportage* nor narrative *invention*, neither solely "historically accurate" nor entirely an imaginary assemblage. Images of London are presented, a static camera recording the movements in a given place, such as a bus stop, the forecourt of a pub, the checkout isles of a supermarket, or the window front of a driving school.

Counterposed to these images is a first-person narrative involving an anonymous narrator. The narrator is a cruise ship's photographer, who, on visiting London, spends time with an old friend, Robinson, a part-time university lecturer, who, in the words of the narrator, "was searching for the location of a memory." The question of the invisible countersignature to a visible reality is most clearly foregrounded through the persistence of the narrative—the voice is of a figure never seen, speaking of another character also never present, yet all the while commenting directly or otherwise on that to which the audience is witness. We see, in effect, through the eyes of ghosts, our perceptions conditioned through the doubling spectral mediation which narrative and imagined character makes possible. When we are told that Robinson listens to the stone gateposts of a municipal garden in Vauxhall, we comprehend, albeit dimly, certain ghostly histories invoked by location.

Robinson's narrative is woven into historical events, including the general election won by John Major in 1992 and various IRA bomb attacks on central London. Robinson's narrative involves the unearthing of a series of alternative London moments, such as the temporary residence in the capital of

FIGURE 11.3. Brick Wall 2. Courtesy of Julian Wolfreys.

Rimbaud, or the possibility that Montaigne had once visited the city. The function of narrative perception is, then, within Keiller's film, to place us "within memory, where the present is determined by the past. For memory," Bernard Cache remarks, "has two aspects: inscription on the one hand, and contraction on the other" (144). Contraction and inscription occupy many of the film's scenes, even as the scenes are themselves inscriptions of imaginative contraction. A brief exploration of two such scenes should suffice to illustrate this, as acts of what Keiller's narrator calls "psychic landscaping, drifting, and free association."

The first shot in question is a street corner in Soho, the corner of Wardour Street to be precise. We see pressboard hoardings covering a building, into which is let a temporary door. The door and hoarding announce the "Montaigne School of English." Robinson, we are told, reads Montaigne. A citation surfaces: "It is good to be born in depraved times for, by comparison with others, you are reckoned virtuous at little cost." A policeman walks in front of the hoarding, and the narrator offers the following commentary: "It is not generally agreed that Montaigne lived for a time in London, in a house in Wardour Street, the first of a number of French writers exiled in London." These include, significantly for Robinson, Mallarmé, Rimbaud, Verlaine. We are told that though Baudelaire never lived in London, his mother was born there and spoke English as a child.

The second shot brings back Baudelaire, this time through a quotation given the narrator by Robinson concerning romanticism: "'Romanticism,' writes Baudelaire, 'is precisely situated neither in choices of subjects, nor in exact truth, but in a mode of feeling.' For Robinson, the essence of the romantic life is in the ability to get outside oneself, to see oneself as if from outside." The image accompanying this citation is of a McDonald's restaurant, on the roof of which an inflatable Ronald McDonald bobs about in the breeze, while, nearby, a large union jack flutters.

The city is clearly figured, in these as in other scenes, through the chance and random concatenation of "found objects," where it is the eye of the camera that obviously locates and transforms through the act of filming. Possible significations are transformed in the process of recording material reality, while the invisibility of the narrator and his words, those of Robinson relayed through him, and the layers of already translated quotation from Montaigne to Baudelaire, further affect experience and reception. Particularly interesting in both these scenes is the play between visible and invisible: not only is there the translation within the visible—Montaigne becomes the signature for a language school, the union jack and Ronald McDonald in proximity are suggestive of various genealogies of colonial and corporate expansion—but, against what is visibly there, there is, whether through citation or narration, an emphasis on negation which it would be easy to overlook. Thus the very possibility of representation is transformed,

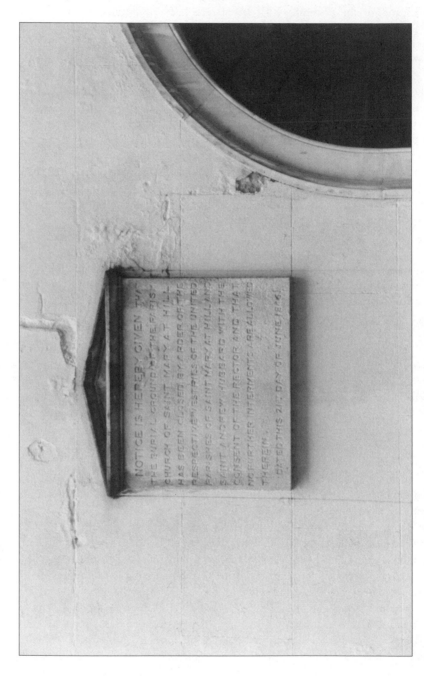

FIGURE 11.4. Notice Is Hereby Given. . . . Courtesy of Julian Wolfreys.

tensions between the voices of the city and the city's images serving to undo and fragment the experience of London; which experience is itself the experience of fragments, there being only the possible ghostly trace of Baudelaire to bring together Ronald McDonald and Soho.

Each image demolishes as much as it reinvents, making any epistemological assumption about place suspect, any interpretive activity impoverished. Moreover, the relatively static condition of each shot is interestingly solicited by the act of narration as a certain temporal otherness mediates against the constant present and presence of the image. Which is not, of course, to suggest that the image, what it represents, is simply undifferentiated within the frame or field of vision. As the "signature" of Montaigne juxtaposed with the policeman on the beat, or the flag and the fast food restaurant suggest—in a manner perhaps indebted to Henri Cartier-Bresson's dictum concerning photography that one records whatever is there, seeking to leave nothing out—this is just the city. What gives the lie to any possible documentary verisimilitude, of course, is that, in being framed, captured, the moment is translated irrevocably. Chance elements are made to operate rhetorically and tropologically, confusing, blurring, and disintegrating: topographics becomes *tropographics*. And what we come to understand from Keiller, as from Sinclair, Moorcock, and others, is that (to cite Stephen Barber) "the transformation of the city is a restless process of negation. . . . The city is perpetually invested with a dynamic jarring and upheaval of its configuration" (29). While this is arguably the case if one were to speak from certain perspectives of local government acts of demolition and rebuilding, of relocation of the city's inhabitants and the political justifications accompanying such acts, what is interesting is that the writers and artists in question take on what appear to be similar processes of transformation yet for wholly different ends. The imaginative and perhaps dissonant processes of imaginative undoing and demolition come from within the very same structures of urban reconstruction as the most politically motivated and cynical of acts. Yet, as the risk entailed in the aesthetic-epistemological acts with which I am here concerned, what the various texts maintain in the face of the politicians' makeovers in the name of uniformity and homogeneous identity and the attendant obliteration of memory which such makeovers desire, is the maintenance of memory, of alternative memories occluded by history and ideological "necessity." It is thus possible to read negation differently, to see, again to quote Barber, "[d]emolition of the city's elements [in the poetics of various recent texts as that which] strengthens what remains and [which] also strengthens the sense of vital damaging through which the city takes its respiration" (29).

Keiller's film thus makes explicit the formal condition of fraught epistemological contest as intrinsic to the registration of the nature of London shared by the writers and artists considered here; although, it has to be stressed, such representation and response is always singular even within a particular text, as the example of Keiller's film makes clear. This shared response to the city, which allows for the inscription of London as so many heterogeneous texts along with, constituted from, the resonances on which such texts, textures, and architectures rely, acknowledges London as what Kojin Karatani terms "the self-differential differential system as a formal precedent" (83). The formal radicality of difference, beyond or before any absolute law of difference is, for Karatani, that which the city makes possible. Karatani's "self-differential differential system" is an invaluable concept, acknowledging as it does how difference is excessive, irreducible to any recuperation into an economy of the self-same or the program which the term "system" implies. Difference is thus other than itself; it is plural, not simply inscribed by a multiplicity belonging to a single determinable or delimitable order. Differences differ and defer, differing and differentiating itselves from within itselves; coming to terms with Karatani's formula, a formula which allows for the experience of the aporetic within the logic of the very idea as system, we may provisionally and with caution take up the idea of the "self-differential differential system" as an unruly figure or historical and spatio-topographical precept by which the city maps and remaps itself, which then comes to govern Keiller's formal praxis. Thus, we can suggest, the response of Keiller to London is an act of letting the city write itselves onto his text, however improbable his various figural, historial, and topographical contrapuntal moments might appear. In short, what we see, and what we come to see we have not seen, what comes back while remaining unseen, is nothing other than so many Londons taking place, undoing London in the process. What Keiller's film gives us to see as a countersignature to the ideologies of representational unanimity, is that the "visual arena of the city *must* move through concurrent acts of construction and obliteration, extrusion and intrusion" (Barber 29), in the name of memory itself.

The double process of transformation and negation particular to an alternative perception of urban identity through time within and yet distinct from dominant representations of the city is caught in my final example, the work of Rachel Whiteread. Whiteread has responded in a number of places to acts of demolition, as area after area of what were once working-class neighborhoods undergo transformation. A series of photographs, included in the Tate Gallery's "Century City" exhibition at the beginning of 2001, capture the instance of destruction. *Demolished: A Clapton Park Estate, Mandeville Street, London E5; Ambergate Court; Norbury Court, October 1993*, offers the viewer the precise moment at which tower blocks begin to collapse, immediately following the controlled detonation, attested to in the suspension that photography enacts by clouds of smoke. Paradoxically, the event and its experience are rendered permanent, transformed by the camera into an impossible experience of immutability: the city, always already fixed in the act of passing away, and fixity punctuated further through the chronicling effected in that

ghostly trace, the title, whereby topography, location, coordinates, and naming become irrevocably translated. No longer the signifiers of location, they
have been reinvested as the inscribed memories of that which is no longer
there as such—hauntological tropes figuring invisible maps. The *punctum* of
the image estranges the viewer's relationship to the event. Indeed, we are witness to that which we cannot see in the moment of its taking place, but which
has now assumed, if not an afterlife, then, at least, an afterimage. The photo-
graphic event speaks beyond the singular instance of demolition to a paradoxical permanence and fleeting transience of the material. At the same time,
it also brings into view, through the artifice of aesthetic permanence manifested in the materiality of the photograph, the invisibility of the city's constant processes of passing beyond the immediacy of any perceivable present.
Demolition, the politically driven instant of obliteration, is transformed
through photography into the memory of one aspect of an otherwise invisible urban experience. Such experience is translated into another form, which
calls for witness.

At the same time as Whiteread was photographing the demolition of the
council estate, she began what in retrospect has become her most visible project, *House* (1993–94), a concrete cast of the interior space of an East End
house. Once again, as with the photograph, the transformation of place, the
destruction of domestic space, becomes fixed, perhaps as memorial. In this reinvention of "the nineteenth-century *realist* house into an abstract composition" (Vidler 145, emphasis in original), we witness how "the traces of former
patterns of life [are] now rendered dead but preserved" (146). The effect is
curious, estranging, and, yet again, paradoxical. While place becomes memorial, what is also preserved—or, perhaps more accurately, suspended, hovering
between past and present, the visible and invisible, and blurring, in the process,
all such distinctions—is not the past as such, as is usually the work of the
memorial effect, but instead an act of bearing witness, of testimony. We witness or, at least, are encouraged to witness, a negotiation or tension between
visibility and invisibility, between that which art can represent and the unrep-
resentable, the hidden, forgotten lives of working-class and immigrant inhabitants of the East End. This is perhaps all the more poignantly made plain by
the fact that the cast is of course that of the hitherto invisible domestic space,
the architecture of the house displaced by the reinvented, materialized location of "home," idea made concrete as it were. (A brief note: interestingly,
shortly after the completion of the casting and the demolition of the house,
an act of ghost writing, an instance of graffito took place, proclaiming "Homes
for all Black + White" appearing on one side; see photograph in Vidler 144.)
Thus, the ghosts return, as Whiteread renders habitation permanent and simultaneously uncanny or "unhomely," as Anthony Vidler correctly suggests (147).
The "temporary act or event" of the cast resonates with all it cannot represent

FIGURE 11.5. Stonework 2. Courtesy of Julian Wolfreys.

directly, thereby constituting itself "as a memory trace of former occupation and a traditional notion of dwelling" (Vidler 148). Whether in the case of photographs or sculpture, Whiteread transforms urban architecture and topography into nothing less than belated memory otherwise articulated.

To return to where we began then, in conclusion: the condition of reading, writing, representing London introduced in this chapter amounts, in Peter Nicholls's words, to "a forgotten history [which] has the power to shake the social and metaphysical forms against which it breaks . . . the idea of history as a violent intrusion from somewhere else" (52). The acknowledgement and incorporation of the chance and the random, the various acts of listing, the creative chaos of colliding disparate images and events—all resurrect and engage in the archaeological exhumation of what was always there, yet, seemingly, always forgotten, with regard to London. However, there is to be read in these acts a constant tension between the aleatory and the desire for the conjuration of specific narratives: to allow events of urban revenance through textual conjuring, and to direct, as a minimal structuration dictated by the specificity of place through time, narratives as the work of mourning the city, in a form of textual and textural *Nachträglichkeit*. "The provisionality [that productive tension between randomness and singularity, where the singularity, the multiple singularities of the submerged traces of forgotten events within a place] of such construction suggests that it will remain open to later *re*construction, not in the sense of rebuilding of a ruined city, or of restoring the past 'as it really was,' but as a continuous process of revision and retranslation" (King 16). The narratives of the past, loosely assembled through chance, doxa, anecdote, and so on, along with the ironic, if not paradoxical, juxtapositions (the flag over McDonald's, the reference to romanticism and nineteenth-century French symbolist poetry; the proximity of Ryvita and an edition of Homer), enforce through the modalities of assemblage and the work of ensemble memory-making (whereby the city itself figures itself and is refigured as so many mnemotechnic sites, given visible articulation through the medium of the artist who brings back the difference within and as the condition of past) the understanding of the city text as always just the structural experience of urban textuality as *Nachträglichkeit*. Through this experience, London is being undone constantly, its fragments resonating beyond any determinable whole. And the reader, sensitive to the ineffability of the urban, comprehends the condition of the city's past and present selves, without the possibility of apprehending or moving towards any desired homogeneity of either representation or experience.

WORKS CITED

Ackroyd, Peter. "Introduction." In *The East End: Four Centuries of London Life*. By Alan Palmer. 1989. New Brunswick: Rutgers UP, 2000. xi–xvi.

Baer, Ulrich. *Remnants of Song: Trauma and the Experience of Modernity in Charles Baude-laire and Paul Celan.* Stanford: Stanford UP, 2000.

Barber, Stephen. *Fragments of the European City.* London: Reaktion Books, 1995.

Cache, Bernard. *Earth Moves: The Furnishing of Territories.* 1983. Trans. Anne Boyman. Michael Speaks, ed. Cambridge, MA: MIT P, 1995.

Derrida, Jacques. "Limited Inc. II." Trans. Peggy Kamuf. In *Material Events: Paul de Man and the Afterlife of Theory.* Tom Cohen, Barbara Cohen, J. Hillis Miller, and Andrzej Warminski, eds. Minneapolis: U of Minnesota P, 2000. 178–244.

Dexter, Emma. Senior Curator, Tate Modern. "Century City: Art and Culture in the Modern Metropolis: London 1990–2001: City as Found Object." 1 Feb. 2001. <http//www.tate.org.uk/modern/exhibitions>.

Fisher, Allen. "The Mathematics of Rimbaud." *Gravity as a Consequence of Shape.* Int. Robert Sheppard. In *Future Exiles: 3 London Poets: Allen Fisher, Bill Griffiths, Brian Catling.* London: Paladin, 1992. 42–49.

———. "Six Poems from *Brixton Fractals* (1982–4)." *Gravity as a Consequence of Shape.* Int. Robert Sheppard. In *Future Exiles: 3 London Poets: Allen Fisher, Bill Griffiths, Brian Catling.* London: Paladin, 1992. 65–104.

Frey, Hans-Jost. *Studies in Poetic Discourse: Mallarmé, Baudelaire, Rimbaud, Hölderlin.* 1986. Trans. William Whobrey. Stanford: Stanford UP, 1996.

Greenlaw, Lavinia. "Love from a Foreign City." *Night Photograph.* London: Faber and Faber, 1993. 44.

Kant, Immanuel. *Critique of Judgment.* Trans. Werner S. Pluhar. Indianapolis and Cambridge: Hackett Publishing Company, 1987.

Karatani, Kojin. *Architecture as Metaphor: Language, Number, Money.* Trans. Sabu Kohso. Michael Speaks, ed. Cambridge, MA: MIT P, 1995.

Keiller, Patrick. *London.* London: British Film Institute, 1993.

King, Nicola. *Memory, Narrative, Identity: Remembering the Self.* Edinburgh: Edinburgh UP, 2000.

Lichtenstein, Rachel, and Iain Sinclair. *Rodinsky's Room.* London: Granta, 1999.

Lupton, Donald. *London and the Countrey Carbonadoed and Quartered into Severall Charac-ters.* 1632. Amsterdam: Theatris Orbum Terrarum, 1977.

Moorcock, Michael. *Mother London.* 1988. London: Scribner, 2000.

Nicholls, Peter. "The Belated Postmodern: History, Phantoms, and Toni Morrison." In *Psychoanalytic Criticism: A Reader.* Sue Vice, ed. London: Polity P, 1996. 50–67.

Palmer, Alan. *The East End: Four Centuries of London Life.* 1989. New Brunswick: Rutgers UP, 2000.

Schelling, F. W. J. *The Ages of the World (Fragment) from the handwritten remains. Third Version (c. 1815).* Trans. and int. Jason M. Wirth. Albany: State U of New York P, 2000.

Sinclair, Iain. "All Change. This train is cancelled." *London Review of Books* 21 (13 May 1999): 10.

—————. *Lud Heat*. 1975. In *Lud Heat and Suicide Bridge*. Int. Michael Moorcock. Maps by Dave McKean. London: Vintage, 1995. 7–142.

Smith, Ken. "Encounter at St Martin's." *The London Poems*. In *Terra*. Newcastle: Bloodaxe Books, 1986. 53.

Vidler, Anthony. *Warped Space: Art, Architecture and Anxiety in Modern Culture*. Cambridge, MA: MIT P, 2000.

Virilio, Paul. *A Landscape of Events*. 1996. Trans. Julie Rose. Foreword Bernard Tschumi. Cambridge, MA: MIT P, 2000.

CHAPTER 12

London 2000:
The Millennial Imagination
in a City of Monuments

MICHAEL LEVENSON

BATTLES OF TRAFALGAR

*D*uring the fall of 2000, the newly elected mayor of London, Ken Livingstone, found himself reflecting on Trafalgar Square and the meaning of its statuary. As control of the square was passing from the national Department of Culture to the newly elected London authorities, Livingstone was asked about the Victorian monuments to Major General Sir Henry Havelock and General Sir Charles Napier, who occupy two corners of the square, while George IV takes a third. "I think," said the mayor, "that the people on the plinths in the main square in our capital city should be identifiable to the generality of the population. I have not a clue who two of the generals there are or what they did." He supposed "that not one person in 10,000 going through Trafalgar Square knows any details about the lives of those two generals. It might be that it is time to look at moving them and having figures on those plinths that ordinary Londoners would know" (Kelso).

Livingstone's comments stirred a predictable tempest in the media. Leader writers came forward to inform him of Havelock's service in Burma, Afghanistan, and India, and of Napier's role in combating Chartists and defeating the Indian tribes of Sindh. The *Guardian* reported the comments of Colonel Alastair Cumming, the regimental secretary of Havelock's old regiment, the 78th

Highlanders, who asked, "Where do we stop? Are they planning to rip Nelson off his column? This really is indicative of where we are going as a country isn't it—consigning our history to oblivion." The Conservative shadow minister for London, Bernard Jenkin, accused the mayor of "trying to erase a fundamental part of our nation's heritage from the heart of our capital city" (Kelso). In some corners of the press Livingstone was painted as a cheerfully ignorant iconoclast; elsewhere, good fun was had in imagining where the statues might be moved (to the New Zealand towns of Napier and Havelock North?) and which figures might take their place (Richard Branson? Liz Hurley? Ken Livingstone himself?).

In this same millennial year, Trafalgar Square attracted the attention of the media in other ways. First, there was the question of the vacant plinth on the fourth corner on the square, which had stood empty since William IV had tried (and failed) to raise money for a statue of himself. For several years Prue Leith of the Royal Society of Arts had campaigned for an end to the embarrassment of the empty plinth, and finally a Vacant Plinth Committee, under the chair of John Mortimer, decided that the space should be occupied by a succession of contemporary sculptures, each installed for a period of months (fig. 12.1). The decision carried a self-conscious refusal of the demand for more traditional works on the model of the equestrian statues of the two generals and the king. A delighted Mortimer called it a victory for "Art" over "History" (Hilty).

The jauntiness of the episode—complete with forced wit and the usual har-har-har of popular journalism—shouldn't distract us from its larger resonance. Contention over the display of public symbols is as old as public life, but what has occurred in millennial London and what gives the initial focus to this chapter is the distinctive turn in the politics of urban symbolism: a newly self-conscious sense of London as a post-imperial metropolis that must now reinvent the symbols by which a community understands itself.

The depth of the question became clear in another visible episode that impinged on Trafalgar Square, the May Day demonstrations led by the group Reclaim the Streets. Pictures of angry protestors naturally circulated in the press, but strikingly, the narrative of bruised bodies and persons under arrest also included the fate of monuments, especially in Parliament Square and along Whitehall. The daubing of paint on the statuary incensed Prime Minister Blair, who commented that "To deface the Cenotaph and the statue of Winston Churchill is simply beneath contempt" ("Police Defend"). The deputy assistant commissioner of the metropolitan police, Mike Todd, tried to explain how the authorities could let such disrespectful conduct occur. His answer was that if the police tried to protect specific monuments, the crowd could simply have moved on to others in the vicinity. The image was of a family of statues, exposed, vulnerable, much loved. Where the protestors remained largely anonymous, a crowd of "mindless thugs," the wounded statuary had names and histories.

FIGURE 12.1. Rachel Whiteread's *Monument* on the once-vacant plinth of Trafalgar Square. Courtesy of Michael Levenson.

From the comic to the bloody, these incidents expose an entrenched agon and a familiar narrative. In repeated episodes, a group of modernizers cast monumental London as a clutter of ancient deposits surviving in bronze heaps—unwelcome relics of the imperial past. Activists on the left—whether cultural (the Vacant Plinth Committee), political (Reclaim the Streets), or cultural/political (Ken Livingstone)—contest this saturated field of ancient imagery. The voices of tradition shout back against the symbolic assault, and the press happily represents the opposing views, extracting the last drops of controversy. What is invariably at stake is a definition of the metropolis that is at the same time a definition of a populace. When Livingstone invokes the great social mass that is indifferent to Havelock and Napier, the mass in which he places himself, he builds the picture of a modern, collective, urban solidarity resisting those elites who cling to obsolete symbols. On the opposite side, the traditionalists offer a community extending not in space but in time, a London citizenry constituted by all those who are signified by the symbols of past glory.

Symbolic public action becomes most active when the content of politics loses force. At a time of convergence among the leading political parties—especially with the success of Blair's Third Way in enshrining a powerful middle term—the contest is increasingly fought on the terrain of imagery. The management of expectations replaces the distribution of resources. Then beyond the neutralizing of 'content' achieved by the centrism of Third Way politics, there is the transforming narrative of Britain's post-imperial destiny. In the last decade of the millennium, a dominant narrative of decline was overlaid by a story of triumph enacted under the banner of "Cool Britannia." London, of course, was at the center of the changing story. As late as 1995 Roy Porter could end his history of the city by observing that "London seems to be becoming one of the historic towns of Europe: a museum piece—even a dinosaur—and in some ways an irrelevance" (Porter 385). Five years later an unbridled civic boosterism could point to the stream of affirmative images in the press and the endless current of tourists. A resurgent narrative of civic triumph depended far more heavily on the play of symbols—images of Young British Artists, of trendy clubs, and street fashions—than on any documentary realism, and as the millennium approached, the apparatus of symbol-making began to chirrup in earnest.

Still, the boosterism of the press and politicians could never suppress all signs of disruption, nor could the play of symbols quiet all critics. Homelessness, street crime, and ethnic and racial violence not only persisted, but they possessed their own attractions for the media. Nothing seems better than the story of London's triumph unless it is the story of London's fall. A vast city with an aging infrastructure, a multinational population, a rickety transport system, and an unsurprising measure of drug-dealing, petty theft, and the rare spectacular murder, was always able to furnish a story of catastrophe whenever an editor decided that the mood was right.

Efforts to take a measured view and to construct a balanced picture often became riven on the double narrative. When in the spring of 1999 *Granta* published a special issue on *London: The Lives of the City*, its editor, Ian Jack, composed a preface clearly aiming to be inclusive and judicious. He describes the beginning of the new period in the middle 1990s when the metropolis became a media success on a new scale, and in a recognizable literary/intellectual gesture, he draws back from the sloganeering that made London the world capital of urban cool. "There are reasons to be sceptical," writes Jack. "British culture has become addicted to branding and marketing, and the eagerness with which British politicians seized and touted a phrase coined on a newsdesk in New York did not inspire trust. And what, exactly, did it describe? A few conceptual artists, a young prime minister, a rock musician or two, some nightclubs, shoals of restaurants: is that what it amounted to?" Then immediately he adds, "Still, the slogan isn't completely empty."

> London has changed and promises to change further. Large stretches of the inner city have been colonized by the young, abandoned warehouses and factories have been knocked into flats, anything without a job (an old brewery, a disused power station) gets one as an art gallery, the streets are fuller for longer into the night, there is a lively, enterprising sense about the place (even if people do seem to drink too much). Some of this optimism may not last; the money which fuels it may run out; the economy may plunge into recession. But something more permanent has been discovered, or so I like to think. London has a fresher, more assertive identity. . . . A place of strange and often unprofitable profusions: which other city in the world contains thirteen different railway terminals, some small region of the hinterland served by each, or ten different daily newspapers?
>
> No, nowhere else will really do. (Jack 6–7)

The *Granta* volume following this preface comprises a series of contemporary stories that represent city life unsentimentally: its traffic, its anomie, its violence, its carelessness. And yet as Jack's introduction suggests, the portrait of urban failure is accompanied by an almost involuntary affirmation. Some people shoot bad drugs into their veins; others get divorced or stabbed; and yet there remains the sense of a profuse metropolis which requires our vitality. Lives may be broken, but the city breathes and blusters.

This chapter will address public, monumental London in its post-imperial and new millennial aspect. It will consider how built objects are determining the imaginative condition of the community; it will ask questions about the circulation of symbols within the built environment, and the fate of urban solidarity; and throughout, it will return to the millennial year and the workings of an overheated media culture that has become such a prominent actor in the metropolitan drama.

THE FINE ART OF REAL ESTATE

The millennium itself, a prodigious invitation to public gesture, was one cause of the symbol-laden architectural boom throughout the capital, but other significant forces had been gathering for several years. The financial success of the national lottery through the '90s meant that vast resources came available for building in London. During the same period, the economic expansion brought private money back into urban investment, and star architects, most notably Norman Foster, turned their hands to London, after years of creating architectural spectacle elsewhere around the globe. At the same time, political discourse underwent perceptible change. The return of the Labour Party to power in 1997 depended upon a new (and fully Americanized) strategy of media discourse and the manipulation of imagery.[1] Journalists acknowledged, reported, and even enjoyed, the story of politicians attempting to influence their work. The subject of "spin" traveled east across the Atlantic and became both a ceaseless labor for the politicians and an inexhaustible topic for the journalists.

In all these respects, the production of symbols has become itself a leading industry in post-imperial Britain, and the urban field, the London field, is the natural site for the manufacture of symbols. Within the long-standing British division between industrial and financial capital, London has of course been the center for finance. As the workings of finance became ever more intangible, increasingly based on the flashing circuits of information, as private and corporate fortunes grew more "fictional" within the gyrating markets, money seemed to become, not the grittiest reality, but more the master symbol in a capital of symbolism.

The most illuminating example here may be the elaborate choreography of money, property, and art in the later '90s. Within the bubble of prosperity, the art market and the real estate market floated upward together. A construction by Tracey Emin or Damien Hirst, a sculpture by Rachel Whiteread, a painting by Gary Hume or Jenny Saville—these contemporary works became not only challenging gestures within a sophisticated art world, but also forms of currency, new aspects that money could wear. After decades of neglect, interrupted only by a relatively few committed collectors, contemporary art suddenly became a cherished commodity. The press found an interest of its own, creating the Young British Artists (YBAs) as celebrities, inventing a superstardom that helped to increase both the price of artworks and the visibility of feature stories in the newspapers. Charles Saatchi, who turned his advertising fortune to the purposes of collecting, became an emblem of a new agitated market in contemporary work. As Martin Coomer has put it, "For young artists, having work bought by Saatchi can mean the difference between affording a studio and continuing, or on the dole" (Coomer 9.2–9.4). He recalls the notorious case of the Italian painter Sandro Chia, dozens of whose paintings

Saatchi acquired, lifting their value overnight. Saatchi then sold them off en masse, depressing their price and lowering Chia's reputation through a few brisk transactions. Saatchi's investment career in the YBAs reached a kind of apotheosis right at the end of the millennium when he purchased Damien Hirst's giant bronze anatomy toy for one million pounds.

At the same time, real estate prices recovered, rose, and then simply soared. In itself, this was no novelty; the London housing market would always be a hypersensitive economic register. What emerged in the later '90s, however, was a new, and uncanny, relationship between the currencies of speculation in art and real estate. In a much-documented cultural migration, artists moved their studios to the east and south as prices rose in central London. Then as the press lifted the fortunes of many new artists, property investors and speculators followed the trail of the art community, because nothing could add luster to a neighborhood more quickly than a gleaming new gallery containing well-dressed viewers prepared to buy. But in one of the signal urban ironies of the decade, the real estate investments brought an increase in rents on studio work-space, driving out those many artists who didn't share the spoils and who had to pack up and continue the trek further away from the center of fungible values.

MAKING A SPECTACLE OF LONDON

> The Millennium Wheel was late. The Millennium Bridge was late and even then only lasted two days. The Millennium Dome is a disaster. Thank God, New Labour didn't give us the Millennium Nuclear Reactor.
> —John W., "Millennium Wheel"

The Millennium Dome was the massive material provocation, looming at the start of the millennial year. A project begun under the Conservatives, reconsidered and then reaffirmed by Labour, uncertain in its funding, confused about its contents, wavering in its leadership, taunted by a press eager to measure any misstep, the dome was born to fail, which it quickly and spectacularly did. The embarrassment began in earnest with the invitations to the New Year's extravaganza which didn't arrive in time. It continued with long queues at the attractions and a nearly unrelieved series of negative reviews. There were resignations, off-the-record character assassinations, and unseemly shiftings of blame. When the projections of twelve million visitors in the year dwindled toward the reality of five or six million, voices in the media began to cackle. As the painful narrative played out in 2000, it became the newspapers' favorite morning routine: to dramatize the failure and to lead the search for the culprits. One question seemed just irresistible: Why had Labour opened its throat to such eviscerating instruments?

The answer isn't far to seek. A government that came to power through an understanding of symbolic action was naturally drawn to the workings of public spectacle. Its strategists believed, and its victory seemed to confirm, that to build a political constituency, a national community, was to construct a symbolic field fit for the new age of media. Costs were calculated; risks were assessed; projections were made and revised. Despite the long deliberations and the worries of naysayers, the publicity attractions of the dome seemed irresistible. As the prime minister was moving to make up his own mind, a rumor spread that he still had a last question. What would make him want to take his children to the dome? In response to the apparently apocryphal question, Simon Jenkins (of the *Times* and the millennium commission) composed a document that came to be called the "Euan letter"—in a reference to Blair's oldest son. Here's how it begins:

> Dear Tony
>   I understand you are eager to know what will make your children want to go to Greenwich. Let me tell you.
>   Greenwich will be the world's one big Millennium celebration. The site is acquired, the Rogers Dome designed, the Foster station under construction. German, French, Italian and American planners all concede Britain's leadership here. Every child, including many from abroad, will want "to see Greenwich in 2000" and tell it to their grandchildren. Such events are milestones in a nation's history, but also in a child's life. ("New Labour, New Dome")

The Festival of Britain, held half a century earlier, was the precedent within living memory, but it's plain that the symbolic imagination flew further back in time, lighting always on the Crystal Palace. Later in his Euan letter, Jenkins wrote that just as "Every Victorian machine said, 'Shown at the Great Exhibition', Every new one should say, 'Shown at Greenwich'."

When the *Independent* published its exposé of the Labour meanderings, including the excerpts from Jenkins's letter, it paraphrased exchanges from the Ministerial Committee on the Millennium Dome, including this defense from Peter Mandelson:

> It would provide a national focus. It would bring the country together. Secondly, it would project strength and confidence in Britain to the world, and would quite clearly be a showcase for a Labour government. And thirdly, to cancel it now, which would throw some £25 million down the drain and show that the government couldn't rise to the occasion, would mean that the symbolism would work against them. ("New Labour, New Dome")

Of course, the symbolism worked against them anyway. Abjectly dependent on the media to promote the dome and to ensure large crowds, the organizers were helpless when the reviews turned negative. A parliamentary report in the summer castigated the project for relying on free attention in the press, an approach that "proved to be disastrous when the press coverage became largely hostile" ("Dome 'Lacks Wow Factor'"). Bob Ayling, head of British Airways and golden boy of New Labour's alliance with enlightened business, began the year as chairman of the New Millennium Experience Company, but by the end of the year he was another celebrated casualty. After his resignation, he rounded on the press, claiming that while other countries welcomed expenditure on signature projects, in Britain, the "stories are about Millennium failure" and how "the Millennium bug has struck again": "We are just pathetic" ("Dome Support").

By the time Ayling uttered his lament, the string of embarrassments had widened from their source in Greenwich. The Millennium Ferris Wheel, a private initiative, had had a series of delays in opening, and more embarrassingly (and more comically) the much-admired Millennium Bridge was forced to close after only a few days of use (fig. 12.2). The bridge was the product of a celebrated partnership between the distinguished architect Norman Foster, and the eminent sculptor Antony Caro; Foster had billed it as a "blade of light across the river" ("Norman Foster"). Unlike the dome, there had been no premonitions of failure. Yet in June, when it began swaying beneath the tramping pedestrians and when no quick structural fix could be found, the same mechanism of media satire began to whirr and hum. Was it a failure of the architect? Or was the engineering firm to blame? How could everyone have missed the instability in the design? Was there a Millennium Jinx? Or did Ayling have it right—were the British "just pathetic"?

What gave edge to the polemic was exactly just this sense that the failure lay not in the buildings, but in Britishness—especially the world-aspiring Britishness that finds its epitome in London.[2] The life of the community became bound to its expensive new monuments. Moreover, everything seemed to turn on the collective will to believe. A community that flocked to the dome would have made its success true. Contrarily, when people stay away in droves, they ensure not only the failure of a project but their own public humiliation.

In the sudden defensive posturing, it was observed that a bridge in Japan had suffered a similar problem. While this case was little known, at least the British didn't keep their embarrassments in the dark but talked about them, openly and awkwardly. As an attempt to excuse the failure, this was weak. But it did emphasize what became inescapable during the millennium year: that within the hyper-mediated conditions of London civic life, the effects of symbolic action would always elude any actor. The dimensions of "spin" had become incalculable and uncontrollable. Those ten daily newspapers mentioned proudly by Ian Jack constituted an apparatus of perpetual opinion that is the counterpart to agitated financial markets. With a metropolitan workforce so heavily dependent on the London underground, the shared spaces of the trains became crowded with bold-faced headlines charting the rise and decline of those who live out their fates within public discourse.

228

FIGURE 12.2. Millennium Bridge 1. Courtesy of Michael Levenson.

Everything fell into place, then, for the familiar pattern of a concentrated journalistic assault on a vulnerable target. The failing dome, the wobbly bridge, the broken wheel—it was easy to see how a story of pride and fall could nearly write itself. And yet one of the striking features of the millennium year was the change in the course of the story. The fiasco of the New Millennium Experience Company was not forgiven; the insults were unrelieved. But the dome itself, with its odd antlers and the pale stretch of space-age materials, was increasingly distinguished from the collapsing enterprise that had spawned it. The *Guardian* captured the mood in a year-end column by Jonathan Glancey, who described the dome as "a rather likable rogue, especially by night" (Glancey). The wheel ran often enough, and its views were spectacular enough, that the odd malfunction was forgiven (the early failures softened by free airline tickets from British Airways) (fig. 12.3). Although the Bridge spent the rest of the year empty of pedestrians, waiting for an engineering solution, the ribboned sleekness of the design had many admirers. As in the case of Rogers's dome, Norman Foster's bridge was separated from the practical embarrassment, and, in any case, critics who may have wanted to feast on the engineering folly had their attention turned by the other public buildings soon to be unveiled.

Indeed in this last point we have a key to the strange trajectory from scepticism to boosterism that marked the course of the millennial year. The sheer, staggering number of monumental projects overwhelmed the sense of particular failure, even the particularly massive failure of the dome. At a certain point, the consciousness of the media became infatuated with the architectural multitude:

> London is in the grip of a frenzied rebuilding the like of which it has not experienced in 50 years. Later this year we will see the completion of the last of the big Lottery projects. The millennium bridge, the first completely new crossing of the Thames for a century, the great court at the British Museum, the Welcome Wing at the Science Museum, and the Tate Modern will all join the Royal Opera House and the Dome on the roll call of London's millennial trophies. (Sudjic, "Boom Town")

In the face of all that stone and glass, critics simply gushed: "Without anybody knowing quite why or how it has happened, self-deprecating old London is suddenly revealed as being bent on transforming itself into a city that has not just the civic grandeur of Paris, and the stylish bustle of Barcelona, but the glamour of Manhattan as well" (Sudjic, "Capital's Master Builder").[3] Here is the affirmative current that began to swell through the course of the year: the vision of London as returning to the elite group of world cities, the great culture cities increasingly defined by their monumental built environment.

Nothing could be plainer than the link between the affirmative tone—shown not only by the endorsements in the press but also by the throngs of citizens and tourists who moved through the Tate Modern, climbed onto the

FIGURE 12.3. The London Eye. Courtesy of Michael Levenson.

London Eye, or pressed into the Great Court—and the excited sense of *profusion*, the same infatuated sense of plenty that overcomes Ian Jack in *Granta*. Repeatedly, one finds the media chanting out the names of the new projects. It's not that every building is praised—savage critiques still attach to individual designs—but these are swept away by an exuberant image of the fertile metropolis, sprouting buildings like new crops.

MODERNISM REDUX

The lottery was the deus ex machina, the swooping, scarcely precedented incitement to metropolitan ambition. It became possible to imagine a dome, to renovate an opera house, to recreate a museum; throughout central London, it became possible to build on the grand scale. Decades of paper design and unemployed architects, of idle dreams that never needed to test practicality, suddenly converted into commissions and deadlines. The artifice of "2000" gave a theatrical quality to time: the boundaries of the year became frames on a stage. Not only did this encourage developers to finish their projects within the terms of the special calendar; but it also, and just as importantly, encouraged a collective stock-taking, a metropolitan self-consciousness. If the millennial year failed to concentrate on the spiritual life of Britain (a neglect that repelled Prince Charles), it concentrated relentlessly on the fate of London.

Indeed, what became clear during the year is that for those privileged enough to move about the city, to take up its invitations, and to feel either the rights of citizenship or tourism, the new London offered distinctive forms of urban pleasure. Much of the satisfaction, of course, lay in the contemplation of national, and more specifically metropolitan, identity. Post-imperial London enjoyed the reversal of a narrative of decline, and the reassertion of a pre-eminence relying neither on political domination nor economic supremacy, but on what we may call a *community of style*. The vision of a city more richly and self-consciously stylized than any other—stylized in its dress, its food, the circulation of its wealth, the flow of its tourists—and more alluring because these intensities are *visible*: this was the real millennial attraction. The luminous prestige of London would not be abstract but sensuous; it must be available to bodies moving through its central districts; and it must be monumental, not simply because monuments will excite the senses, but because they will organize space into the form of exhilaration.

Yet, despite the competitive temper shown in the appetite for a pre-eminent city, the world city—an appetite that pervades the tourist brochures—one of the most striking features of the new monumentalism is its symbolic neutrality, the impersonality of its designs. When Norman Foster spoke proudly of the Millennium Bridge as "a blade of light across the river," he did more than coin a catchphrase for the journalists; he laid out a principle of imagery. It would not be an heroic gesture or a national project that would inspire the design; it would be the play of aesthetic forms: color, texture, scale, and light.

The Tate Modern inhabits the shell of a muscular power station, and precisely what the building achieves is the conversion of utility into aesthetics, of electric power into touristic energy. What was once a referent to practical civic progress is now the home of non-referential modernism, hundreds of artworks suspending the claims of practicality. Much as the new Tate plays against the great power station that it inhabits and *shuts down*, so does Richard Rogers playfully refer to Christopher Wren's great domes. The *Sunday Times* reported Prince Charles description of the Millennium Dome as a "crass waste of money," resembling a "monstrous blancmange"; and the paper indicated that while attending a recital at St. Paul's, the prince sniffily remarked that "This is the real dome" (Morgan). No doubt the comment delighted Richard Rogers, whose dome depended on measuring its distance from the "real dome," refusing the imagery of tradition and religious belief in order to display its look, its vast size, its featherweight. So, too, when Norman Foster designed the much-praised Great Court in the British Museum, he carefully placed his work within the Victorian framework designed by Robert Smirke. But the effect was neither to celebrate nor to reprove the neoclassic precedent. Foster accepts what Smirke gave him and then goes on to pursue his own characteristic aims: a liberation of space, a play of forms, a volume (not merely a blade) of light.

These are characteristically modernist values—the formal values of texture, color, and scale—but set within a cultural mood that remains recognizably postmodern. The intense consciousness of, and cool distance from, the past—this is what had incited the postmodern turn. But in its earlier manifestations, for instance, in Rogers's Pompidou Center and his Lloyds Bank, architectural postmodernism throve on jaunty references to the past-that-was-superceded, on a literary awareness of the wit, the irony, of the building. The past is still there. Wren looms behind Rogers, Smirke behind Foster, the power station behind Herzog and de Meuron. Yet what has strikingly changed—and what made Norman Foster the figure of the millennial moment—is that a new tonality has perceptibly arrived. The game that postmodernism played with the past has engendered a renewed game of modernist form. We might indeed see this as a final postmodern irony: the liberation of possibility conducted against the tyranny of modernism has ended by liberating modernism too. When John Mortimer proclaimed that, by deciding to exhibit a series of contemporary sculpture, his Vacant Plinth Committee marked the victory of "Art" over "History," he was referring to a triumph over the imperial statues on the other corners of Trafalgar Square. But Art versus History also gives a way of describing the revival of modernist values within a postmodern milieu. In fact, of course, there can be no question of modernist triumph. But what makes millennial London at once so agitated and so interesting are the complicated tones of modernism-within-postmodernity, the prominence of modernist forms within a saturated historical self-consciousness.

THE ENTERPRISE OF STYLE

The impersonality of millennial London, its formalism, even its aestheticism—this is not only opposed to the promiscuous personalizing of urban space in the later Victorian period (the remaking of the Mall as a triumphal processional for the Queen being only one extravagant example); it is also distinguished from the mid-twentieth-century epoch of urban planning. In 1960, London County Council (LCC) published a celebration of its scheme for a rebuilt metropolis, an unabashed, unapologetic strategy to furnish the housing needs of the metropolis by building quickly and building high. Here is how the pamphlet began:

> London is growing up. For centuries it has been spreading outwards over the surrounding countryside. Today it is pushing upwards. Londoners, who have spent contemplative lunch-hours gazing at great excavated holes, now see high blocks of offices and flats rising to heights undreamed of twenty years ago in the City, the West End, Islington and Camberwell, Roehampton and Poplar and all points east, west, south and north. (London County Council 15)

These contributions to the public good were unadorned buildings, squat despite their height, whose leading features were rectangular windows within rectilinear designs. The repetitive patternings, prefabricated materials, colorless facades, and high population densities made these buildings celebrated targets of architectural and social critique. The management of populations had merged with the management of building costs.[4] The unhappy result has been tirelessly rehearsed: an administration of urban space that too often solved a problem of housing by creating the problem of social estrangement.

But for all the vulnerability to stylistic and social critique, the building projects of the LCC grew from a coherent urban vision, a "grand design to turn the amorphous mass of London into a pattern of inter-related living centres" (London County Council 23). Indeed, the LCC well understood the social exchanges required by its comprehensive building scheme. *New Sights of London* acknowledged that "With all the admitted advantages [of the tower flats], two-thirds [of residents] said they would prefer a little house of their own with a garden" (26)—to which the voice of the council responded that "in overcrowded London some people must live aloft to make room out of doors for themselves and everyone else" (29). Between the Victorian image of royal and military personhood and the LCC conception of social totality, there is, of course, the greatest contrast. And yet both ideals share an image of coherent urban space, not yet achieved but beckoning in the distance. Where the first emanates from exalted individuals invoked through statuary, the second founds itself on shared identities, to be represented through the administrative body of the London County Council. An arch dedicated to the Queen signifies a hierarchy of value sanctioning community from above, while a block of council flats represents a dream of urban solidarity in which even an undesirable place in the city's expanse—a small flat in a crowded building—can be seen as a contribution to the "person" that is London as a whole.

It is against this background that we need to locate the late-twentieth-century transformations in the city. If we look for a decisive moment of change, it would be the reinvention of Docklands in the '80s and '90s. The Thatcher government made the area an Enterprise Zone, freeing it from local control and inviting private companies to pursue nothing but the logic of investment. The recession of the early '90s looked as if might be devastating, but by the end of the decade, Docklands showed itself as a full-scale city within the city, a vast expanse of lustrous buildings, utterly without stylistic unity.[5] Hard alongside still depressed local communities, the new towers sprouted, each following a spatial logic of its own. Docklands began as a kind of anti-community, a building zone founded on the principle of liberation from communal needs. What the freedom of the Enterprise Zone permitted was an architectural free-for-all, which was open to savage attack, both politically and aesthetically, but which has turned out to be uncannily prophetic of Lottery London.

If the Docklands development was a risky adventure in private capital, the Thatcher government did offer some soft cushions of reassurance. Its contribution was in infrastructure: roads, services, and, most spectacularly, the extension of the Jubilee line from central London to the Docklands. Boomed as the largest engineering project in Europe, the Jubilee extension encountered some difficult cost overruns and long delays. Like the dome toward which it was digging, it became an easy target for the satiric press. But when it was finished, just in time to carry passengers to the millennial festival, its fortunes revived in a single stroke, and it became one of the focal points for London boosterism (fig. 12.4). The clever idea had been to assign each of the new stations to a different architect, freeing each for large-scale ambition with an ample budget. One after another, new cavernous spaces became not drafty halls to pass through, but places to linger in and gaze upon. As one doting critic put it, "The line has become a tourist attraction in its own right. It is a truly great achievement; the sheer scale of some of the lonelier stations, such as Canada Water, suggesting future development around them in what, in parts, are still very poor areas of London" (Glancey).

Together, Docklands and the Jubilee line established a principle of stylistic relativism. Within Docklands the jumble of styles, the clash of different scales

235

FIGURE 12.4. Canary Wharf. Courtesy of Michael Levenson.

and competing colors, created some strange and eccentric vistas. The lure of the Jubilee line, on the other hand, was that its diversity was dispersed throughout the underground, so that each new design along the tunnel could be a visual tableau unto itself. Speaking of his solar-energized egg-shaped design for the Greater London Assembly, Norman Foster noted that, with its "unusual shape," it is "not likely that you will mistake it for any other building" ("Work Begins"). And yet, this apt remark might be made of scores of other projects, either built or soon to come. What the emerging monumentalism has exposed is the force of Difference, the value of the "inimitable" structure—dome, wheel, bridge, etc.—that can't be mistaken for any another and so establishes its unforgettable singularity.

CITIZEN TOWERS

If the new Jubilee line stations encouraged the doctrine of extravagant individuality, each ambitious station distinguished from every other, at the same time it recalled another vision of the urban expanse. After all, the Jubilee Line not only exhibited new architecture, it carried its passengers across a long swath of space. If its architecture was a triumph of difference, its practical purpose was to integrate—not to separate. To connect the vast eastern spaces of Greenwich and the Docklands to the center of London—this raised again the vision of a London that worked and *moved*, a coherent city that could be traversed reliably and rapidly.

But elsewhere, the state of transport was a glaring problem only aggravated by the Labour government's conspicuous failed promises of improvement. Violent crime works on the imaginative lives of Londoners, but it takes no imagination to see the problems of the tube. In the resigned words of the *Times*: "Mini-seizures are now an almost daily occurrence" (Parris). Late in the year, Ken Livingstone used his new mayoral power to contest New Labour's plan for the underground, which relied on government partnerships with private capital. Livingstone formulated a counterplan, appointing as his transport commissioner Robert "Bob" Kiley, the American credited with saving the New York City subway. As the millennial year reached its waning days, Livingstone and Kiley were actively resisting the Labour cabinet and laying the ground for a possibly ugly struggle between the mayor and the prime minister.

The row over the London underground only enforced the sense of the unintegrated city—the city of traffic and crowds that places impasses to movement and obstructs a vision of urban coherence. Delays and breakdowns on the tube were not only gratingly literal occurrences; they also evoked an imagery of the fragmented city, the metropolitan space that will not hold together but breaks into partial views, discontinuous movements, self-enclosed communities.

As London tries to imagine a new millennial future, it holds to a vision of the total metropolis, the splendid, but also the intelligible, city—a fit site for a liveable community. Late in 2000, Richard Rogers published a book called *Cities for a Small Country*, a kind of literary pendant to his Millennium Dome. The book decries the failure of urban solidarity and the need to "counter the fragmentation of the post-industrial age." For Rogers this means "planning compact, connected, textured new developments that minimise environmental impact and maximise cohesion" (290). In the same spirit, Norman Foster talks reassuringly of the links between all those singular, soaring buildings, and Ken Livingstone speaks for a London of the millions, not the few. These images of flourishing civic life still hover in the exhaust-laden air. Only suppose that the transport problem can be solved, that ethnicities can mingle without strife, that homelessness recedes, and that solidarity among London's working citizens can accommodate all the new buildings gleaming against the sky.

The lived experience of London 2000, however, its millennial urban phenomenology, was not the experience of the orderly space, finally resolving into coherence and susceptible to synthetic judgment.[6] It was rather a more radically dispersed city, sprouting monuments which suggest another, perhaps more likely, future. Drawn to the ideal of singularity, each vastly different from the other, the buildings are stand-alone wonders. They create an expanse that resembles an open museum traversed by endless crowds. Even those too busy to lift their eyes or too hard-pressed to explore an interior must still sense the uncanny profusion. More than ever, millennial London is a spectatorial space, a touristic theater even for its workday citizens.

The higher towers, the extravagant shapes, the unprecedented technologies, the new materials, the sheer number of architectural scenes—these are crystallizations of wealth, engineering skill, and (often enough) aesthetic discrimination; they are the physical precipitates of those resources that only a world city can muster. Evoking no heroic past, no celebration of named individuals or communities, the buildings take on the aspect of new autonomous "persons," and become strange exemplars of citizenship in a transforming London. Self-dramatizing and up-to-date, independent and brazen, enjoying their difference, paying token homage to collectivity while asserting their own singular attractions—the monuments are part of a community of isolates, gazing at one another from a distance.

The media, always quivering and ready to pounce, will no doubt continue to swerve wildly between tales of doom and triumph. A week of stories about breakdown along the Northern line will give way to cheery reports of a faster river ferry. The combination of limitless ambition, visible change, and the relentless public discourse creates a collective unreality. Is this beauty, or is it decadence? Is London growing together or hardening apart? Whose monuments are they?

NOTES

1. It is important to remember that while the Labour campaign of 1997 became marked as the work of new media Machiavellis, obsessively concerned with the control of imagery, the Conservative Party had pointed the way. Since the early '70s, their reliance on the advertisers Saatchi and Saatchi to promote their cause had already raised the stakes in the political struggle for the control of persuasive imagery.

2. Compare Durrschmidt's discussion of the relationship between ordinary life and the experience of globalism.

3. Richard Rogers unashamedly links architectural innovation with the new urban boosterism:

> Ken Livingstone hustled to be mayor. He has great vision and he loves London. I want to see the Thames used better. For many years it has been the barrier between the rich north side and the poorer south. I want to create new districts on its shores, like beads on a string. And I want boats, not the tin cans you have to travel in at the moment. Paris has those glorious bateaux-mouches, for goodness' sake. Why can't we have the same? We must help London's poorest boroughs, we must have inspirational things like the Dome and the Millennium Wheel that brand the city. (*Times*, 21 Oct. 2000)

4. "Why a plan?" ask the writers of the London County Council. "The word has suspicious undertones for people who think it natural to plan a holiday, a children's outing, a bride's trousseau, the production line of a factory, or a military campaign. The solution of any problem needs a plan; and the stupendous confusion of London has needed one badly for years" (London County Council 15).

5. In this light, consider David Harvey's working definition of urban postmodernity:

> In the urban context, therefore, I shall simply characterize post-modernism as signifying a break with the idea that planning and development should focus on large scale, technologically rational, austere and functionally efficient "international style" design and that vernacular traditions, local history and specialized spatial designs ranging from functions of intimacy to grand spectacle should be approached with a much greater eclecticism of style. (258)

6. See Jameson's reading of the Bonaventure Hotel, where he describes the "originality of postmodern space": "a mutation in the object unaccompanied as yet by any equivalent mutation in the subject" (38).

WORKS CITED

Coomer, Martin. *Art London*. London: Ellipsis, 2000.

"Dome 'Lacks Wow Factor,' Say MPs." *BBC News Online* 1 Aug. 2000. <http://news.bbc.co.uk/>. 7 Jan. 2001.

"Dome Support 'Pathetic,' Says Ex-Boss." *BBC News Online* 2 July 2000. <http://news.bbc.co.uk/>. 9 Jan. 2001.

Durrschmidt, Jorg. *Everyday Lives in the Global City*. London and New York: Routledge, 2000.

Glancey, Jonathan. "Arts: Reach for the Skies: Architecture Scaled the Heights This Year." *Guardian* 30 Dec. 2000. <http://www.guardianunlimited.co.uk/>. 10 Jan. 2001.

Harvey, David. *The Urban Experience*. Oxford: Basil Blackwell, 1989.

Hilty, Greg. "The Battle for Trafalgar." *Guardian* 18 Dec. 2000. <http://www. guardian-unlimited.co.uk/>. 10 Jan. 2001.

Jack, Ian, ed. *Granta* 65 (Spring 1999).

Jameson, Frederic. *Postmodernism: Or, the Cultural Logic of Late Capitalism*. Durham: Duke UP, 1991.

Kelso, Paul. "Mayor Attacks Generals in Battle of Trafalgar Square." *Guardian* 20 Oct. 2000. <http://www.guardianunlimited.co.uk/>. 6 Jan. 2001.

London County Council. *New Sights of London*. London, 1960.

Morgan, Christopher. "Charles Says Dome Is 'Monstrous Blancmange.'" *Sunday Times* 16 Jan. 2000. <http://www.sunday-times.co.uk/>. 15 Jan. 2001.

"New Labour, New Dome." *Independent* 9 Dec. 1999. <http://www.independent. co.uk/>. 18 Dec. 2000.

"Norman Foster: Building the Future." *BBC News Online* 9 May 2000. <http://news. bbc.co.uk/>. 7 Dec. 2000.

Parris, Matthew. "I'm With You Ken, Right Down the Line." *Times* 11 Nov. 2000. <http://www.thetimes.co.uk/>. 11 Jan. 2001.

"Police Defend May Day Tactics." *BBC News Online* 2 May 2000. < http://news.bbc. co.uk/>. 15 Dec. 2000.

Porter, Roy. *London: A Social History*. Cambridge, MA and London: Harvard UP, 1995.

Rogers, Richard, and Anne Power. *Cities for a Small Country*. London: Faber and Faber, 2000.

Sudjic, Deyan. "Boom Town." *Guardian* 23 Apr. 2000. <http://www.guardianunlimited. co.uk/>. 9 Jan. 2001.

———. "The Capital's Master Builder." *Observer* 11 June 2000. <http://www. observer.co.uk/>. 15 Jan. 2001.

W., John. "Millennium Wheel." *BBC News Online* n.d. < http://news.bbc.co.uk/>. 5 Jan. 2001.

"Work Begins on Mayor's HQ." *BBC News Online* 17 Mar. 2000. < http://news.bbc. co.uk/>. 6 Jan. 2001.

Contributors ⌒

JOHN EADE is Professor of Sociology and Anthropology at the University of Surrey Roehampton. His main research interests are urban ethnicity and global/local processes. He has authored two books, *The Politics of Community* (1989) and *Placing London: From Imperial Capital to Global City* (2000). He also edited *Living the Global City* and co-edited *Divided Europeans: Understanding Ethnicities in Conflict* and *Contesting the Sacred: The Anthropology of Christian Pilgrimage*. He is currently co-editing *Understanding the City: Contemporary and Future Perspectives* for the Blackwells' *Studies in Urban and Social Change* series. He is a founding editor of *Journeys: The International Journal of Travel and Travel Writing*.

ISABELLE FREMEAUX is currently completing her Ph.D. thesis, undertaken in the Communications Department at London Guildhall University under the supervision of Professor Jerry Palmer. This research explores the discursive status and potential strategic dimension of the notion of community, especially as used in the institutional framework of urban regeneration. The investigation focuses on arts projects organized in this context and is principally based on case studies of two festivals organized in the Bengali community in the East End of London. Her article "The Influence of Community in Cultural Projects" has recently been published in *Rising East*, a sociological journal from the University of East London.

DAVID GARBIN is a Ph.D. student in the Department of Geography of the University of Tours, France, and currently a visiting researcher in the Centre for Bangladeshi Studies, University of Surrey Roehampton, London. His doctoral research is focused on the transnational dynamics of the Bengali community in London and based on fieldwork both in the United Kingdom and in rural Bangladesh. His interests include contemporary migration processes, identity politics, and global-local dialectics.

DAVID GILBERT is Senior Lecturer in Geography at Royal Holloway, University of London. His recent work has concerned the geographies of the modern city, particularly the influence of imperialism on the landscapes of London, and the development of tourist cartographies and understandings of London and New York. His publications include *Imperial Cities: Landscape, Display and Identity* (Manchester University Press, 1999, with Felix Driver) and *Class, Community and Collective Action* (Clarendon, 1992).

PAMELA K. GILBERT is Associate Professor of English at the University of Florida, and series editor for State University of New York Press's Studies in the Long Nineteenth Century. Her book *Disease, Desire and the Body in Victorian Women's Popular Novels* was published in 1997 by Cambridge University Press. *Beyond Sensation, Mary Elizabeth Braddon in Context*, a collection co-edited with Marlene Tromp and Aeron Haynie, appeared in 2000 from State University of New York Press. Her work has appeared in several journals, including *Nineteenth Century Studies, Nineteenth Century Prose, Women and Performance, English, LIT: Literature/Interpretation/Theory, Essays in Literature*, and *Victorian Newsletter*, among others. She is currently finishing a book that traces the construction of the social body and public health in England, especially London, from 1832 to 1866.

FIONA HENDERSON is a graduate student in the Department of Geography at Royal Holloway College, University of London. Having written her Master's thesis on the changing representation of the English landscape in twentieth-century British art, she is currently working on her Ph.D., examining the changing tourist landscapes of the European capital city in the latter half of the twentieth century. Working in London, Paris, and Berlin, Fiona's research explores, among other things, the construction of the American tourist, building site tourism in Berlin, bomb-damage tours of London, and the romantic experience of Paris.

HEIDI J. HOLDER is Associate Professor of English at Central Michigan University. In the areas of Irish, British, and Canadian drama, she has contributed to journals including *Essays in Theatre* and the *Journal of Modern Literature*, and collections ranging from *Acts of Supremacy: The British Empire and the Stage, 1790–1930* (Manchester University Press, 1991) to *Women and Playwriting in Nineteenth-Century Britain* (Cambridge University Press, 1999). She is currently at work on a book on the Victorian theaters of London's East End.

MORRIS B. KAPLAN teaches philosophy and lesbian/gay studies at Purchase College in the State University of New York. He served for several years as a trial attorney with the Legal Aid Society of New York and as the inaugural

Rockefeller Foundation Fellow in Legal Humanities at the Stanford Humanities Center. In 1997 Routledge published his *Sexual Justice: Democratic Citizenship and the Politics of Desire*. The chapter in this volume grows out of research for *Sodom on the Thames: Love, Lust and Scandal in Wilde Times*, forthcoming from Cornell University Press. He is the author of numerous articles and reviews, including "Who's Afraid of John Saul? Urban Culture and the Politics of Desire," which appeared in *GLQ* in 1999.

MICHAEL LEVENSON is the William B. Christian Professor of English at the University of Virginia and the author of *A Genealogy of Modernism* (Cambridge, 1984), *Modernism and the Fate of Individuality* (Cambridge, 1991), and *The Spectacle of Intimacy* (Princeton, 2000, co-author Karen Chase). Professor Levenson has written numerous articles on nineteenth- and twentieth-century literature and culture; he is the editor of the *Cambridge Companion to Modernism* (1999), and is currently chair of the English Department at Virginia. His next book, *What Was Modernism?*, is forthcoming from Yale University Press.

ALEXEI MONROE recently completed a Ph.D. in the interdisciplinary field of Communication and Image Studies at the University of Kent, Canterbury. His Ph.D. research concerns the Slovene group Laibach and the associated cultural movement NSK. He is currently preparing the first major book on this subject. Besides maintaining an active interest in the art, culture, and politics of former Yugoslavia, he works on the aesthetics of electronic music and is now also active as an experimental DJ and musician. He writes on popular culture for the Internet journal *Central Europe Review* and has also written regularly for the Slovene music magazine *Muska*. He has published several articles on electronic music, art, and popular culture for various publications in Britain, Slovenia, and Yugoslavia, including the 1999 Routledge anthology *Living Through Pop*.

DAVID L. PIKE teaches in the Department of Literature at American University. He is the author of *Passage through Hell: Modernist Descents, Medieval Underworlds* (Cornell University Press), which received the 1997 Gustave O. Arlt Award in the Humanities from the Council of Graduate Schools. He is currently at work on a book-length study of changing images of underground London and Paris since the early nineteenth century. In addition to the urban underground, he teaches courses on modernism, Dante, and film. From 1993 to 1995, Professor Pike was Mellon Postdoctoral Fellow in the Society of Fellow in the Humanities at Columbia University.

GAUTAM PREMNATH teaches Twentieth-century British and Postcolonial Literature in the English department at the University of Massachusetts, Boston. His other publications include "Remembering Fanon, Decolonizing

Diaspora," in Benita Parry and Laura Chrisman, ed., *Postcolonial Theory and Criticism* (D.S. Brewer, 2000), and "The Weak Sovereignty of the Postcolonial Nation-State," in Amitava Kumar, ed., *World Bank Literature* (forthcoming from University of Minnesota Press). He is a member of the editorial collective of *Ghadar,* the journal of the Forum of the Indian Left. He can be reached at <gautam.premnath@umb.edu>.

MICHELLE SIPE is completing her dissertation in the English Department at the University of Florida. Her research explores nineteenth-century British women novelists' appropriations of landscape discourses and their use of eighteenth-century aesthetic principles such as the picturesque in their representations of the rural poor and working classes. Her study focuses particularly on the influence of Victorian landscape and gardening encyclopedias, manuals, and periodicals on women's literature of the period.

JULIAN WOLFREYS is Professor of English at the University of Florida. His most recent publications include *Readings: Acts of Close Reading in Literary Theory* (1999) and *Victorian Hauntings: Spectrality, Gothic, the Uncanny and Literature* (2000). He is also the author of *Writing London: The Trace of the Urban Text from Blake to Dickens* (1998) and *Being English: Narratives, Idioms, and Performances of National Identity from Coleridge to Trollope* (State University of New York Press, 1996) and co-author (with Jeremy Gibson) of *Peter Ackroyd: The Ludic and Labyrinthine Text* (2000). He has edited and co-edited numerous volumes, including, also for State University of New York Press, *The French Connections of Jacques Derrida* (1999). He is currently working on a second volume of *Writing London.*

ANGELA WOOLLACOTT is a Professor of History and teaches in the Women's Studies program at Case Western Reserve University. Her current research fields include feminist approaches to the study of empire and colonialism, the construction of whiteness as racial identity, and the new historiography of the British Empire. Her books include *On Her Their Lives Depend: Munitions Workers in the Great War* (University of California Press, 1994), *To Try Her Fortune in London: Australian Women, Colonialism, and Modernity* (Oxford University Press, 2001), *Gendering War Talk,* edited with Miriam Cooke (Princeton University Press, 1993), and *Feminisms and Internationalism,* edited with Mrinalini Sinha and Donna J. Guy (Blackwell Publishers, 1999). She is currently at work on a book titled *Gender and the Politics of Empire.*

Index ✑